TO HULL
AND BACK

ON HOLIDAY IN
UNSUNG BRITAIN

TOM CHESSHYRE

pp. 18, extract from 'Here' by Philip Larkin printed by kind permission of Faber & Faber

pp. 36, extract from *Coasting* by Jonathan Raban printed by kind permission of Pan Macmillan

pp. 43, extract from 'Slough' by John Betjeman

pp. 145, extract from 'Poem in October' from *The Poems* by Dylan Thomas printed by kind permission of Dent

pp. 205, extract from *Kingdom Come* by J. G. Ballard

pp. 225, extract from *English Journey* by J. B. Priestley

pp. 315, extract from 'Friday Night at the Royal Station Hotel' by Philip Larkin printed by kind permission of Faber & Faber

To Emma

To Hull and Back

Derry

South
Shields

Hull

Salford

Coventry

Norwich

Milton
Keynes

Port
Talbot

London

Slough

Croydon

Hell Bay

Scilly Isles

CONTENTS

1

EAST COAST MAIN LINE: NEVER DULL IN HULL?

Standing on the concourse at King's Cross station, a quarter of an hour before my train north, I get a strange sensation. Around me are hundreds of people, mainly commuters judging by the suits and laptop bags, as well as others catching trains to go home, and students with huge rucksacks. But here I am with my black roll-along case *about to go on holiday*.

I peer around, feeling like an outsider: what am I doing taking a long weekend break in Britain by train? Everyone else seems to be bustling with purpose; absorbed in their routines. *They* don't look like tourists. But I am one: about to visit a place I'd never have thought of seeing for anything but work (a dull trade conference perhaps, or a last-minute business meeting). It almost seems old-fashioned, I suddenly realise as I gaze towards the platforms, as if I've stepped back in time: I'm taking a break in the UK to a spot that somehow feels forgotten and that's certainly not what most people identify with 'holiday', travelling along rail tracks laid down in the nineteenth century before planes had even been invented.

Next to the departure board, there's a large television. 'WATCHDOG SLAMS HEATHROW AND GATWICK' says a headline. Britain's Competition Commission has attacked airport authorities for 'failing to manage security queues, causing unacceptable delays to passengers, crew and flights', the presenter announces, in a weary tone that seems to suggest: 'Yes, they've messed it all up again.' The authorities, the presenter continues, have acted 'against the public interest'. I look about the station again, glad not to be stuck in a security jam at Heathrow or Gatwick. There's a long row of strawberry-red 'Fast Ticket' machines, without a soul at them. There's a quirky florist selling sunflowers, a Marks and Spencer and a sandwich shop called Ixxy's from where I've just bought an expensive bagel and a drink for the trip. A couple of very camp middle-aged men pass by. One is in charge of a bright white, fluffy poodle that looks as though it's just been put through a washing machine. He theatrically says to his companion: 'The one thirty to Darlington. That's the one you want, dear!' A young man with a bushy beard, a waistcoat and spectacles is reading a slim book of poetry (T. S. Eliot) by the ticket machines. He's leaning against a wall with his legs stretched out casually, looking as though he's waiting for an English literature lecture.

There's an almost bohemian feel to the place. It's laid-back, simple to navigate, and a far cry from all the airport queues. I'd probably still be at check-in at Heathrow. Here I'm walking towards a small, shiny green train, already on my way.

So begins my journey into Unsung Britain, on a sunny early October day. I'm heading for Hull and I'm on a mission: to see the parts of the country that most people choose to ignore. I'm soon to become very well acquainted with Britain's train stations (not always quite as relaxed as King's Cross on my first morning) as well as some of the country's most overlooked, least celebrated spots: places that I know from newspaper reports, but have rarely, if ever, seen in the travel section pages. Am I mad? After all, as a journalist working for the travel desk of a national paper I have access to some of the most exotic, exclusive and downright glamorous locations on the globe. It's my *job* to fly to sunny, far-away locations.

So why am I waiting for a train to Hull at 10 a.m. on a cold Friday morning? I suppose I could just pretend I'm bored of hot climes, pristine beaches and living it up, but that wouldn't be quite true (although once you've been to one all-inclusive resort with palm trees and pools with swim-up bars, you've really been to them all). What it comes down to is that I'm simply very curious about the parts of Britain that so often get passed by. What goes on in the bits of the country that so few people bother to see: the parts so few ever reach? After spending six months travelling through the 'unspellable', off-the-beaten-track parts of Eastern Europe for *How Low Can You Go?* – a book on places you can't pronounce, but can reach on dirt-cheap budget flights – I've realised that one of the best ways to get to know a country is to take yourself to the less touristy, less obvious destinations. And let's face it: things don't get much less touristy than Slough (waiting for me with its famous trading estate a couple of weekends away). Finding out how these places sell themselves as 'tourist sights', how they chase the increasingly important tourist pound, will give me an insight into life in Britain that I just wouldn't have got in traditional holiday spots.

At least, I hope so. This will be an 'off-duty' adventure for me – unlike the trips I take for my travel writing work, I will be doing this one purely out of personal curiosity. I want to see what I can as a 'holidaymaker', but I'm interested in more than just the obvious attractions: I intend to be nosy… very nosy. I'll use the skills and contacts I have from being a reporter in my day job to unearth stories the casual visitor might well miss. And who knows what characters I'll bump into and discoveries I'll make along the way (or, for that matter, what mishaps and misunderstandings await).

What's going on in Derry, Salford, Croydon and Milton Keynes? I want to know – even if my (very understanding) girlfriend Anne thinks I'm definitely going round the bend this time. When I announced the idea, which came to me when I was in the office one day writing an article on the latest boutique hotels in the Indian Ocean, she commented in a tone that seemed to be pushing me in a slightly sunnier direction: 'But aren't the Maldives quite nice at this time of year?'

To which I replied: 'That's not the point. The Maldives may be nice, but they're boring.'

At this, she cocked an eyebrow and gave me a steady look: 'And Slough is interesting?'

My parents simply could not get their heads round it ('Are you sure, Tom?'), while friends reacted either with 'rather you than me, mate' or with a barely contained look of glee that appeared to be a mixture of good old-fashioned *Schadenfreude* and: 'At least he's not off somewhere hot this time.'

But I've decided to do it now: to go to Hull and Slough, on a series of weekend breaks over the next four months. What the hell: give it a go, it'll be an adventure... even if it is a peculiar one. What, if anything, might visiting all these unsung places reveal about life in Britain? What will I learn about the country that I wouldn't have if I'd just mooched about at home? It's only four months of unusual weekends in the UK, it's not as though I'm quitting everything and heading around the globe for a year with a backpack, or sailing round the world in a dinghy. What will my weekend jaunts throw up for me? Will going to the places everyone loves to overlook be the adventure I'm hoping it will turn out to be? And if I can have a good time in Hull, could I begin to think twice about the whole nature of 'taking a holiday'? Is 'home' (Britain) the new 'away', as so many people seem to say these days? Anyway, will we be able to afford much 'away' in the future? Does being green mean learning to love Milton Keynes? If we open our eyes to the delights of the places we usually ignore, might we actually be delighted?

Or is all this thinking about things too much?

Just about everyone has a joke at the expense of places like Croydon and Coventry. There are even books with titles like *Crap Towns* and *Don't Go There* that mercilessly poke fun. But I'm setting off to prove them wrong. I'm planning an eclectic and, I hope, fun journey starting in Hull, travelling to places I never dreamed I'd visit, and ending in Hell (Hell, in this instance, being a bay with that name in the Scilly Isles). From Hull to Hell: what's happening in Britain's 'backwaters'?

I didn't have a clue. And that's exactly how it should be. If travel is about adventure – a trip into the unknown – that's precisely how it feels as I set off from King's Cross on my way to Hull.

The train surprises us by leaving right on time. A dapper elderly man in a tweed jacket sitting beside me taps his watch to confirm this – 'Right on time,' he says, looking pleased and slightly amazed – as we roll slowly out of North London past council estates, red-brick terraces and building sites piled with rubble. Soon we're racing away. The capital disappears in a flash, and before I know it lovely biscuit-coloured fields materialise, criss-crossed with hedges and dotted with haystacks. Tiny villages with churches and cosy-looking pubs come and go. Cricket pitches, copses and lakes fly by. As I look out, I'm reminded of John Major's comment on Englishness, in which he drew on the words of George Orwell: 'Fifty years on from now, Britain will still be the country of long shadows on cricket grounds, warm beer, invincible green suburbs, dog lovers and pool fillers, and as George Orwell said: "old maids bicycling to holy communion through the morning mist".' There is no mist, but the sun breaks through the clouds and the fields turn golden. Solitary trees in vast cornfields cast thoughtful shadows. I lean back in my seat as the English countryside in all its glory unfolds: mustard fields, clusters of cows, chestnut horses, hedgerows lined with cow parsley, farmers in red tractors quietly going about their business with bounding black-and-white dogs in tow.

I buy a coffee from a friendly cafe assistant – 'You're having a weekend break in *Hull*?' she asks, as though she hadn't quite heard me correctly – and take in my carriage. A tall, studious-looking man with cropped hair has fallen fast asleep with his legs poking into the aisle and his laptop in view. An odd screensaver message reads: 'Physics is my friend.' Opposite, a busty woman with dyed-red hair is reading a novel called *Tell Me Your Dreams*. A loud man with a Yorkshire accent is having a mobile phone conversation about betting on football matches. 'A hundred to thirty, a hundred to thirty. That's what it is. Not bad, eh?' he says in a voice that suggests he's definitely got the bookies on the run this time. 'I might lose you. I might lose you. It's cutting out. No it isn't. Are you there? Last game of the season. Worth a punt. Are you there? Yes, to win the Champions League!'

Peterborough passes in a blur of B&Qs, Asdas, train depots, cement plants and fields of sheep. Grantham's spire peeks beyond the red, white and blue facade of Sportsdirect.com's warehouse and a shop called Pets at Home. Then comes a shanty-town of allotments, followed by rugby pitches and a tunnel in the lead-up to Doncaster, where there's a warehouse with men in orange uniforms and hard hats, a canal full of crumpled shopping trolleys and a wall covered with graffiti... Not exactly your usual holiday fare, perhaps. An advert at Selby station is for Thomson-fly.com: 'FLY AWAY ON OUR LOW-FARE FLIGHTS FROM DONCASTER-SHEFFIELD!' it says in big red letters. But who needs flights, I'm thinking, as we shoot past Selby across a pancake-flat landscape? The sun is out. Steam coming from the cooling towers of a power station makes the whole vista look like the deck of an enormous ship heading out to sea. The power station is, I suddenly realise, really quite beautiful (if you squint your eyes a bit). Travelling as a *tourist* on my way to a place so disassociated with tourism is already making me see the country differently.

I'm actually beginning to feel like I'm on holiday as the Humber comes into view: a huge mercury swirl under a strangely matching sky. Again I try to work out where I would have been if I had been travelling on a plane. We're a quarter of an hour from Paragon station in Hull. At Heathrow or Stansted I'd probably not have taken off yet; instead I'm a few minutes from my destination. No security queues to come. No carousel scramble. No costly taxi or confusing buses into town.

Thank God for that. The Humber Bridge emerges, its suspension cables seeming delicate and spider-like. A survey, I've just read, has put the bridge at number six in the 'Seven Wonders of the UK' behind Big Ben, the Eden Project, the Millennium Wheel, Buckingham Palace and the Angel of the North (but ahead of Wembley Stadium). I've never had a good look at it before. What a fantastic structure. What a feat of engineering. Not bad: just a few hours after leaving home I've already seen a 'wonder of the UK'. Beyond the bridge, the river is vast and solemn. We slide slowly by a road with lorries carrying pale-blue cargo containers marked Finnlines and Maersk. We pass a gravel depot. A yellow digger is destroying a derelict terrace. There's an industrial chimney, a large red-brick building, a 1970s estate painted pink and a wavy-roofed Tesco. A jolly voice clicks on the loudspeaker and tells us that 'Marie-Anne, Ruth and driver Jim' would like to thank us for travelling with Hull Trains. The carriages pull in to a quiet station with a green and white iron roof. We have arrived in Hull. We're five minutes early. King's Cross feels a very long way away. What, I'm wondering, happens in Hull?

I guess I'm about to find out.

2

HULL: POEMS AND PARTIES BY THE HUMBER

I've been in Hull less than an hour and I'm sitting in the kitchen of a Victorian terrace, drinking coffee with the woman who discovered Philip Larkin. At King's Cross, I hadn't expected that. But at Paragon station, I received a call: the meeting I had been trying to fix was on. Could I make it by 3 p.m.? I took a taxi straight over and pressed a buzzer.

Larkin lived in Hull, where he was head librarian at the university, from 1955 to his death in 1985. There is no Larkin Museum: 'Not enough interest,' said a tourist official when I asked before coming, 'though you do get a few people who want to see where he lived.' Local tourist brochures fail to mention Larkin. There are no Larkin T-shirts or booklets in the information centre near the train station. And I can't help feeling that the city is not especially fond of its best-known modern poet (Andrew Marvell also lived here when he wrote 'To His Coy Mistress' in the seventeenth century).

Perhaps that is understandable. Shortly after moving to Hull, before he had settled in, Larkin wrote to a friend saying: 'I wish I could think of just one nice thing to tell you about Hull – oh yes, well, it's nice and flat for cycling: that's about the best I can say.' Later in 'Here', a poem based on the city, Larkin described it as having 'a cut-price crowd, urban yet simple, dwelling / Where only salesmen and relations come'. In other words: not many tourists or people who don't have to visit – people like me. The poem goes on to mention 'the slave museum' (Wilberforce House, where William Wilberforce was born), 'a terminate and fishy-smelling / Pastoral of ships up streets', 'residents of raw estates', 'tattoo-shops, consulates, grim head-scarved wives', 'loneliness' and 'removed lives'; leaving what some might consider a depressing impression.

Jean Hartley, a sprightly woman in her early seventies with auburn hair and sparkling eyes, would disagree. Before setting off for Hull, I'd come across a slim book entitled *Philip Larkin's Hull and East Yorkshire*, written by Jean, who still lives in the city. I'd called, left a message, and just now she had cheerfully agreed to meet, tickled by the idea of me heading off to so many out-of-the way spots. 'Are you sure you want to come to Hull?' she asked jokingly.

In the 1950s, Jean and her then husband George, both twenty-one, ran a small-circulation poetry magazine called *Listen*. Its remarkable list of contributors included Kingsley Amis, Elizabeth Jennings and Philip Larkin. The couple decided to publish a book from one of them. 'Why Larkin?' I ask, after Jean leads me into her eclectic and bright kitchen, which has bookshelves to one side overflowing with recipe books, except for one volume: *The Collected Larkin*. Pictures fill almost every space on the walls, with a beautiful watercolour of the Humber and the outline of the Lincolnshire coast under a dark sky next to an unusual pastel of geese drinking from a puddle. 'I painted that one, after I came back from a trip to Africa,' says Jean, seeing my eyes drawn to it. And before she answers my question about Larkin, she is telling me how the poet used to sit at this very table: 'He sat in your chair, oh yes, lots of times when he came round for meals.' A photograph of Larkin, looking enigmatic next to his bicycle, which he would have used to cycle to visit Jean, hangs by a neat row of mugs on hooks.

'His poems just stood out, being first of all accessible and wry, and humane and funny,' Jean says smiling kindly, passing me a mug of excellent fresh coffee, and generally making me feel at home. She still, she says, reads the poems regularly, which is why she likes to have a volume close to hand in the kitchen. 'Both of us felt that Philip Larkin's were the poems that we liked best.'

'George and I formed Marvell Press,' Jean says – the name obviously playing on Hull's Andrew Marvell connection. At the time, Larkin was thirty-one, working in Belfast, about to move to Hull. 'How did you get him to agree to work with two twenty-something Hullensians?' I ask, wondering why such a 'great' had been so overlooked by everyone else.

'It was very difficult to get noticed as a poet back then, just as it is today. He was delighted to be taken on and thought being near his editors would be a good idea. But he had a proviso: he'd only come with us if we could assure him that we wouldn't sell any copies in Hull. Which wasn't difficult,' Jean says with another smile.

'Really? I would have thought as many sales as possible would have been his aim,' I reply.

'Larkin didn't want to mix his public and his private lives, which is what led to his "hermit of Hull" nickname. We sold all over the world but not many in Hull,' Jean says, laughing brightly. The book was called *The Less Deceived*.

'Had you not spotted him, what might have happened?'

She pauses for a moment or two, deep in thought, gazing at a row of paper Chinese lanterns above her bookshelves, then says: 'I think he would have carried on but it would have taken longer. I think he was quite demoralised.'

Jean's book on Larkin's old haunts in the city mentions all sorts of pubs including Ye Olde Blackboy; the Marks and Spencer in the Old Town (the subject of 'The Large Cool Store'); Paragon station (from which Larkin begins a train journey to London in 'The Whitsun Weddings'); the Royal Station Hotel (which inspired 'Friday Night at the Royal Station Hotel'); the Hull Royal Infirmary ('The Building'). About 'Here' and its cut-price crowds and grim head-scarved wives, Jean says warmly: 'Actually, I think of that as a kind of love letter to Hull.' She describes a group of 'Larkin tourists' who once visited, and who told her they'd asked the tourist office 'What about Larkin?', only to be misheard and informed: 'Oh yeah, the parking's very easy.' Jean has another chuckle about this, and pours more coffee.

'So how do you think Hull remembers Larkin?'

She turns serious at my question. 'The poet has been shamefully shoved in a corner in Hull. There should be a poetry centre for him – and I know the Larkin Society would dearly love it to be in Larkin's Pearson Park flat, if only the City Council would do something. He'd think that would be a giggle but I think he'd think he was worth it,' she says. Then Jean goes on to tell me, apropos of nothing, that Larkin went shopping at Mr Big and Mr Tall, 'because he had a very long body and very short legs: it was very difficult to get shirts that were long enough.'

Not a lot of people, I reflect, are likely to know that.

After leaving Jean – who could not have been kinder – I take a short walk to Larkin's old flat. It's an eye-opener: in a terrible state. A creaking gate leads to an overgrown arbour. Junk blocks the path to a door with chipped white paint. A dented gas cooker, a crumpled plastic Christmas tree and an ancient bed frame are heaped in the front garden. The blue heritage sign is almost totally hidden behind creepers. It looks like a doss house, like something out of a Harold Pinter play: it's hard to imagine this ever becoming a tourist sight. I peer up at the large windows of his top-floor flat, which inspired the title of the poem 'High Windows'. According to Jean, Larkin used to spy on people in Pearson Park using binoculars. I'm in for a shock. A man with a long grey beard is staring down from the first-floor window. He doesn't look pleased to see me. For a moment, I have a strange sensation: that Larkin's ghost is watching. I give the 'ghost' a nod and a thumbs-up. He replies with an almost imperceptible nod, and disappears. I ring the buzzer, but there's no reply.

I walk up Newland Avenue, where Larkin used to shop. It's pretty rough and ready. A poster screams 'REMOVE VIOLENCE FROM HULL'. Shops with 'stock liquidations' are selling sofas. An off-licence is called 'Bargain Beers', and a sign for a gospel mission tells me: 'THE TRUTH IS OUT THERE'. Further on, I come to Hull University and the cube-like library that Larkin helped design. In a room with slatted blinds on the first floor I discover a portrait of the poet. He stares back at me, somehow managing to be searching, stern and slightly amused, all at the same time. He is buried in Cottingham Cemetery, a short bus ride away. I decide to investigate and catch a bus there; I find a plain white headstone to the left of the entrance to the cemetery that says plainly: 'Philip Larkin 1922–1985 Writer'. Nearby are the graves of Monica Jones, the woman with whom he had an affair, who died in 2001, and Maeve Brennan, who died in 2003, his long-time girlfriend. Jean had said: 'Oh yeah, go to the cemetery – there's this sort of love triangle.' And there it is. A few hours in Hull and I've already learned about one of the best-known, best-loved (and most mysterious) poets Britain has ever produced. Exactly what I'd hoped for in Unsung Britain: an encounter with someone with a story to tell and a reason to visit a place that's so often overlooked.

As I catch a cab back to Paragon station to pick up my bag (the driver asks 'Philip who?' when I mention Larkin), I turn my mind back to the matter at hand: Hull. To say that Hull gets a terrible press is an understatement. Hull gets a stinking, lousy, almost hopeless press: just about everyone seems to want to have a go at the South Yorkshire city (population 253,000). Just before I came here, it was judged to be the second 'worst place to live' in Britain by the television programme *Location, Location, Location*. This was based on crime, drug use, education and health records. Only Middlesbrough was worse. Previously, in 2005, Hull had been number one on the don't-go-there list, with the programme citing 'sixty-nine crimes a day'. This moved John Prescott, then deputy prime minister and MP for Hull East, to defend the city's honour. 'It is arrogance beyond belief to proclaim Hull the worst place to live,' he countered. 'I challenge them to come to Hull and I will personally show Phil and Kirsty [the programme's presenters] that it's a great northern city and a great place to live and work.'

We pass a nondescript row of kebab, fried chicken and fish and chip shops. One of the criteria for the 'worst places' survey was the quality of diet. In 2004 Hull was found by two separate studies to be the 'chubbiest' city in the UK. *Men's Health* magazine reported that Hull men were the 'fattest', eating an average of ninety-five grams of fat a day. Another report put the city at the top of an obesity league table on the basis of hospital admissions for Type 2 diabetes; 'white, working class families that do little exercise' were shown to be the most at risk. Meanwhile, a survey in 2002 named the city as having the highest number of snorers in Britain. Commenting on Prescott's own lifestyle, the editor of *Men's Health* optimistically suggested: 'Maybe he could set us an example with a five-times-a-week exercise programme.' Even the *Hull Daily Mail* is downbeat. 'DISPOSABLE INCOME AMONG THE LOWEST' runs a headline in today's paper. It says that 'in 1997 the average household in Hull had £7,475... 40 per cent of their overall income, to spend freely. Today the average household in Hull has £8,875, just 37 per cent of total income, to spend on non-essential items.' The national average is, the report says, almost double: £16,262.

So, if you accept this evidence, the city is not a particularly nice place to live, full of overweight people, criminals and people struggling to make ends meet. What can you do in Hull? Get fat, get mugged, get flooded. A few months earlier, more than 10,000 homes had been badly damaged by flooding in the city, much of which is below sea level. All this was depressing: the 'Hull is dull' rhyme seemed to ring true, I reflected as the cab pulled into the station. Yes, the tourist office talks about 'the gem in Yorkshire's magnificent crown', but *Crap Towns: The 50 Worst Places to Live in the UK*, which describes itself as 'The Domesday Book of misery', is not so sure. At number one on its list?

Hull.

On my way to my hotel, I'm beginning to understand why: I walk past a 'Poundland: yes everything's £1', a warren of damp malls, desolate streets by empty car lots, an odd restaurant called The Omelette, and a group of youths hanging about on bikes. Clyde House Hotel consists of two houses on a red-brick terrace converted into 'three-star guest accommodation'. I've booked a single. 'The bathroom is down the corridor,' Janice, the owner, had warned when I'd phoned. I'd paused when she'd said this. But then she'd told me the price: £27 a night, B & B. For three nights the bill is £81: how can I go wrong with that? You can hardly afford a single night in a Travelodge by a roundabout in London for eighty quid. I ring a buzzer. A short man with a crew cut and thick glasses who introduces himself as Richard opens the door. 'All right mate,' he says.

We pass through a minuscule bar with pink wallpaper and navy carpets. 'It's the smallest bar in Hull,' Richard says. On the wall there's a framed collection of 'historic golf balls'. Sport is flickering on a television in front of a white sofa set. Light filters through lace curtains. A rack with books holds *Images of Victorian Hull* and *A Tribute to Hull's Fishing*. A picture of KC Stadium, where rugby league and football is played, sits on the mantelpiece. A notice says: 'House rules: no swearing, no drinking, no gambling, no loose women! Enjoy your stay!' Clyde House Hotel is not exactly pitched at the trendy mini-break brigade.

Richard is chatty. 'We've got lots of contract workers in right now,' he says, as we ascend a narrow staircase. 'They're refitting flood victims' housing. They've been ripping everything out. Most of the donkey work has been done. Now we're getting the fitters, the joiners, the plumbers and the electricians.' He drops my bag in a tiny room with a single bed, a faded Monet print, a sink, a thin wardrobe that reminds me of a coffin, and a view of a graffiti-covered wall by a busy road. He bustles about like a bellboy at The Ritz, pointing to a light above the sink. 'It's not working. Apologies for that,' he says matter-of-factly. 'Here's the bathroom,' he adds, nodding to a cramped room with a shower just outside the bedroom door. On my budget – I'm trying to keep costs on these adventures as low as possible, with the occasional extravagance thrown in – I'm going to have to get used to a few bathrooms down the hall.

We go downstairs, where Richard leads me to Hull's smallest bar and offers me a pint. He seems pleased when I say yes. 'What's that?' I ask, pointing at a strange, spaghetti-style diagram on a wall close to the 'historic golf balls': it looks like a warped version of the London Underground map. Richard squints, mole-like, at the poster and grins. 'It is a map of Hull's pubs,' he says, suddenly coming alive. Hull, it appears, has an awful lot of pubs. 'Some have been knocked down since this was made,' Richard says, staring fondly at the poster. 'Ah yes, Ye Olde White Hart, now you must go to Ye Olde White Hart. Unfortunately the Heritage and Oberon have closed 'cos it's all being developed down there.' By 'down there' he's referring to an area south of Hull's Old Town by the Humber. 'There's only the Green Bricks that way now. But you could try the Paragon or the Hull Cheese,' he says thoughtfully. I sip my pint. Richard and I are getting on just fine. Clyde House isn't so bad really, as long as you don't think too much about the room (or spend too much time in it). I like it – it feels homely.

'So I'm guessing you must have worked in one of these pubs at some point?'

'I used to be behind the bar at the Hull Cheese,' he replies. 'It was funny: you used to get these old fellows coming in and they'd ask: "Do you still have the rooms upstairs with the ladies?" From years ago they were: old-timers who used to work on the docks. I said to them: "We still have the rooms upstairs but the ladies have gone." They just laughed at that.'

We have a laugh about that, too, examining the pub map. 'Oh yes. The Earl de Grey… the Earl de Grey. That was shut down once for ladies-of-the-night type reasons,' he says. Then he adds: 'Yes, I like to go round the pubs. I was very keen on them from a young age. I liked to listen to all the folk talking about life. I've always been one for pubs, never for shopping. Now you've got all these major designers and shops in town. You used to have to go to Leeds and Manchester for all that designer stuff: not any more.' Outside it's begun to drizzle. It looks grey and unpromisingly dreary. My pint is almost finished, and Richard's gaze is still on the map – which seems to have some sort of transfixing effect. 'Ah yes,' he says dreamily, adopting a butterfly collector tone all of a sudden. 'Some lovely ones here. Some absolute beauties.'

But before trying the lovely, beautiful and plentiful pubs of Hull – which seem to be a local must if Richard (and Larkin, for that matter) is anything to go by – I stumble upon the city's connections to Robinson Crusoe. Daniel Defoe's adventures at sea begin in Hull. There's a small bronze of him dressed in furs and carrying a sunshade made of palm-tree fronds in an easy-to-overlook corner of a park near my hotel. Crusoe took to the high seas in September 1651, quickly hitting a violent storm on the way to London and watching his ship sink. After seeing his vessel disappear into the North Sea, he reflects: 'Had I now the sense to have gone back to Hull, and have gone home, [I'd have] been happy.'

In the run-up to Hull I'd tried to fix a day trip on a trawler, in search of the city's seafaring and fishy side. This was not a good idea for two reasons: (1) fishing trawlers usually go out for longer than a day; and (2) there are virtually no fishing trawlers in Hull any more. Surely a fishing trip would be possible in Hull, I'd asked the information centre people? 'Sorry, no,' replied an exasperated official.

'Everyone thinks Hull is a fishing village, but that is just plain wrong,' says Bob Stones, manager for Associated British Ports, which runs the city's working docks on the outskirts of town. In the absence of trawlers he is kindly taking me on a docks tour in a shiny Citroën – providing an insight into Hull life that the average tourist just does not get. Bob wears a pinstripe suit and has sandy hair and a tan. His job is to oversee the port's security. He began on the docks in the 1960s as a messenger boy 'doing the rates': checking ships' profit and loss sheets.

The Fishing – as the fishing industry is referred to locally – is yesterday's story, he says cheerfully; everyone I've met so far in Hull seems cheerful, no matter what the *Crap Towns* book says. But Hull is 'not a quiet place, like so many people think'. Quite the contrary, Hull is 'a thriving port with lots of imports and exports'. It is the principal UK port for imports of timber, mainly from Russia and the Nordic countries, Bob says. Hull City Council figures show that 18.5 per cent of all UK imports come through the port, with 15 per cent of seaborne trade leaving the country from here.

'So what happened to The Fishing?' I ask. Its decline has been almost absolute. These days, Albert Dock, to the west of the Old Town towards the Humber Bridge, is usually empty. We drive round a vast enclosure of dark water. Inside, there are just a handful of vessels.

'It all began with the "cod wars" of the 1970s,' Bob patiently explains, as we pause to look out across the coal-black expanse. From 1975 to 1976 Iceland and Britain came to blows because Iceland believed British trawlers were encroaching on its waters. For Iceland this was a desperate time. The country, having few other natural resources, relied heavily on fishing. It wanted a 200-mile exclusion zone around its coast, fearing that cod could go the way of herring, which had already almost disappeared due to over-fishing. There had been previous skirmishes, or 'wars' with Britain in 1958 and 1972 that had seen the exclusion zone extended to fifty miles. Then in 1975 there were clashes on the high seas, with British nets cut and frigates sent to patrol the waters. Iceland argued that there was an 'international trend' towards 200-mile exclusion zones around countries, and its politicians cunningly threatened to close a strategically important NATO base at Keflavik if it did not get its way. The matter went to the United Nations. And the result, after NATO intervention, was that only twenty-four of Britain's trawlers out of a list of ninety-three could fish within the 200-mile zone at any one time. The amount of cod Britain could catch annually was cut drastically to 50,000 tons, and at least 1,500 fishermen were made unemployed, with big knock-on effects on economies in ports such as Hull.

'But that was a long time ago,' concludes Bob, as we drive into King George Dock. Seagulls are swooping over stacks of cargo containers. A wind swirls through clumps of roadside weeds. And then I notice something. It's hard not to. Across vast lots, hundreds of old caravans and 'holiday homes' are stretching into the distance.

'Why are all those holiday homes there?' I ask, intrigued.

'Oh those,' he says, off-handedly. 'Those are second-hand caravans – for export to Russia. We take their wood. We give them caravans.'

As he says this, we pass a cargo ship comically piled with caravans. 'You see,' he explains, 'these holiday parks only have the same caravans for so many years. They replace them. But the old ones have got to go somewhere.'

'It's quite an extraordinary sight,' I comment, as we pause so I can take a photo of a higgledy-piggledy pile of caravans on another rusty cargo ship.

'The timber we get off them [mainly the Russians and Finns] is made into all sorts of things. Lattice fencing. Lattice fencing is big. All those there.'

I point to two long corridors of wood: 'Who buys all of that?'

'B&Q. That's to supply B&Q,' he replies. 'Lattice fencing has taken off massive style. Well, I suppose it's 'cos they're so easy. You put up the fences and that's it, you're done.' We pass pyramids of pumice, gravel and sand; vats of syrup 'for Tate & Lyle'; colourful containers packed with 'clothes, CDs, beer, you name it'; a mountain of rusty scrap; vegetable oil containers; and a row of old concrete-mixer trucks. 'They're off to Russia as well,' says Bob, pointing at the mixers. 'They'll buy anything, the Russians. You think: "What on earth do they want those for?" But they do.'

Bob pauses to chat to a man on a forklift truck. 'He'll be on the go on that forklift all day,' he tells me. 'Manning levels are right these days: people are not hanging around playing cards all day like they used to. Numbers working on the docks have plummeted over the years, with improved cranes the main reason why so few employees are needed. In the old days ships would be in for three weeks unloading and re-loading. Now it's a day. Back then, every single bit of timber was loose. Now you can take 500 planks at one time. That's mechanisation for you. It's fantastic.'

We stop at the Hull Seafarers' Centre, a Christian charity based in a nondescript building on the King George Dock. I jump out, thank Bob and say goodbye, and I'm soon talking to David Birk, one of the chaplains – who is equally informative about dock-life. He's another jolly chap, with an open, panda-like face and wearing a black jumper and jeans; looking as though he might work on a ship himself. Instead, he provides important support to thousands of crew members, mainly from the Far East, who pass through each year. We're in a low-ceilinged room with a pool table, a row of Internet terminals and a counter selling chocolate bars, toothpaste and deodorant. A doorway in a corner leads to a cupboard full of woolly hats, scarves and overcoats that sailors can pick up for free.

'What's the scale of work on the docks?' I ask.

'We get about 4,000 vessels here a year,' David replies, 'but the way of life for sailors has changed massively. Ships used to dock for three or four weeks. Now forget it: it's more like twelve to eighteen hours. Containerisation means bigger vessels and a quick turn around. We get lots of Eastern Europeans as well as Asians – from the Philippines, Burma and Indonesia.' There are very few British seamen, and the atmosphere on the docks has altered beyond recognition in recent years. 'The people we get here are on fifteen-month contracts. That's a long time to be away from friends and family. You can imagine the fatigue, the isolation and sometimes the depression.' Short moorings mean that 'the days of boozy stopovers are over. A lot of ships are "dry" and if you get caught drunk there's a chance of dismissal.'

'What do you think of the negative reputation Hull seems to have?' I ask, mentioning the comments my friends had made about going to Hull.

At this David puts concerns about conditions for seamen on cargo ships to one side and quickly launches into a 'defence' of the city. 'Yes, there's a lot of unemployment here,' he says, looking at me steadily, 'but this city's on the up! It's difficult to get rid of the "it's dull in Hull" image. OK, there are a lot of problems with alcohol. And the town can be quite rough and tough at night. But we're striving to be a top ten city – in ten years' time, that's what we want. That *Crap Towns* book was unfair. Coventry and London were given money to recover from World War Two. But Hull never got a thing.' He pauses. Then he says again: 'Yes, Hull is definitely on the up!'

Maybe. But the city has definitely always been *different*. In perhaps its most dramatically different moment, back in the seventeenth century, Hull denied Charles I entry through the city gates. On 23 April 1642 the Beverley Gate drawbridge was raised, and the king was sent into a fit of anger when Sir John Hotham, who had been appointed governor by Parliament, turned him away. The king had hoped to seize Hull's armaments to strengthen his military position. The moment is seen by many as an important event in the lead-up to the English Civil War.

Some regard this as the start of an 'independent streak' in the city. Later, the local MP William Wilberforce (1759–1833) continued the streak with his campaigns to end the slave trade. Add to this Hull's geographical isolation (York, the nearest city, is more than 30 miles away) and you have a place that generally likes to 'think for itself' and 'considers itself apart'. That, at least, is the view of Paul Schofield, a guide I meet at the small Tourist Information Centre near the remains of Beverley Gate by Princes Dock. I am the only visitor. Decorative coffee spoons with Hull's crest, plates printed with pictures of the Humber Bridge, key rings, rubbers, pens, stickers and badges are on sale – all with 'Hull' written on them. T-shirts are on offer with the slogans 'It's never dull in Hull' and 'Hull of a night'. There are 'Hull' hooded tops, and 'Hull' posters. Selling objects with 'Hull' written on them appears to be a booming business, though where all the customers are, I'm not sure.

Paul has led city tours for nineteen years and is a fount of local knowledge. He tells me about Beverley Gate over beers in a bar near the tourist office and the few stone remains of the old gate, where he expands on his theory of the city. 'People from here have always been radical. People like Wilberforce,' he says. 'Because this is a port, we've imported ideas from other countries. We are not in the middle of the establishment here. Oh no: there's nothing establishment about Hull. That's why people like Philip Larkin loved it: he could do whatever he wanted. Intellectually we're not in the centre of what's going on – of what's fashionable at the moment.' He pauses and sips his drink. 'But we don't care.'

I order more beers. 'Fashions come and fashions go: other people can have fashion!' Paul says, getting expansive. 'In Hull we stand apart. We've always stood alone and have always stood up to authority. We don't take kindly to authoritarian demands. That's just the way we are round here.' We finish our drinks. It's early evening on Saturday. Paul and I cheerily part. Then I take my hotel manager's advice and do what everyone else seems to be doing on Saturday night in Hull: I go on a pub crawl.

First stop is the Banks Harbour, not far from the hotel, where pop music is playing and the first person I talk to is Dave, an unemployed decorator wearing a Ralph Lauren shirt, aged twenty-six. 'How long have you been unemployed?' I enquire, not sure whether it's good etiquette to ask questions like this in the Banks Harbour (it's a little rough around the edges). 'I've been unemployed a year. You know, I just wanted a rest,' he says, not seeming at all perturbed. 'Now I'm seeking [work] 'cos my girlfriend's pregnant. Obviously the worst thing is not having the money. That's been the worst.' His friend Luke, a twenty-four-year-old electrician wearing a pink Lacoste polo shirt, is more downbeat: 'I want to move to Canada. There's **** weather here and this town is full of grunts.'

'Full of grunts? What's that?' I ask.

'We call the unemployed "grunts",' he says, looking at Dave, though Dave doesn't mind in the slightest.

Danny and Tara join us. Danny, thirty, introduces himself as an 'erection specialist' (he's a builder), and Tara, twenty-one, is an accounts assistant. She says: 'In 'ull you get big groups of blokes and women going out: forty of them sometimes. We all go drinking and dancing. Everyone slags off 'ull. But we can take the piss out of ourselves.'

Not far away at the New Clarence pub I meet Eamonn one of the flood contractors from my hotel. He recognises me from the breakfast room, and calls me over: it's easy to make friends in Hull. Eamonn, a skinny man in his forties from Luton, is a foreman, and has been here for two months. 'Some of the flood damage is horrendous,' he says. 'Some people had three feet of water in their living rooms. Lives have been wrecked. When I tell them everything has to be ripped out, it's like saying to Van Gogh: "That's crap. You've got to do it all again."'

He's wearing a blue polo neck and has a copy of the *Hull Daily Mail*. Pictures on the front page show flood damage alongside a story about insurance payouts. He points to a particular picture:

'Those are sleeper walls. They take the pressure of the room. Any builder who removes those should be shot.' Eamonn buys me a Tetley's. He's in a confiding mood. He recently split from his wife in Luton, he says. But he'd been on a date with a local woman the previous night. 'I couldn't believe it,' he says. 'She took me to a gay venue. There was a drag queen on stage.' He raises his eyebrows. 'It was a hoot!' As he says this, Chris, who owns the Clyde House Hotel with his wife Janice, enters. He is selling the hotel, he tells me, as Janice was recently assaulted in their backyard: 'She said to me: "I can't do it. I can't live here any more."' Kelly, the blonde barmaid, joins in: 'The problem in Hull is that everyone moves out. There's better education outside. Better quality of life, everything. People downsize to get out in the suburbs.' She says that this makes studies of education standards in Hull unfair.

Chris surprises us by suddenly announcing: 'I've been rejected four times from *The X Factor*.' And before we know it we're all, including Eamonn and a few other flood contractors who've just been introduced, heading to a karaoke bar, where Chris wants to show off his singing. Soon he's crooning away to Snow Patrol. We order more Tetley's. The flood contractors start dancing to Chris's dulcet tones. Whiskies are downed. More pints of Tetley's are consumed. The flood contractors keep on dancing. Chris hits a creaky high note. We wince a bit, and sip our beers. Time slips by. The songs get worse. I'm having fun with my new flood contractor friends. I won't forget my Saturday night by the Humber in a hurry.

But I wake up feeling awful, staring at the wardrobe that looks like a coffin in my box room, quivering slightly and wondering what I'm doing in Hull. Did I really meet a group of dancing flood contractors last night? Feeling dazed, I go to the tiny shower down the hall, and then take a brisk walk to The Deep. This is Hull's big 'tourist attraction' and one of Europe's deepest aquarium tanks, ten metres deep, in an extraordinary building shaped like an enormous fish. It opened next to Hull's marina, part of the old fishing docks, in 2002 as a Millennium Commission project, costing more than £52 million and helping to regenerate a part of the city that had fallen badly into decline. The Deep is, apparently, one of the most popular new attractions in the country.

My head hurts as I take in the (many) fish. There are more than 3,500. I stare at them. It's not a bad hangover cure, I suddenly realise. Jacks, cod, moray eels, reef sharks, potato-groupers and small yellow fish glide past almost soothingly. I wonder for a while why the bigger fish don't eat the little ones, before meeting Linda Martin, the attraction's communications director, who tells me that the sharks are so well fed they don't bother to attack: 'Every day we feed them at two o'clock. It stops them snacking.'

In his 1982 travel book, *Coasting*, Jonathan Raban dropped by Hull on his journey round Britain by yacht, mooring close to the spot where The Deep is now situated and considering the city's tourist possibilities: 'I was The Fishing's first foreign tourist – a portent maybe. After me, the deluge. You could land coach loads where you used to land cod, and make a Rye-style killing out of History and desolation. Even now there were plans to turn the Humber dock into a yacht marina. Perhaps... perhaps... Could Hull turn into the Lymington of the North, with riggers' shops as seafood restaurants, the chandlers as nautical boutiques? Clearly someone was hoping so.'

Now there *is* a marina, and The Fishing has as good as disappeared, but from talking to Linda, the magical tourist deluge has clearly yet to arrive. 'Before The Deep, Hull was short of a tourist attraction. Now Hull has a hook, a reason to come,' she said, adding pleadingly: 'People should come to Hull!'

We go to the top of the building, where there are sweeping estuary views, with the Humber Bridge in the distance. In the foreground weeds grow amid the foundations of old buildings in bulldozed plots of land; not looking particularly tourist-friendly (there are no tourists walking towards The Deep). This is known as Sammy's Point, on the site of a nineteenth-century shipyard run by Martin Samuelson, who built dozens of iron ships at a time when only Liverpool was growing at a faster rate than Hull. The aquarium is also on the site of defences built by Henry VIII. This was on the edge of the old walled city of Hull that first became important; gaining the name Kingston-upon-Hull (originally King's Town), when Edward I chose the location to launch campaigns against the Scots. For several centuries it was the second busiest port after London.

I gaze across the city. About 90 per cent of Hull's buildings were damaged or destroyed during World War Two bombing raids. This, I've learned, was on a par with damage caused by bombs in Coventry, which is more famous for its flattening as it was named at the time in the media, whereas Hull was only referred to as a 'north-east town' for national security reasons. Yet a surprisingly large part of Hull's Old Town survived including Holy Trinity Church, a splendid structure that is said to be the largest parish church in England. Up on the balcony, looking across the city, my head begins to feel much better, and I decide it's been a good couple of days in Hull. When I'd called the tourist office before coming, I'd been told that the city has a terrible time selling itself. A spokeswoman told me about a recent tourism campaign: 'We wanted to attract tourists from Derbyshire. But they didn't want to visit. So we offered "mystery tours".' These, she said, worked by selling a coach trip, with the customers boarding without knowing their destination. 'It was the only way we could sell Hull,' she admitted, sounding frustrated at how hard it is to convince the outside world of the delights of the city. 'People loved it... once they got over the mindset of "this is Hull".'

But I would recommend a visit – mystery tour or not. With a final couple of hours to kill before moving on, I take Linda's advice and join the Trans Pennine Way where it runs along the Humber next to old docks that are not far from the station. It is not the most auspicious neighbourhood, tucked away behind Kingston Retail Park, with its Carphone Warehouses and Sportsdirect.com buildings, along a road lined with crumbling brick walls, weeds, litter and a tiny blue sign that says: 'PUBLIC RIGHT OF WAY' next to graffiti that reads: 'RICHARD, DANNO, JAMIE'. So begins the couple of miles of paths along the Albert and William Wright Docks following the Humber.

It's a revelation. While the Trans Pennine Way, which was completed in 2001 with yet more Millennium Commission cash and runs for 207 miles from Southport on the Irish Sea to Hornsea on the North Sea passing Liverpool, the Pennines, Selby and Hull, is incredibly popular in places, very few people make it to the section at Hull's docks. I am on my own as I cross a small bridge next to a 'RABIES PREVENTION' sign and look across the dock, which seems to spread out forever, the size of a hundred football pitches or more. In this vast space, there are eight vessels, most looking rusty and forgotten, with a couple of tugs, a coastguard ship of some sort and a solitary fishing boat (the second-hand caravan export boom takes place elsewhere). A silvery sun shines on disused warehouse roofs by the brown, muddy estuary leading to the distant pencil-thin line of Lincolnshire's coast. I am literally the only person along the whole vast dock. This, I'm thinking as I look out across the empty water, is what Hull has been up against since the end of The Fishing: the almost total collapse of its major industry.

In the most unlikely of places (Hull's docks), I feel as though I have hit upon a winner. The trail is easy to access from the city, the free map I picked up from the tourist office in town informative and clear. But on my visit I get the sense that few people come to take advantage of the trail... they should. The walk is beautiful, without overwhelming me with signs explaining 'The Fishing's decline in Hull'. There aren't any, as they're not necessary: the decline is self-evident. Merely walking the trail and seeing for myself the huge empty dock brings home the enormity of what the old trawlers used to mean to the city. The setting is also wonderfully peaceful. As I stroll along this forgotten stretch of a usually overlooked part of the country I find it incredibly calming. Perhaps it's the sensation of imagining the bustle that once was here and comparing it to what I see before me. There is a smell of sea, salt and fish. Gulls are squawking. The sun is getting stronger

(I'm in danger of getting a tan in Hull). Then I pass a sign on a lock with a shopping trolley embedded in a bank of mud, and an old fence with graffiti that says: 'BRING BACK THE BIRCH.' That's the thing about Unsung Britain, I'm learning: it constantly throws you surprises.

Later, as I catch the train onwards, I consider how crazy, and just plain wrong, all these 'worst places to live' lists can be. Hull, despite its well-chronicled drawbacks, didn't feel like a 'worst place' to me. If you count friendly, interesting people and a city with character, a colourful, often-rebellious history, lots of great pubs, an enormous aquarium that could hold its own in Florida, jazzy new shopping malls near the docks, a strong association with one of Britain's favourite poets (a statue of whom, I later learn, is to be unveiled in Paragon station on the twenty-fifth anniversary of Larkin's death, showing that Hull does really love its 'hermit'), the hauntingly beautiful docks, the excellent Ferens art museum (free, and full of masterpieces), the lively Hull Truck Theatre (where I saw a sharp-witted play written by the resident director John Godber) and the salty sea-dog Maritime Museum (also free), as the 'first or second worst place' to live, something must have gone wrong in the calculations. I have enjoyed Hull, its sights and especially its people. I turned up a stranger, but I made many friends. I also enjoyed its sense of independence, its cut-off feeling of not caring what others think: the atmosphere that seems to have attracted Larkin.

My next (slightly random) stop-off is down south; all visits to Unsung Britain are a little random, I'm learning, it's the nature of the journey. It will be very different, I know… and it has a lot to live up to.

3

SLOUGH: 'WE MUST CELEBRATE THE TRADING ESTATE!'

To say I don't know what to expect in Slough is putting it mildly. Before coming, I'd called the council to ask about the town's attractions. An almost comically downbeat official had simply said: 'Slough is not really a tourist place right now.' There is no tourist office, she'd added, sounding as though she didn't want me to visit. After talking to the council official, I'd examined the *Rough Guide* and *Lonely Planet* guidebooks: neither mentioned Slough. But then I'd checked the council website. And there was hope. Under its 'About the Town' section, the site listed 'Slough's ten claims to fame'.

In number one spot was Sir William Herschel – the man who discovered the planet Uranus in 1781, and who lived in the town when he was the King's Astronomer. Next was the fact that Charles Dickens' 'unpublicised mistress' Nelly Ternan lived there, and Dickens visited frequently. Queen Victoria made her first ever train journey from Slough to Paddington in 1842. Cox's Orange Pippin apples were first grown in the borough. Britain's first black female mayor was appointed in the town in 1984. There is the 'largest trading estate in Europe in single ownership'. The Slough Ice Arena has been used by ice-skating stars including Olympic champions Jayne Torvill and Christopher Dean. And Mars bars have been made in Slough since 1932.

As I make the short train journey from Paddington into Slough on a bright, sunny Friday afternoon – a fortnight after Hull – I look out at leafy suburbs in the run up to my destination and wonder whether they were around when Queen Victoria made this trip. Maybe they were brand new then, or perhaps this was all countryside. Whatever it was like, it's not exactly exciting – no beautiful Humber Bridge and estuary on the outskirts of Slough. Just suburbia, followed by traffic-jammed roads and a few warehouses. I'm feeling a little doubtful about what lies ahead, but am also enjoying the sense of not knowing what Unsung Britain will deliver next. It just feels like an adventure: going to a place that seems so far removed from what you normally expect of a 'tourist destination'. What will Slough deliver, I'm wondering? I'm not totally sure. But it's a bright day and I've got a weekend to find out. Bring it on Slough, I'm thinking, as the train comes to a mysterious and lengthy halt next to a derelict lot, and I look over the list from the council website. New planets, illicit literary liaisons, famous train journeys, undiscovered apples and much-loved chocolate bars don't sound like a bad start at all. I realise I'm looking forward to my weekend… warts and all, whatever happens.

But then, of course, there is 'that poem', as the website described it. I feel reluctant to mention 'that poem' because apparently it's a terrible cliché to do so when writing about Slough. At least, that is the message coming from two articles by journalists who have lived in the town – which I'd discovered earlier, planning the trip. In *The Times,* Greg Hurst launched an attack in the paper's Thunderer column: 'Enough is enough. It is time someone took to the barricades to defend the most maligned town in Britain. It is time someone spoke up for Slough.' He describes the 1937 poem in question as a poisonous ode, and accuses those who are rude about the town of suffering from 'snobbery at its worst, cloaked in ignorance, taking pleasure in the lot of those less fortunate'.

Meanwhile in *The Guardian,* under the headline 'COME TO FRIENDLY SLOUGH', Michael Hann criticised the 'lazy stereotypes' about the Berkshire town that come from 'that poem'. Still staring out at the derelict lot (and still wondering why we're not moving), I read Hann's attack on those who use the famous verse as a way of writing off the place. They are, he says, usually 'snide London hacks who can't see beyond their Fairtrade Polynesian tofu yurts designed by Philippe Starck and think 120,000 residents living in a town they've never visited don't need to be treated like normal human beings'.

John Betjeman's poem 'Slough' – which I've also brought with me – begins: 'Come friendly bombs and fall on Slough / It isn't fit for humans now.' It continues: 'Come, bombs, and blow to smithereens / Those air-conditioned, bright canteens.' And goes on to mention: 'the mess they call a town', 'bogus-Tudor bars', 'wives [who] frizz out peroxide hair', 'boring dirty joke[s]', and 'a man with [a] double chin... who washes his repulsive skin'. Its effect, along with comments from the Queen Mother – 'wasn't it nice before Slough was here?' she once mused from nearby Windsor – has made Slough into a long-standing joke. Add to this the television programme *The Office*, which features the grim central roundabout, the depressing bus station and a dull office block, the name (literally meaning 'mire' or 'morass'), plus John Bunyan's 'Slough of Despond' in *The Pilgrim's Progress*, and Slough seems generally to have its work cut out for itself. Almost every time the town is mentioned in the press, as Slough has been often of late in reports on immigration ('COME TO SLOUGH, EVERYONE ELSE HAS' and 'PRIDE AND PREJUDICE OF SLOUGH, THE TOWN IN POLE POSITION'), the easy jokes are rehashed.

We arrive and I step out of the station to find myself facing a bland forecourt with a taxi rank, a series of pedestrian walkways leading towards warren-like shopping malls, and one of the largest Tescos I've ever laid eyes on. For a moment or two I feel genuinely at a loss. Am I really about to spend a whole weekend here? But at least I've got one appointment already set up: a visit to the Slough Trading Estate. I realise this may not exactly sound super-exciting. Slough Trading Estate may not be everyone's idea of a top tourist attraction. But it is in Slough. Members of the public, admittedly usually local students, can request guided tours.

It's a kind of trading estate tourism, and I walk along the A4 from the station – it's not too far but the sun is still shining – on my way to Slough's number one 'sight'. The estate, I've read, employs 17,000 people in more than 400 companies on a sprawling 486-acre site. In the 1960s before improved mechanisation, there were as many as 33,000 jobs here. The Slough Trading Estate is a key local employer, helping keep unemployment in the area below the national average of 7.9 per cent (as I write).

I turn off the A4, pass through a giant car park and find myself in a shiny lobby with leather sofas and tropical plants, where I'm met by Neil Impiazzi, the estate's sharp-suited leasing manager.

'Thanks for agreeing to show me round,' I say. 'I have to admit I never imagined I'd visit the Slough Trading Estate.'

Neil is quick to correct me. 'It is called Segro now,' he says.

'What do you mean?' I ask, a little confused.

'The estate recently changed its name to Segro. Foreigners can't really pronounce Slough – it doesn't translate well,' he explains.

'It wasn't because of the associations connected to Slough? Betjeman? Friendly bombs?' I ask.

'Absolutely not,' replies Neil, feigning annoyance at the suggestion, as he leads me to a bird's eye photograph of the estate on a wall by the reception.

Here he tells me about the estate's history. The story starts in 1920 when Sir Noel Mobbs, an entrepreneur, led a group of investors to buy a 600-acre site known as The Dump, where thousands of old World War One vehicles had been deposited. 'Mobbs acquired the site to recondition and sell off the vehicles,' says Neil. 'It was a very successful venture.' But once the vehicles were gone, he was left with 600 acres of land, close to London on the railway. With businesses short of capital to invest in property at the time, Mobbs decided to rent plots. So began the trading estate, which is considered the world's first. Soon Citroën, Gillette and Johnson & Johnson were on board, bucking the Depression, attracting migrant workers (many from Wales, some of whom walked across the country in their desperation for employment), and setting the wheels in motion for a long-running economic success story. The estate went from strength to strength. The output after World War Two was such that an on-site coal-fired power station was built to keep up with electricity demands.

Neil drives me round the grid-like streets pointing out the international firms: Ferrari, Maserati, LG (the Korean electronics company) and Dr Reddy's ('India's largest pharmaceutical firm').

'What it's like to live in Slough?' I ask.

'There are a lot worse places,' he says, sounding a touch huffy. He must get asked this a lot: I soon get the impression that the residents of Slough are very used to questions about the town. 'It is a good place to live. There are jobs. We've always said that the real reason people come to Slough is to do one thing: to make money.'

The trading estate certainly appears to be doing that. As well as O2's British headquarters and the huge Mars factory (where I asked in advance to be shown round, but was told 'we don't do tours'), there are smaller companies selling model railway trains, while another offers security shutters for garages. We pass the offices of 'Rollover: the best hotdog in the world' (who would have thought Slough could claim to be home to that?), a software company, a firm that makes the moving adverts at football matches, and the power station that generates electricity to keep everything going. Lorries and vans slide by. Workers walk to fetch lunches. The sweet smell of chocolate wafts across from the giant Mars bar factory. As I look around, it suddenly strikes me as unusual to see all this evidence of industry and things actually being made: the world's best hotdogs, Maseratis, model railway trains, Mars bars. There's a feeling of bustle, of productivity, of entrepreneurship, of action – I could imagine this bit of Slough being somewhere in the United States, the outskirts of Houston or Atlanta, perhaps. It feels invigorating and switched on in a way that I just hadn't expected in Slough (I admit, I must have had negative preconceptions). A delivery vehicle passes on the way to the shiny LG headquarters, as a woman listening to an iPod jogs past, looking as though she's on an office break. If everywhere was as industrious and up for it as the Slough Trading Estate seems to be, I'm suddenly thinking, Britain would surely be booming. In fact, it really doesn't feel like Britain at all here. It just seems too well run and successful for that.

Then we reach the estate's best-known building. Apparently tourists often come to take pictures of Crossover House, the uninspiring block that features in the credits for *The Office* – home of Wernham Hogg, run by David Brent, the hapless, harassed, but highly amusing stationery-supply office manager played by Ricky Gervais. Slough does, it appears, get a few holidaymakers no matter what the council official says.

I hop out in a car park and find myself outside a mini-supermarket talking to Ben, a twenty-eight-year-old project co-ordinator at a telecommunications company. He has a matter-of-fact style that reminds me of Tim Canterbury, the downtrodden sales rep from *The Office*. I ask if he sees many tourists.

'From time to time,' he says, at first sounding a little downtrodden himself. 'They stand on the corner trying to get the right angle for their pictures.' He points to the spot.

'So do you think the programme's portrayal of the town is fair?'

'I think it's probably quite good for Slough,' he says, suddenly sounding brighter about things. 'It creates a point of interest. It's an amusing programme, a mockumentary, a mick take. I like it.'

A couple of slightly shifty looking figures are lurking by a fire exit to Crossover House. On closer inspection I see they're eating sausage rolls and drinking bottles of Coke; dressed in hooded tops and trainers.

'Are you tourists?' I ask, extremely doubtfully (it would be nice to find a real live Slough tourist, but my hopes aren't set too high).

They are not. 'I work here,' says Kathleen, pointing to the building from the TV show. She is employed in customer services for a furniture company, and is clearly incredulous that I've come to see the estate.

'I'm currently unemployed,' says her friend Stephen, aged eighteen, who seems a bit sullen. 'I wouldn't mind a job in mechanics or security though,' he says, as though I might be able to help.

They find my presence peculiar, but are happy to answer questions. 'What do you think of *The Office*?' I ask, expecting them to object to the programme.

Quite the opposite. Sounding like a television critic, Stephen perks up and replies: '*The Office* is a good programme. The script is funny. It's good as it shows us a part of Slough that other people do not get to see. All publicity is good publicity.'

He pauses and considers what he's just said. Then he qualifies it: 'Actually, all publicity is good publicity – as long as it doesn't involve the police.' As he says this, he gives me a look.

I go back to the car, and Neil drives me to the front entrance by the A4. I've enjoyed my tour. Not long after leaving home, I've learned for myself about the trading estate that seems to symbolise the town that Betjeman made so famous: the source of so many of the jokes and fuss. Without quite realising it was happening, I've become a trading estate tourist in Berkshire, and discovered a little pocket of Britain where things appear to be going very well indeed.

I'm on holiday, having fun, Slough-style.

From the trading estate, I catch a cab. I'm about to see my second Slough tourist sight in quick succession. And it's a world-famous attraction. While the compilers of lists of the top English poems sometimes overlook Hull's Larkin, Thomas Gray (1716–1771) is almost always there with 'Elegy in a Country Churchyard'. It's littered with phrases that have passed into common usage: 'far from the madding crowd', 'paths of glory' and 'kindred spirit' being among the best known. But rather than make a big deal about this, the council fails to mention Gray in its claims to fame. This is because the church that inspired the poem is in the village of Stoke Poges, effectively a suburb of Slough, but just outside the town boundary.

I show a taxi driver the church on my map. The driver says nothing. He glances at the map and, before I've fastened my seat belt, puts his foot down. Soon we're tearing along and I'm wondering: what's the rush? Then the driver demands: 'What is the name of the church?' I explain that it's the one I've just shown on the map – there's none other close by. 'Where? Which one?' he demands, sounding aggressive. I point to the map again. 'Yes, but what is its name?' he barks. 'The one on Church Lane,' I say. 'There are many Church Lanes,' he says dismissively. I show the map once more. 'Where? Where is this?' he grunts. It's as though he just won't accept the map. He looks angrily at me.

'Are you having a bad day?' I ask, beginning to get fed up. What have I done to upset him?

'I'm having a very good day, thank you,' he replies, sounding sarcastic. We drive on. Then he stops on a street with nothing in sight. The church can't be far from here, so I say I'll walk. He abruptly says: 'Oh I know the church. I know this place very well.' Then he speeds round a corner towards the entrance, as though I should have told him it was this church to start with. We shudder to a halt. I hand him £5, which he says is the fare (though the meter isn't on). He grabs the note, doesn't say a word, and accelerates away. I watch as the car disappears down the hill, feeling completely at a loss.

The entrance to Stoke Poges Church is through a neat wooden archway surrounded by ivy bushes with bright orange berries. Next to this is a faded poster warning drivers not to leave valuables in cars. There's birdsong, and no one else is about. The trading estate feels a very long way away. I step through the archway and walk along a flagstone path... and suddenly there is calm (inexplicably irate taxi drivers totally forgotten). In 1750 Gray finally completed his masterpiece. He had begun 'Elegy' eight years earlier after the death of a childhood friend, which had moved him to put his feelings down on paper. But he was famously neither a fast nor a prolific writer: his entire lifetime output was about a thousand lines.

'Elegy in a Country Churchyard' was an immediate hit, helped initially by publicity from his old school friend Horace Walpole, son of Britain's first prime minister, Sir Robert Walpole. Another reason for its success was its common touch: the way Gray used the churchyard setting at Stoke Poges to meditate on everyday lives. 'Some mute inglorious Milton here may rest, / Some Cromwell guiltless of his country's blood': in other words, some person of potential note or notoriety who led a quiet countryside existence. Re-reading it before coming, I'd liked the way that 'Elegy' seemed to speak on behalf of the unspoken – it felt that the poem somehow fitted in neatly with the whole nature of my offbeat trip.

It's approaching dusk, just as it is in the poem's first few lines: 'The curfew tolls the knell of parting day...' A drizzle is falling on the rows of headstones. There are rhododendron bushes, pink roses and a leaf-scattered lawn. The pretty church is made of red bricks and flint stones. There is something very special about the place: being in a churchyard that cannot have changed all that much in appearance since Gray looked around (despite all the bustle of modern life not so far away). I spend a few moments just soaking in the calm and imagining the poet sitting somewhere here thinking about things. At the front of the building I find Gray's mottled tomb, which stands by a plaque saying that he was buried on 6 August 1771. He died of an attack of gout in Cambridge, but had asked to be placed alongside his mother in Stoke Poges. The setting by the tomb is indeed 'far from the madding crowd's ignoble strife'. And light is really fading now, just as it does in the poem:

'Now fades the glimmering landscape on the sight,
And all the air a solemn stillness holds,
Save where the beetle wheels his droning flight,
And drowsy tinklings lull the distant folds...'

There are no droning beetles now, just the occasional drone of traffic from somewhere not so far away. From the edge of the churchyard, I look down the hill to Slough. Above a line of trees, I can just catch the cooling tower of the power plant on the trading estate, where 400 companies and 17,000 employees are still hard at work. Today's 'Elegy' would have to take in a Mars bar factory and Rollover Hotdogs... these days the madding crowds are moving slowly in. Yet Gray's churchyard still feels like a magical, secretive place.

A bit like my digs for the weekend (though in a very different way). Slough, I'm quickly discovering, is full of secrets. After my contemplative time at the Stoke Poges church, I make my way by taxi to a guest house that's more like 'somebody's house' in Langley, a suburb full of detached properties surrounded by hedges on the east of Slough. It costs £30 a night and it's called Wit's End.

Yes, I'm in Slough and I'm at my Wit's End.

Not many people stay here. Wit's End is run by a large, jovial woman named Marion. She initially tried to put me off when I called. 'We're in the middle of decorations,' she said in a nasal voice. 'There's nowhere to spare.' Are you absolutely sure, I'd asked? I really wanted to stay at Wit's End – this was my one and only chance. Marion had sounded hesitant. 'We've got relatives round, you see,' she continued unconvincingly.

Then she relented: 'Yes, I suppose we could squeeze you in.' And later Marion told me, when I arrived and discovered there were no decorations in progress, no relatives and no other guests, just her and her son Tim, a thirty-eight-year-old who worked at a local railway station: 'We've virtually given up on taking guests, to be honest.'

Wit's End is a bungalow on a side street. It has a gravel drive and two rooms for guests: a double and a single. There's a living room with a television (often on, usually loudly), a gas fireplace decorated in 'rustic style with Dorset stone' (so says Marion), two red leather armchairs and a collection of porcelain pixies on a shelf. A large black cat with owl-like eyes sits on the kitchen table overseeing proceedings most of the time. Marion explains that the guest house name came from when she and her late husband were painstakingly doing up the rooms. We have cups of tea, and soon she's telling me about one of her last guests; she does not seem to have had many. He was a 'disaster', she says. He had taken my room, a single with a door that doesn't quite shut properly. 'It was a disgusting mess. Disgusting,' she says, sounding disgusted.

'What was?'

'His room. We've had to redecorate it since. He stayed for six months. There were potions and lotions all over the place. He used to shave his legs in the bathroom. He was obsessed with himself. Obsessed with his potions and lotions.'

She sighs loudly. 'He'd forget his keys and start banging on windows in the dead of night.' She sighs again.

'I won't mess about with potions and lotions, or shave my legs,' I assure her.

Marion sighs a big sigh… and keeps on going. 'He fell behind with the rent. When he finally left, the bills started arriving. Fines. Bills for hiring a dance studio. He disappeared without a word. He was a complete nutcase.' She pauses for breath, and says: 'If I'd had a machine gun I would have shot him.'

I get the feeling that Marion really did not like the guy.

Then Tim arrives. He leaps into the spare armchair, hangs a leg over one of the arms, sips on a pint of Rebellion ale, brewed in nearby Marlow ('Excellent stuff, excellent,' says Tim), and begins to tell me about Slough.

'There's nothing to see, nothing,' he says bluntly, staring at me.

'Don't be silly, Timothy,' Marion intervenes. Tim is momentarily distracted. He sips his Rebellion again.

'There's some good shopping. The Queensmere and Observatory malls near the station.' After a pause he adds, 'Oh yes, and you can see Wembley Stadium.'

'What do you mean?' I ask, confused.

'You can see Wembley Stadium,' he replies.

'Sorry, I don't understand,' I say.

'You can see Wembley Stadium,' he repeats, somewhat annoyingly – while I just look at him.

'Timothy! He's not from round here!' says Marion.

'OK, sorry,' Tim relents. 'The old Wembley Stadium. The rubble. It's in Upton Court Park. It's been used to level the ground. Apparently there's some nuclear canister or something under there as well.'

'Timothy!' warns Marion. And he says quickly: 'But that's just gossip.'

Soon Tim, who's wearing a white T-shirt and jeans, and resting his Rebellion on his belly, is telling me about his plans. 'Ideally I'd like to move to Prague. I like it out there,' he says. 'I'm not sure if I'd live there full-time. Maybe if I met a nice Czech girl. It would be an investment though – I'd buy property. I've got friends out there. There are still some decent prices.' He used to go out with a Slovak woman who worked in Slough. 'It all went badly wrong. It's a shame really. She's married now.' He recently sold his flat in Chalvey, a part of Slough near the M4, and moved back to the family home. He later tells me, over another Rebellion, that: 'I made a tidy profit on Chalvey. Tidy. I could go down the road and buy a Porsche.' Though he admits: 'It's not an ideal situation living at home aged thirty-eight: but it's temporary, you know. It's not that bad.' We talk about the royals. Slough is a five-minute train to Windsor and even closer to Eton, where Princes William and Harry studied. 'I've seen Harry at Slough station. I've met Queeny a couple of times, and the other half, what's his name? Philip. And I've seen Charlie.' Tim used to carry the royal luggage. 'You'd get a crisp ten-pound note for that. Yes, I've had the odd tenner for carrying the Queen's luggage. Do you know how you can tell the Queen has arrived?'

'Paparazzi?' I suggest tentatively.

'No, no, no!' Tim says. He likes teasing questions. 'Unplated Rolls-Royce – that's how. No road tax. No number plate. The only car in the country like that: the only one that's legal anyway.'

Marion has lots of local royal stories, and remembers Harry and William at Eton. 'I used to see them quite often in the streets with friends, or you could watch them playing games

– no problem,' she says. 'Not recently, but I've seen the Queen at polo and in coach and horses at Windsor park. I've seen Andrew cycling round. Zara on horseback.' Royals rolling by on bikes and trotting casually past on horses: yet another reason, for some people, to visit Slough!

After our chat, I settle down in my tiny bedroom and call home to say hello to Anne and describe my new digs. 'It sounds lovely,' she comments wryly, not offering to come and join me. I try to convince her that poking about in Slough is fun, that I'm finding out about things: trading estates, *The Office*, Thomas Gray, the remains of the old Wembley Stadium, the Queen's unplated Rolls-Royce. 'It sounds lovely,' she repeats, and then there's a muffled noise down the line, which sounds distinctly as though she's hiding laughter. 'Are you laughing?' I ask, to which more muffled noises echo on my mobile – our last two trips have been to the slightly more glamorous Seychelles and the wilds of the Masai Mara game reserve in Kenya. Both were dream breaks that we'd planned for months. 'I've got to go now,' she says, amid muffles. 'Hope you have a good time…' Muffle, muffle. '… in Wit's End.' Muffle, muffle, muffle.

Yes very funny, I'm thinking, as I take a look around my bedroom. It's full of piles of magazines with Princess Diana and other royals on the covers. There's barely enough room for the single bed, and there's a little sink not much bigger than a dining plate by a mirror in a corner. The door to my room, which doesn't have a lock, does not quite shut properly. I shove my shoes against it so there's no gap into the hallway to let in the cat. Then I pick up one of the magazines. It's devoted to the late Queen Mother and is full of God-bless-her editorials and pictures of her unveiling plaques. Sure, she may have been rude about Slough when looking down from Windsor Castle, but all is clearly forgiven in Wit's End. Just as I found at the cheap and very cheerful Clyde House Hotel back in Hull, I like it here. Marion and Tim could not have been more welcoming. I drift off to sleep, listening to the faint sound of a game show on the living room TV.

Tim's talk about Chalvey got me thinking. In the morning, in my tiny room, I begin reading through articles I'd printed out about the town back home and I'm amazed by the number of stories about its immigration problems. Chalvey, a neighbourhood to the south-west of the town centre, is usually mentioned as being where many of the immigrants live. 'Slough is threatening to become a nightmarish model for mass immigration,' roars the *Daily Express*, quoting locals who describe gypsies urinating in the streets, and a local PC who says they are 'society's worst nightmare' and 'a plague to their own countrymen'. Meanwhile the *Daily Mail*, under the headline 'TRUE COST OF IMMIGRATION' says that as many as twenty Romanians live in some houses: 'Some sleep on kitchen worktops, others in garden sheds.' There have been at least 10,000 Polish incomers in Slough since 2004, the paper adds.

It is hard to ignore all the controversy. So even though this is not a tourist part of Slough – and without wanting to talk down the town – this is how I find myself walking along a dreary street towards Chalvey. My curiosity, for better or for worse, has drawn me here. It's a cold, grey morning. A brisk wind is blowing across the M4, with clouds scudding towards London. Planes from Heathrow soar noisily above, carrying holidaymakers off to sunny climes (well away from Slough). Derelict houses with broken windows and tattered curtains, others covered in metal grills, line the street. There's an Adult Centre with smoked-glass windows. A pub with a St George's Cross advertises: 'LATE NIGHT HERE FRIDAY AND SATURDAY: FOSTERS.' This is absolutely, definitely not holidaymaker territory. What on earth am I doing walking along here, I wonder? But I keep on going, passing a police station and a skinhead wearing a tracksuit. A pyramid of silver cider cans is standing next to an old sofa in a disused garage lot. Beyond – tucked behind a large blue metal crate – is a filthy caravan. I knock on the door to see if one of the Roma families lives here. There's silence. The caravan's curtains are drawn. I detect a very faint movement. Then nothing.

Further on, I meet Alma, forty-three, from Lithuania, who is standing in the small front garden of a terraced house. She's wearing a denim jacket and jeans, has blonde hair with highlights, and bright blue eyes.

After she gives me directions, I ask: 'What's the best thing about Slough?'

'I find a good job – that is best,' she replies.

'What do you do?'

'I do housekeeping at hotel.'

'Do you like the area?'

She pauses for a moment. 'This is not England,' she says, echoing the thoughts I had about the trading estate, but with a different meaning. 'It is Poland and Muslim. It does not feel like England here.'

Further on, outside a shop selling Polish sausages and beers as well as a wonderful array of spices, chapatti flour, curries, lentils and vast packets of rice, I fall into conversation with Przemek and Ola, after asking them for directions, too. They are in their twenties and from Glogow in Poland. Przemek says he has worked as a chef, a builder, and 'lots of jobs, so many jobs, from an agency'. He is tall and upright with a short back and sides. Ola is wearing a leather jacket and jeans. They've been in Slough three years. 'It is not too bad here,' says Przemek. 'I like it that you can buy many Polish articles.' He's referring to the Polish food in the shop. 'There are so many Poles in Slough. Official figures say there are about one-point-two million in Britain. The Home Office is wrong,' says Przemek, when I ask how many Poles he thinks are in the UK. 'It is more like three million.'

I keep on walking, wondering who I'll bump into next. There seem to be so many different nationalities in Slough. The council estimates that 37 per cent of the population is BME, black and minority ethnic, the highest mix outside London. Down a side street there's a cheap second-hand car dealer, a pub with a sign saying '25 AND OVER, NO OVERALLS, SOILED CLOTHES OR SHOES', and Chalvey Working Men's and Social Club. Close by, a dozen children are playing in the middle of the street: tiny kids on plastic tricycles and older kids on bikes. I walk towards them: is this one of Slough's Roma families? It is. The children crowd round and follow me along brightly saying things like: 'No understand mister... what want mister... problem mister?' A large woman with gap-teeth comes out of a council terrace, another woman in a headscarf stands in the entrance next

59

door. Lace curtains in both houses are pushed aside. Lots of faces peer down.

'The manager is not home,' says a grinning boy. The large woman says: 'No understand,' when I enquire whether anyone speaks English. On her instruction, the children scamper inside. 'What the problem, what the problem?' she asks. I say: 'No problem, no problem,' not wanting to frighten her. I walk back up the path, past a wheelie bin overflowing with rubbish. Then as I move away, a woman in a brown skirt rushes up. 'The boss has gone to Tesca,' she declares, flashing gold teeth at me. A tiny child dressed in green clings to her leg.

'Tesca?' I ask.

'Yes Tesca! Tesca! Get food!' She points at the rubbish and says: 'When go? Problem!' I try to explain I don't work for the council. She begins to berate me in Romany – so I walk away. By the time I reach the end of the street, they're all out playing again. A couple of the older boys are keeping watch on me.

My detour through Chalvey has certainly been an eye-opener (just what I want Unsung Britain to be), but now I'm keen to get back to the task in hand. I turn and venture back into 'holiday-land' Slough.

The centre of the town, a short walk away, is small, shaped like an anvil squashed between four main roads. It's dominated by two shopping malls. These run on to a high street that seems to be an advert for successful multicultural Britain: Eastern Europeans, Asians and Africans mixing together in a buzzing atmosphere. There are market stalls, shops offering wigs and hair extensions, £1-a-slice pizza outlets and agencies where you can send money abroad.

Slough Museum stands at the end of the high street, housed in a 1960s block that used to be a carpet shop. Before the trading estate became so important, brick-making was the big local trade, a display says. Apparently '2,469,000 bricks went towards the construction of Eton College by 1551'. Another local industry involved large nurseries producing fruits, roses and herbs. A big nursery in Langley was owned by Sir Harry Veitch, founder of the Chelsea Flower Show. I talk to Nadia, the twenty-something curator, who shows me about.

'So do many tourists come to look around?' I ask.

'We get a few,' she says, hesitantly. After some thought, she adds: 'A lady from the Netherlands phoned to ask about her granddad the other day.'

There's a big section on William Herschel, who discovered Uranus and lived in Slough from 1782 to 1822. Herschel initially called his new planet, the first to be detected beyond those visible with the naked eye, George's Star, in honour of George III, but this upset the French and it was eventually renamed. He was born in Germany – he was originally named Wilhelm – but came to the UK aged nineteen, I learn. And he was a man of many talents: writing symphonies and concertos, playing the oboe and the harpsichord, naming several moons and discovering infrared radiation.

'I notice there is no sign of a certain Betjeman poem,' I say.

'Yeah, that poem,' she replies. 'BBC Berkshire called to ask me about that the other day. Maybe people laugh too much for us to be tongue-in-cheek about it.'

Fiona MacTaggart, MP, has more to say about the poem. She's come to speak at the museum's AGM, which just happens to be on the afternoon I arrive. A group of dignitaries including the mayor is crammed into a side-room with fluorescent strip-lighting. 'Everyone in the world seems to patronise Slough,' says MacTaggart, who has been the local MP since 1997. 'My fellow MPs ask: "How's Sluff?" Then there are all the old jokes about bombs and going down to *The Office*. One of the ways to deal with people who "diss" us is to talk about our heritage. This is a serious place with a serious role in history. Stagecoaches stopped here. We've had the first black mayor in Britain. We've got the trading estate. We should celebrate the trading estate! It's still the biggest trading estate in single ownership!' She pauses for a moment. 'If Betjeman's horrible poem about bombs dropping on Slough happened, there would be no trading estate,' she continues. 'When people say nasty things about Slough, I say "Do you know we've got four grade one-listed buildings?"' I've seen these dotted about the city centre, looking almost out of place amid all the modern shopping centres and offices. MacTaggart pauses, then adds with aplomb: 'I say that Slough should aim for the stars!'

Upon this, there's a burst of applause. Then a man holding a drum and wearing an African headdress goes to the front of the room. It is Black History Month and the man, a Zimbabwean, is singing a song in honour of this. He begins beating the drum and closes his eyes as though he's being transported. He sings: 'I don't know about this world. There's so much going on. It's all mixed up. Whoah. Whoah. Whoah.' The lyrics may not quite be in Bob Dylan's league, but the tune is good and the song goes down well. Afterwards, slices of pink cake are handed out. I have a moment with MacTaggart, and she tells me she's upset about the council's reaction to Polish immigration. 'The council acts as though it is a bit helpless: "Oh, oh, oh, there are so many Polish people." But we've got a long-standing Polish community here. [Many of whom fought for the Allies in World War Two]. Polish workers have been a huge shot in the arm for us for a long time. And that's a good thing.'

We finish our pink cake. Then I go round the corner to a ninety-nine pence shop: 'Quality Products Under a Pound'. This is one of the busiest high street shops – and it hides yet another Slough secret. It is also almost exactly where Charles Dickens, whose marriage had already failed, took clandestine lodgings with his mistress in 1867. It is believed he stayed at Elizabeth Cottage, which burnt down long ago, for several months with Ellen 'Nelly' Ternan. This actress was eighteen when they first met in the 1850s, the same age as his daughter. He was aged forty-five.

There is nothing in the museum about the affair. But at the local library, a book by Felix Aylmer entitled *Dickens Incognito*, published in 1959, sheds some light on the meetings – which is how I found the location of Elizabeth Cottage. In *Dickens Incognito* Aylmer describes stumbling across Dickens's pocket diary for 1867 at a public library in New York. Dickens had lost the diary during a reading tour. When Aylmer saw it, only a handful of American scholars had previously laid eyes on the small book.

They had all missed something. The diary contained one-line entries using initials that described Dickens's strange movements that year – including a series of journeys from 'P' and 'W' to 'Sl' and 'W'; trips to 'Off' and 'G. H.', with regular meetings with 'N', and an 'Arrival' on 13 April. Aylmer makes a convincing case that Dickens lived with Nelly in Slough, and that she may have given birth to an illegitimate son while she was here. Aylmer recognised 'Sl' as Slough, 'P' as Paddington, 'W' as either Waterloo or Windsor, 'Off' as office, 'G. H.' as his family home in Gad's Hill in Kent, and 'N' as Nelly. 'Arrival' was, possibly, the arrival of a child. Aylmer had looked through council records and discovered that Dickens used an alias in Slough – Charles Tringham. It was possible that he chose this name so that a false birth certificate could be acquired to allow a baby to be adopted. A search of birth and marriage records backed up this story. Details also showed that Dickens tended to catch trains *in* to Slough station, and *out* of Windsor, thus avoiding recognition at the station near his secret home.

Not many ninety-nine pence stores hide stories like that. Inside it's jam-packed with people buying toothbrushes, 'adult novelty slippers', raincoats for dogs, energy-saving light bulbs, tool boxes and bags of jellybeans. A whole new curiosity shop... on the site of the man who dreamed up the old one.

There's lots to discover in Slough, after all. I take in the labyrinthine shopping malls – which apparently attract visitors from miles around – and find myself buying an evening ticket to a Bollywood film called *Saawariya*. There are several Bollywood options, and I've never watched one before. The film turns out to be so long there is an interval, and the plot is about a man who falls in love with a woman who does not want him. He tries singing and dancing, but still she is not interested. In the end it begins snowing in India, and the man decides to shadow-box his unhappiness away. 'Life is a boxing ring. Unhappiness is your opponent,' he declares, jabbing in the air. And with that motto ringing in my ears, I return to my Wit's End.

After a good night's sleep, I head off to my final appointment, just on the other side of the M4, a short walk away in Eton.

It doesn't take long to go from most-definitely-not-posh Slough to perhaps the epitome of posh. I pass Slough Baptist Church, a new home sales centre and a McDonald's, before strolling under the motorway and finding myself in the flat expanse of the playing fields of Eton. They almost come as a shock to the system after the busy town centre in Slough. So this is where Waterloo was won (in theory at least)! There's a cricket pavilion to one side and I try to imagine the likes of Prince William, Prince Harry and David Cameron chasing cricket balls about here (not so far away from Chalvey). Then I reach the centre of Eton, where I enter a courtyard next to a large chapel. Dozens of folders and books with titles like *The History of the Peloponnesian Way* are strewn under an awning. A group of pupils rushes out in the distinctive black and white Eton College uniforms, starched white collars standing up smartly. They gather their books and disappear to classes. At the centre of the courtyard there's a statue of Henry VI, who founded Eton in 1440. Beyond is another courtyard. I go up some steps and along a blue corridor hung with pictures of Old Etonians including Thomas Gray and Percy Bysshe Shelley, and enter the headmaster's office – feeling as though I've done something wrong.

Before corporal punishment was phased out in the 1970s, students might well have felt frightened entering this office. But I'm offered coffee by a smiling secretary and led to Anthony Little, the headmaster. Little has a grey moustache, glasses, and a manner that suggests he's weighing up the evidence you present. Behind his desk, a rowing oar is propped on a bookcase. From the windows you can see Gray's 'silver-winding' Thames. I've arranged to meet him because it feels as though Slough and Eton are so close (yet so different). I'm simply interested in the contrast between the two. I can't think of two neighbouring places anywhere else in the country that have such starkly differing reputations.

'Does Eton look down its nose as its neighbour? What does Eton really think of Slough?' I ask.

'It's hugely varied,' Little replies smoothly, sounding like a politician. 'It depends who you ask. I think it's an extraordinary place. It has its dark side. And there is some element of threat about it.'

'What do you mean by that?'

'Drug-selling on the streets, all that kind of thing. I mean that's all over the place, but it's sometimes more marked in Slough than it is in other areas.'

'Do you discourage pupils from visiting then?'

'They can go where they want,' Little says reservedly. 'They can go to the cinema with a group of people. An awful lot go to Slough simply to get the train. It's a town like any other. In the daytime it's pretty much fine.'

'Do you give pupils advice on how to avoid drug dealers?' I ask – realising it feels as though I'm asking Eton's headmaster twenty questions.

'No less or more than I would anywhere else. A lot of these boys live in London. But these are canny young people. They've not been swathed in cotton wool.'

Eton has 1,300 pupils aged between thirteen and eighteen, of whom about 20 per cent receive scholarships of some sort. There are 160 masters. The annual fee is, as Little admits, astronomical, at £26,000. This is more than the average wage for a full-time employee in the UK: £23,746. We talk about the uniforms, which Little says act as a disguise for even the most famous pupils. Prince Harry used to walk unnoticed past tourists taking pictures of other students, he says.

'But is all of this fair? Is spending £26,000 a year to give your kid an advantage in life right? In some parts of Slough that would seem like madness.'

His reply goes like this: (1) British independent schools are the best of their kind in the world; (2) to get rid of them would be dumbing down, and that would affect the quality of all schools, both private and state-run; (3) is this dumbing down worth it for the sake of 'achieving egalitarianism, one version of fairness?'; (4) he thinks not. Little admits: 'Eton is still of course a privileged environment. It's privileged for the people who can afford to pay it and it is privileged for people who are given scholarships.' Then, reflecting on the proximity to its less privileged neighbour, he says: 'But I think Eton benefits hugely from being a mile up the road from Slough.' In what way? He pauses for a moment, then replies carefully: 'Because it's a context. It's "the world". You know, one of the things that most surprises people when they visit Eton is that there's no gate. There's no wall. There's no security check as you come in. We're in public streets, in walking distance from Slough.'

Outside, students in starched collars are making their way to their next lessons. I stand by the statue of Henry VI, thinking how very unusual it seems that this world is so close to Slough's world. Then I check out a little museum with pictures of former pupils including George Orwell, Ian Fleming and Wilfred

Thesiger, take in pretty cloisters and the courtyard where the famous racing scene from *Chariots of Fire* was really filmed (not in Cambridge), and look at the elegant interior of the chapel, where a flag hangs that was retrieved from no-man's-land during World War One by an Eton boy who was later killed – there are organised tours of the grounds that are open to the public. I stroll along Eton's charming high street to the small bridge separating Eton from Windsor, with Slough now well behind me. Swans paddle by. The sun comes out. Students stroll past. As I walk towards the train station in Windsor I'm thinking how, despite the jokes and the headlines, I've had an interesting time in Slough, with my unusual trading estate tour, the wonderful hideaway of Gray's church, the peculiar but cosy Wit's End, the story of Charles Dickens' lover, the amazing melting pot of nationalities, the quirky museum, and just the sense I kept on getting of: whatever next? What secrets were waiting round the corner? I've been to my wit's end, literally, and I've come back in one piece. I've also enjoyed the sense of being in a bustling town full of industry, where people clearly take pride in their work and where a wide range of people with different backgrounds seem to get on – often against the odds (and against what the papers say). I've had an admittedly odd, but rewarding, time.

Next I'll be heading for somewhere that even people back in Hull were rude about.

4

SALFORD: 'THE REAL CORONATION STREET'

The train north slides out of Euston on time. We're on Virgin Trains in an almost empty first-class carriage on a Saturday afternoon in early November. 'We' consists of me and Anne. Yes, I've persuaded her to venture into Unsung Britain. It hadn't been easy. 'But isn't Salford just like Slough, except it's up north?' she'd said. 'Are you going to visit trading estates and neighbourhoods known for their immigration problems?'

I assured her not. 'Slough was a one-off,' I say, explaining that I enjoyed it, but that Salford would be totally different. 'It even has a tourism strategy. Salford *wants* tourists to visit. There's lots to see and do: the tourist people have sent me brochures about the attractions.'

'Are you sure? We're not staying at Wit's End are we?'

I assured her not, again. 'Wit's End was very definitely a one-off. I've found somewhere a bit grander this time...'

Anne gave me a look that seemed to say: 'I'll be the judge of that.'

Selling Unsung Britain to the unconverted (i.e. my girlfriend) can be tough at times, I'm finding.

The weather at the start of the trip isn't exactly helping. It is a grey, drizzly day. Multicoloured graffiti on blackened walls announces that 'PSYCHO' and 'LORD' have recently passed this way too. Through a grimy window we can see the backs of tall terraced houses that look squeezed together like books on a shelf. Washing hangs limply in the damp air. Pigeons flutter on rooftops amid rusty satellite dishes. The sky darkens. It begins to rain heavily.

All in all, it's quite a depressing setting. So it feels good to be moving on, moving up the country in our first-class carriage. We've upgraded for £15, and are pretty pleased with the results. We've virtually got the place to ourselves. There's a couple at the far end of the carriage talking quietly, a charming steward who pushes a trolley past every now and then offering free packets of crisps, shortbread and cups of tea and coffee. It's not bad at all. We spread out the papers and take a look at the day's headlines. Politicians have been caught claiming for perks on fancy overseas trips – why couldn't they just take a break back at home, go for a weekend in Salford like us? With London behind us, our mood lifts as the 'PSYCHO' and 'LORD' graffiti is left behind and rolling green countryside emerges. It feels nice to be racing through the Midlands and feeling that we are escaping the usual tourist crowds and doing something that so few people might consider. The carriage is so empty that it's almost as though the train has been laid on just for us: take us to Salford, Richard Branson!

And it's pleasing to see the landscape flash past and get the feeling of covering the country – there goes Rugby, then Nuneaton, then Stoke. Yet more Unsung Britain (unsung to me at least) that's out there just waiting to be discovered. I go to find the steward to fetch more coffee. He's relaxed in a seat in an adjoining carriage that's totally empty, reading a copy of the *Express*. 'No problem mate, no problem,' he says. 'I'll bring them to you.' And he does. It's like we've got our own butler and our own carriage… quite a bizarre set-up after slumming it into and around Slough.

We pass a big red-brick former rubber works and arrive on time at Manchester's Piccadilly station, where a hen party of women with fake tans, mini-skirts and knee-high white socks is waiting on the platform to go south. We walk through a big airy modern station and go down an escalator to a taxi rank. There is no queue and soon we are passing adverts for L'Oréal shampoo and Lexus cars, an 'American Golf' shop, a 'Euro Adult Video' outlet and a Travelodge, before crossing a short bridge into Salford. We drop our bags at our hotel after the ten-minute ride: Salford and Manchester seem almost to merge into each other. Then we jump in another cab and head along a street that does not quite feel as well-to-do as the ones through Manchester into Salford. There are boarded-up buildings, a large advert for the Conservative Party on which someone has painted a Hitler moustache on David Cameron's face and added the message '****ER', and empty lots that look as though they are waiting for developments to come along in better economic times.

This is how we find ourselves in the courtyard at the back of the Crescent pub in Salford, not far from a peaceful bend in the river Irwell – where we have a rendezvous. But first we take in the surroundings. There are sunshades and neat wooden garden tables. Pink flowers peek out of pots with bamboo-stick candle holders. Bright retro adverts for old cigarette companies – Kool, Mild Menthol, Cork Tipped – are on the walls of the yard. And there's a party atmosphere. A slightly staggering middle-aged woman wearing a gold chain has just asked me to dance, making Anne laugh. A jolly, younger couple has spotted my professional-looking camera and wants me to take their picture. They pose beneath an advert for Zippo lighters, grinning broadly. 'Thanks mate: get our good sides,' they say, and then come to inspect the result on the digital display. They turn out to be performance artists who have just finished a show in a new arts centre on the site of Islington Mill, not far from here.

'I deep-fried my socks in batter in my last show,' says Fliss, who has dark hair and bright red lipstick. 'People liked that.'

She smiles as though deep-frying socks is quite a normal way of conducting oneself in these parts. 'I've also waxed my legs with gaffer tape,' she adds, grimacing.

'That must have hurt,' says Anne, grimacing too.

'Yes it did,' admits Fliss. 'I've only done it once.'

She smiles again, and then tells us about her most popular show. 'We iron bacon,' she says. 'We filmed it and it's got a cult following on YouTube.'

We ask what she means. 'Well, a couple of us dress up as cleaning ladies and then we literally iron pieces of bacon on an ironing board and then hang them up as though they are drying out on clothes lines.'

All of this is done to the sound of ethereal music. 'We experiment with sounds too. We're trying to capture the sound of walking in the rain for our next show,' says Fliss.

She grins and returns to her table. Then a bald man with tattoos on his arms sidles up and wordlessly shakes our hands, just because he seems to feel like it. He nods at us, as though conveying an extremely important message in this nod. Then he winks a couple of times. He seems too far gone to speak, but quite content to communicate in nods and winks.

And the next thing we know – in the hectic courtyard of the Crescent pub, where almost anything seems possible – we're discovering the 'real' history of the Russian Revolution. This history comes courtesy of Stephen Kingston, editor of the *Salford Star*, a free local magazine with a circulation of 20,000 and the motto 'With attitude and love'. We've arranged to meet him, and as the early Saturday evening revelry at the Crescent hots up, Stephen sips his lager and begins, in conspiratorial tones, to tell us the story of Mary Burns. 'Without Mary Burns,' he says, peering through his circular glasses, '*The Condition of the Working Class in England* by Engels would never have been written.' This classic account of working-class life during industrialisation, which showed how progress ironically made living worse for people at the bottom of society, was written during Engels' stay in Salford and Manchester in the 1840s, Stephen says. It was incredibly influential at the time, lifting the lid on terrible working conditions and diseases such as cholera, typhoid and smallpox that were connected to people living in housing with poor sanitation.

Stephen draws on his cigarette, pausing for effect, and then tells us how Mary met Friedrich Engels after the German came to work in one of his father's mills in Salford in 1842. She was Irish, from a working-class background, and it is believed that she was employed at Engels' mill.

'They began a relationship that was to continue until her death twenty years later,' says Stephen, going on to explain that they never married because it is understood that Engels was against the institution, which he regarded as 'unjust'.

Stephen has a chuckle about this, and then explains that the arrangement suited Mary just fine. 'She was fiercely independent. She refused to be a kept woman, and she worked long hours in the factory during their time together,' he says.

We're interrupted by the man with tattoos who nods an important nod and points at his cigarette: he wants a light. Stephen obliges. The man shakes our hands again (just as they were in Hull and Slough, everyone seems very friendly in Salford). Then Stephen continues. 'Mary showed Fred the social horror on her doorstep,' he says. She did this by taking Engels, who wore a disguise on their outings, around the working-class neighbourhoods where she lived. He wouldn't have been able to do this on his own, Stephen believes, as 'he was a German toff. They [the locals] would have killed him... kicked his head in.' The result of these perambulations was Engels' *The Conditions of the Working Class*, published in German in 1845 and in English in 1887, followed by his later collaborations with Karl Marx in *The Communist Manifesto*.

'So Mary's influence went way beyond her doorstep?' I ask.

Stephen is in no doubt: 'Without Mary Burns there would have been no *Communist Manifesto*, no Russian Revolution, no Che Guevara, no revolution in Cuba!' he exclaims. 'It's all down to Mary Burns!'

He lights another cigarette – even though we're outside, the cigarette smoke is like a heavy fog.

'Are there any pictures of Mary?'

'No, there are none. And she was so poor, there is no birth certificate for her. No one has found a grave. But I think she should get more recognition. She helped Engels to marry real life with his theories. She showed him the streets of Manchester and Salford.' Without that legwork, without seeing from the grassroots what capitalism was doing to the poor during the industrial revolution, Stephen believes that Marx and Engels would not have had the same courage of their convictions in later writings.

He reaches into a bag and passes one of his magazines – it includes a Mary Burns page. There's a section explaining the importance of both Mary and the working-class people of Salford in the communist movement: 'Marx was absolutely skint... he would have had to get a job stacking shelves in Netto or something, but the money that Engels sent him came from the profits at his dad's mill: the sweat of Salford's workers paid for these history-changing books to be written.' It continues: 'Mary Burns acted to ignite the flame that inspired over fifty worker revolutions across the globe!'

It's rousing stuff... and we're in an appropriate venue to be talking revolution. The Crescent is one of two pubs – the other is the Grapes – where it is believed Engels used to meet Marx for a drink when Marx visited from London. I go to the bar with Anne to buy a round and ask the barmaid if she knows of the communist connection. She looks at me as if I'm mad and calls the landlord.

'Nobody really knows whether that's true or not,' says Stephen Cliffe, the twenty-something, spiky-haired landlord. 'You do get people coming by and asking about it. The Labour Party sometimes comes in. Hazel Blears [the local MP at the time of writing] sometimes holds events here.' We look around the front bar. It's small with a scuffed wooden floor, a piano and posters advertising real ales. There's a Lowry print on a wall. Light filters through smoked-glass window panes. Regulars line the bar, which stocks Belgian beers on tap. 'This really is a very nice old boozer,' I say as we take in the scene. 'Did Marx and Engels really sit here dreaming up the political system that influenced the twentieth century more than any other? I can imagine them sitting by the front window overlooking the crescent.'

'Oh yes, I believe that's quite possible,' says Stephen, smiling, 'even though Engels' factory was in an area of Salford called Weaste, quite a long way from the Crescent.'

We sip our drinks, and Stephen returns to the subject of Mary Burns. The only direct references to her he has unearthed are in a letter from Marx to Engels describing her as 'very good-natured' and 'witty', while Marx's daughter also wrote that she was 'very pretty, witty and an altogether charming girl... but in later years drank to excess'. On pointing this out, Stephen takes a look around the pub, sips his pint, and wryly comments: 'Sounds like she definitely was from Salford!'

As Anne and I catch a cab back to our hotel, she looks out across a row of council estate towers near a wall covered in graffiti and, sounding thoughtful, remarks: 'You know I never imagined myself on a weekend break in Salford.'

She pauses, letting this sink in as we stop at a corner where a group of youths in hoodies are smoking cigarettes. And sounding thoughtful again, she adds: 'Remind me again why we came here?'

I think back on what brought us to Salford – and tell her it was all because of Dave.

'Who's Dave?' she asks in a tone that suggests that Dave has quite a bit to answer for.

I explain that Dave was an unemployed decorator I met back in Hull – the chap I'd bumped into on my lengthy pub crawl that ended with the dancing flood contractors, the one who said he was seeking work because his girlfriend was pregnant.

'And…' says Anne, who has heard all about this pub crawl already and queried the necessity of such in-depth 'research'.

'He was the one who recommended Salford,' I explain. 'He said: "You want to go to Salford. That's where you want to go. It's a right ****-hole in Salford."'

'Oh brilliant, Tom, just brilliant,' she says, laughing and looking towards the roof of the cab as if seeking divine intervention from its beige carpet surface. 'You kept that quiet back in London.'

As we drive on I recall Dave's recommendation, which had prompted me to look up the city on the Internet when I'd got home. I'd begun with Google and discovered a link to a YouTube video. This video was set to the theme tune of 'Eye of the Tiger' by the pop group Survivor. It was a film of a walk around 'the Salford slums – Langworthy Road' showcasing boarded-up buildings, empty streets, piles of litter and graffiti-covered walls. The video ended with a night-time sequence in which a young man punches another young man in the face. The video had a link to another film entitled 'Salford Ramraid' that showed a lorry backing into a shopfront. Another link featured skidding cars, with pictures taken by the 'Salford Boyz', pit bulls growling at one another, and a rap group called the Kersal Massive (Kersal is a district within Salford), whose lyrics shout 'we don't **** about' and boast about 'smoking the reefa'.

At first glance, Salford certainly seemed 'unsung' – and possibly dangerous. I had also come across the Channel 4 property programme, *The Best and Worst Places to Live in the UK*, which had deemed Salford the ninth worst place to live. Website notes accompanying the show said: 'Best known as the basis for Weatherfield, home of *Coronation Street*, in real life the city lacks the homely 1950s values of its fictional equivalent. Educational standards are shocking. Salford's truancy record is the second worst in the entire country.'

From guidebooks I'd learned that the city, which borders Manchester, with which it shares a 'Two Cities' nickname, has a population of about 220,000. It was the birthplace of the Trade Union Congress in 1868, and a centre of industrialisation from before the days of Engels onwards. The opening of the Manchester Ship Canal in 1894, which acted to bypass the Liverpool docks, made Salford one of the busiest places of industry in the country. However, the Great Depression in the 1920s hit the city hard and by the 1970s, general industrial decline had made Salford one of the most deprived parts of Britain.

The estates we are passing do not seem to indicate that much has changed. The streets appear tough and forbidding. Anne is shooting me strange looks (the kind of looks that say: 'let's go home'). On first impression, Salford does not feel as though many people would come here for a weekend break. But that is what my journey in Unsung Britain is all about, I'm thinking, taking on the places that others overlook. I *want* to be challenged. That's exactly why I've picked the city.

Even its songs seem to emphasise its rougher, grimier side. 'Dirty Old Town', written by the Salfordian folk singer-songwriter Ewan MacColl, cropped up early on in my Internet search and somehow feels as though it is constantly playing in the background. Dave in Hull appeared to be right. What am I doing bringing Anne here, I think, looking across at her as she peers out of the window at a boarded-up building? Is our visit to this dirty old town going to be a big mistake? I'm not quite sure.

But while the YouTube clips and the Channel 4 findings were depressing, the bigger picture for the area feels bright and positive, with one key word cropping up again and again: regeneration. And we're about to meet the person who has helped as much as anyone to bring regeneration and the possibility of weekend tourists to Salford – in the salubrious, downright swanky surroundings of the five-star Lowry Hotel. OK, I kept costs down in Hull and Slough, but this time we're staying in a £150-a-night room on the Salford bank of the river Irwell. If there's a chance to live it up a bit in Unsung Britain, it's best to seize the opportunity when you can, we'd reasoned (Anne in particular coming to this conclusion).

Our hotel overlooks the central business district of Manchester, not that far away from many of Manchester's regenerated trendy bars and clubs. And our room could be straight out of a fashion magazine: stripy grey carpet, abstract art, orange leather chaise longue and large flat-screen TV. Copies of *Manchester: An Architectural History* are propped on a coffee table next to a *Vanity Fair* with a lead story headlined: 'HOLLYWOOD NEW WAVE, GOSSIP GIRLS AND SUPERBAD BOYS!', and a magazine entitled *The Luxury Review*. There are cool blasts of air-conditioning, and the mini-bar stocks Côtes du Rhône wine and Bombay Sapphire gin. Apparently, Kylie Minogue, Daniel Craig, David Beckham, Jay-Z and the Manchester United football team have all stayed here. 'Wow,' says Anne, feeling the plush leather of the chaise longue, and gazing across the river to Manchester. Even though we're close to Salford's relatively well-to-do sister city, we're sticking to this side of the Irwell during our stay.

The next morning, Sunday, I meet Felicity Goodey, a former BBC industrial correspondent, in an airy downstairs lounge with cream sofas (while Anne checks out the lavish hotel spa). She's wearing jeans, pearl earrings and red lipstick. Felicity is chairman of the Central Salford Urban Regeneration Company – and has a reputation as being Ms Regeneration in these parts. We order coffees and she begins to fill me in on the schemes to redevelop central Salford, which has already seen the 2002 opening of the giant Lowry arts and entertainment centre on Salford Quays, with two theatres and a permanent exhibition of L. S. Lowry's works. This is to be followed by MediaCity, a series of offices and studios to which the BBC will move its sports and children's shows, bringing as many as 15,000 new jobs. Apartment blocks with penthouses have sprung up overlooking the cleaned-up docks, she is soon telling me, and there's a plan to create a 'corridor of regeneration' from the arts centre to the Lowry Hotel.

'Why is so much regeneration needed in Salford?' I ask – the r-word definitely seems to be the buzzword round here.

'Salford is still struggling with the legacy of the industrial revolution,' explains Felicity. 'That may sound incredible in the twenty-first century, but that past is still alive with us.' By this, she means that the decline of heavy industry has still to find a replacement form of employment. As unlikely as tourism may seem, she says, it is one way to bring work to the area.

I ask Felicity, who is middle-aged and somehow manages to be both laid-back and sparky at the same time, how she got involved with the redevelopment of Salford Quays. It all began, she says, when she reported for the BBC on plans to build the arts centre. The Quays were then derelict and the council had bought them cheaply from the old canal owners, and council leaders did not have the faintest idea what to do with them: 'The water in the canals bubbled and it wasn't oxygen that was making it bubble. It was ghastly. If you'd fallen in, you'd be in serious trouble.'

So when she met the architect Peter Hunter on the edge of Pier Eight in 1989, with her camera crew in tow, she didn't know what to expect: 'It was a drizzly day. But he looked across the water and at the sky and said: "Yes, something can be done here." He had already superimposed a picture of the Royal Albert Hall at the end of the pier. My camera crew fell about laughing. The camera actually wobbled during the report. They couldn't believe what they were hearing. The local news editor said it was bonkers.'

'Did you have to convince your bosses to run the story?'

'Absolutely!' she replies. 'They really did not believe in it at all.'

Lottery cash, however, meant that the plans were not so bonkers after all, she tells me. The dream of the arts centre became reality, by which time Felicity had become inspired by the positive spirit of the project and crossed over from reporter to regenerator, she says, as Anne joins us and we jump in Felicity's gleaming new Jaguar: regenerators, it appears, do quite well for themselves. 'Even Jeremy Clarkson has fallen in love with these,' she says, revving the engine as we head for the Lowry Centre along a street with boarded-up pubs in decrepit buildings with weeds growing out of their roofs. Incongruous adverts on construction sites boast of a 'Fresh Perspective' and mysteriously announce: 'Be Stylish. Be Tickled. With Envy.'

As we drive in her plush car along the not so plush streets, we talk about the BBC's move to Salford. Felicity explains: 'The BBC realised it was seen as London and south-east centric. Yet it has a universal licence fee. Politicians were cutting up rough in the north. The corporation had a political problem on its hands.'

All of this made Salford an attractive choice. We arrive at the Lowry Centre, which looks a bit like a mini metallic version of the Sydney Opera House, next to the Lowry Outlet Mall, full of all the usual high-street shops. Combined with the Imperial War Museum North, just across the river Irwell, and Old Trafford, Manchester United's football ground (about a mile away), the Lowry Centre is now part of an established tourist trail, says Felicity. 'Tourism is worth eleven billion pounds to the north-west and there are two-hundred thousand jobs in tourism!' We enter the main theatre, where she points out: 'No seat in this house has a fully compromised view!' We pass the bathrooms: 'There are more ladies loos than in any other arts building in the country!' The centre is 'the most commercially successful arts institute in the country!' we're told, as Felicity leads us onwards, as though she is showing us rooms in her home.

We gaze out of a window towards the river Irwell – no bubbling waters in sight these days. Felicity looks contentedly at the scene, and then glances at her watch: she has to go.

'But is all this a bit of a pipe dream: is Salford going to feel the r-word for real?' I ask, before she zooms off.

She looks me squarely in the eyes and admits: 'I could take you to places in Salford where plenty of people will say all this is a load of rubbish.'

'So are you worried that things like MediaCity and flashy new apartments will just be seen as being for yuppies working for the BBC and young professionals who cannot afford prices in Manchester? Are you concerned that the local people who already live in Salford will not benefit from recent changes?'

She pauses, seemingly deep in thought. 'Yes, we want locals to prosper, not just people who come in from outside. We've got to make sure we unlock possibilities presented to the local community,' she continues. 'It would be morally indefensible for us not to. There are some of the roughest estates in the country near here. But many of the people I've talked to say: "I may be poor, but I don't want my children to be poor."'

We shake hands and we thank her for giving up so much time on a weekend. It has been a pleasure to meet someone so committed to improving a community.

Then we visit the Lowry exhibition. At the top of an escalator we are met with a Lowry quote: 'You don't need brains to be a painter, just feelings.' Anne is taken by this. 'Isn't it lovely?' she says.

Then we go through to a side-room where we watch a flickering twenty-minute film on Lowry's lonely life (1887– 1976). 'I hadn't known he'd been such an outsider,' I whisper as the film describes how the artist kept to himself, never marrying, venturing abroad or owning a telephone or car.

'It seems as though his relationship with his mother was the closest of his life,' says Anne. 'It's touching, but it's also sad.' He looked after his mother for many years while she was ill, the film tells us.

Until retirement, despite his many artistic successes, most of which came later on, he worked as a rent collector; although few people knew this when he was alive. 'Imagine someone like Damien Hirst living so modestly,' I say.

'Not very likely,' Anne replies, as the film explains that Lowry's decision to paint the factory scenes he saw around him near his home in Pendlebury brought him fame, but not widespread critical acclaim. Asked if he minded when critics said he painted 'matchstick men', he replied: 'I don't mind at all... I paint figures as I see them.'

In another clip, he comments on inner-city life: 'You can't photograph this, you've got to be personal about it,' while of his pictures of down-and-outs, he ruminates: 'What happened to them and how did they get into that state? It could happen to any of us if we got into a crisis.'

After this we enter the gallery. And it is totally transfixing. The scenes of red-brick terraces next to smokestacks open up before us – some of the canvasses five or six feet square, others much smaller, but with every inch of each seeming to tell a story. There are women pushing prams, trade union marchers, quirky little dogs scampering about, doleful fellows with hunched gaits and hands in their pockets. Boys kick footballs. Girls are led by hand by their mothers. Elderly chaps in long coats puff on cigarettes.

'I love this one,' says Anne, as we stand before one of the few pictures that doesn't depict industrial scenes. It is entitled *Portrait of Ann* (by coincidence), painted in 1957, and shows a woman wearing a red roll-neck jumper, with an oval face and a sad look in her eyes. According to the film earlier, this may have been Lowry's idealised version of a woman. He once admitted in an interview: 'I have no close friends at all. I've never been married. I've never had a girl, in fact. And now I'm nearly eighty I think it's too late to start.'

My favourite is *Man Lying on a Wall*, which shows a man doing just that. 'He looks so content. So happy,' I say. And he does: lying flat on his back smoking a cigarette, with his bowler hat resting on his belly and his briefcase and umbrella propped against the wall.

Near this, there's a self-portrait dating from 1925, which shows Lowry peering out from under a floppy flat cap, looking meek and slightly anxious. This is next to a harrowing painting of an older man with stubble and very red eyes, said to be Lowry, although it is not confirmed that this is a self-portrait as well. 'Looks like you after a night out,' comments Anne.

Even though it is quite small, you could spend hours in the gallery. There is something hauntingly beautiful about his work, as well as something bleakly sad and lonely too. If Unsung Britain has an (unofficial) artist, it has to be L. S. Lowry.

Afterwards, we have a pleasant lunch in a Parisian-style cafe at the foot of the escalator and then drop into the flashy, un-Lowry-like sales showroom of MediaCity apartments next door to the Lowry Centre. A woman with blonde hair, who seems surprised to have visitors, tells us that a two-bedroom flat here is £189,000 while a three-bedroom penthouse comes to £340,000. Everything seems to be about half the price you might expect to pay in London. We take a look at a room with a bed with a cream cover, antique-style side tables, a fluffy rug, a charcoal grey sofa and an anglepoise lamp. It's all very tasteful and stylish: a bit like walking into a Habitat display. 'If you buy in MediaCity, I don't think you can go wrong,' she says, admitting sales have been slow due to the economic downturn. It looks as though she's probably right.

Then we catch a taxi to Langworthy – the star of the YouTube videos, and also where Walter Greenwood set his moving novel *Love on the Dole*, which covers the 'soot and grime' of unemployment in these parts in the 1920s – to see another new housing project. Perhaps not a usual tourist activity, but I'd read about the place in a newspaper's property section, and I'd been intrigued to see the development as it seems to symbolise the changes happening in Salford. The driver drops us at the 'Upside Down' development in Chimney Pot Park. His name is Phil and as I pay the fare he says: 'The sad thing round here is the influx of the media. I had my own house in Langworthy and I'd been struggling to sell it. Within two weeks of the BBC announcement that they were coming, it had gone. That's what's sad: that it took that before I could sell it.'

Is it safe to walk around here? 'Well I'd be careful if I was you,' he replies. 'I'm not sure I'd want to bring my young ones up here, let's put it that way. There used to be fist fights in the old days and if you were street smart, you were OK. Now it's knives and whatever you can pick up on the street.'

Anne gives me one of her looks – the type that suggests we head back to the hotel. But we take a walk around, discovering that Chimney Pot Park consists of five red-brick terraced streets which feature in the title sequence of *Coronation Street* as well as in the film version of *A Taste of Honey*, Shelagh Delaney's gritty story of a 1950s single mother: another local literary connection. All the houses have been renovated by the urban regeneration company Urban Splash, and stylishly decorated, after being bought through compulsory purchase orders, I learned before coming. But even though the refitted properties were designed for first-time buyers with priority given to local residents, most have been sold to outsiders. They are also extremely odd. While it feels as though we're walking through *Coronation Street*, the houses are in pristine condition, all looking identical, with holiday home-style decks with mini gardens at the back above garages. They are dubbed 'upside-down' houses as the bedrooms are on the ground floor, while the living areas are upstairs. This arrangement means there is outdoor space as well as room beneath for the garages.

There's hardly anyone about. We walk up and down a couple of streets, feeling totally safe, before finally encountering a local. Paul is a graphic and web designer in his twenties from Dublin, who has just bought one of the houses for £129,000.

'What's it like to live in an upside-down house?' I ask.

'It's a good place here,' he replies, 'very handy to get into town, just ten or fifteen minutes.' By this, he means the centre of Manchester, not Salford. 'I like the old and the new. The exteriors are a hundred years old, but inside it's very modern.'

Further along, we bump into Roy, a retired plumber, and Pat, a retired machinist, who are pushing a shopping bag with wheels past a sign saying: 'SHOW HOUSES OPEN TO VIEW.' They do not feel quite the same way as Paul. 'I don't like 'em,' says Pat, when I ask what they think. 'I know people who used to live in them. They were always too small. They should have knocked the whole lot down or made two houses into one.' Roy adds: 'The people who lived in those houses thought there was going to be a demolition. Our friend got seven thousand pounds for hers.'

We cross a street, pass a tattoo shop, and head into Seedley, suddenly feeling conspicuous. Graffiti on a wall says: 'XXXX is a slag'. Ahead is a terrace with windows covered with metal grills. The slate roof has holes, as though it's been struck by artillery. The terrace stands alone in the middle of what looks like a field, but is in fact patches of grass where houses used to be. Mini fences mark out where the houses were. The land, the size of half a dozen football pitches, looks like some kind of headstone-less cemetery. At its boundaries, houses with barred windows stand solemnly. 'ALL MATERIALS OF VALUE HAVE BEEN REMOVED' reads a notice. Another says: 'WARNING: ANTI-CLIMB PAINT'. There are no youths with knives to be seen.

But two women walk towards us. One pushes a pram and is carrying a black umbrella to keep off the sun – it's surprisingly warm for this time of year. It's a lovely day in sunny Salford! Her companion is older, wearing a red blouse, a black satin dress and lots of make-up. At first they are hesitant to speak, but then Jody, the woman pushing the pram, gets talking.

'I went to college doing catering, I'm seventeen, and I'm a mum on the dole,' she explains.

'What do you think of the upside-down houses?'

'I think it's smart, and it's making a change for the community. But they should have done work on them years ago.'

Emma, thirty, another mum on the dole, has a different opinion: 'We hate it. They're full of idiots. They just think they're better than us 'cos they've got nice cars.' Then, changing subject, she adds: 'I'm not being racist but there's a lot of refugees round here. Russians, Poles and blacks – we don't know where they're from. They get better looked after than we do: bus passes, food vouchers.'

These streets, although a couple of hundred yards from Chimney Pot Park, are a million metaphorical miles away. On a corner, we meet a middle-aged man named John, who has an open expression and is very friendly. He believes that the authorities have been turning a blind eye to lawlessness in the area to speed up the clearing of the old terraces: 'Houses are getting burned up. There's no control. Kids are smashing up houses still. Some people don't feel safe in their own homes.

If you touch the kids, they just tell you to **** off. What can you do?'

His friend Sonia, who works at the local hospital, comes up to us as he is talking: 'We need to do more for the youths. They are just bored. We don't need funny new houses. We need more sports centres.' Tracey, who runs a newsagent, joins us. It feels as though we're having some kind of community meeting: 'The new lot [the ones in the upside-down houses] don't buy things from us. We haven't seen any of them in the shop, and we've lost our regular customers.'

At this point Anne leans over and whispers in my ear: 'As fascinating as this is, I think I'm going to leave you to it.'

She's not cut out for community meetings on the backstreets of Salford – it's one step too far for her in Unsung Britain. Which is fair enough: I guess trudging around boarded-up terraces is not on most people's weekend break to-do list, even if it does provide an insight into the fast-changing way of life in this part of the city. So I call for a taxi from the firm we used earlier (it comes quickly), and she heads back to the Lowry Hotel. 'I'll be in the hotel spa!' she says, as the taxi pulls away.

Then I walk down Liverpool Road alone, past the gasworks that Ewan MacColl sang about. Along the way, I see zombie-like figures who must be drug addicts, so skinny they look as though they have just been let out of a concentration camp: real-life matchstick figures, in the heart of Lowry-land. I look into the face of one and his eyes seem dead to the world. As I turn a corner, a group of three lads in hoodies veers towards me. They look like textbook trouble. I pass by, gazing downwards. One of the lads says: 'BOO!' loudly, and the others laugh. I walk quickly on, and turn to see them staring back at me, their body language suggesting they are weighing me up. How much is this bloke worth, and is he worth the bother? Probably not, seems to be their conclusion. They hesitate, shrug and turn away.

Amid all of this – it's hard to believe – there is a bona fide tourist attraction that I've been heading towards: the Salford Lads Club. The club dates from 1904, when it was opened by Robert Baden-Powell, although he was merely a guest official and the club is not connected to the Scout movement. It is on the corner of Coronation Street, and Leslie Holmes, a cheerful club volunteer who meets me outside and shows me round, says that Tony Warren, the original writer of the long-running soap, 'will deny that he got the name from here. But he did. There was a pub nearby called the Amalgamated Inn. That's long since been knocked down, but that was the basis of the Rovers Return. This here,' he points at the terraced houses, 'This is the real *Coronation Street*.'

But that is not what attracts the tourists, says Leslie, who has a white beard and a bit of a look of Father Christmas about him. The Salford Lads Club was featured as a backdrop for the sleeve of *The Queen is Dead*, a 1986 album by The Smiths. Almost every day, Leslie says, Morrissey fans come to have their picture taken in the same spot as the band in front of the distinctive red-brick Victorian building. According to Leslie, the group, who are from Manchester, originally rang to ask permission for the photo: 'The leader of the club at the time said he didn't want to be associated with a pop group. But they just came and did it anyway. Then the fans started coming. Back in 1986 that didn't go down too well round here.' The group was too effete for rough-and-tough Salford.

But Morrissey donates cash to the club, recently giving £20,000 to replace leading that was stolen from the roof; so all is forgiven.

Leslie shows me a room dedicated to The Smiths. It's full of paraphernalia about the band, with messages from fans on a board saying 'Shyness is nice' and 'If my bike gets nicked while I'm in here, then you owe me Morrissey'. There's also a copy of a postcard from Morrissey to the photographer Stephen Wright, who took the picture outside the club, that says: 'A sweeter set of pictures were never taken. I smiled for a full minute (phone Roy Castle, that's a record). I quite fancy Southport Wet Sands next.' The photograph now hangs in the National Portrait Gallery and is the most famous image of The Smiths.

The lads club is a one-off, and what's so great about it is the sense of timelessness. Inside it looks as though little has changed in a century. There's an upstairs boxing ring, a large pool table room, table tennis, and a tiny five-a-side football pitch. 'It's simple but it's what kids want,' says Leslie. Members have included several Manchester United and Manchester City football players. Eddie Coleman, one of the Busby Babes who died in the 1958 Munich air crash, learned to play the game here.

'The club seems to be thriving,' I say. 'What makes it work so well?'

'Well, the purpose of the club is to get lads off the street and give them something to do. There's precious little of that round here, and we offer kids that,' Leslie says. 'Our motto is: "To brighten young lives and make good citizens." That's been going a hundred years but it's a motto that the government would love to get working now.' Lasses can also join the club, he says, and there's a 'girls' night' on Tuesdays. Everything is run by volunteers, funded by donations.

Leslie shows me a board with historical information about the demolition of nearby terraces: 'This was social engineering on a monumental scale. It happened in every city. It was the solution to housing for the poor, but it didn't work. Now a lot of the tower blocks that replaced the local streets are being demolished and they're trying to get people to live in terraces again.' Then we go outside where I'm met by Paul, the same taxi driver from earlier. I say goodbye to Leslie and we drive off, with Paul telling me about local racial tension, 'a botched assassination in a pub' and an 'Iraqi who fled Iraq to get away from all the troubles and violence who told me that he wished he'd bloody well stayed.'

Salford, I'm learning, is a place of stories and extremes.

Down the street from my next Salford attraction – not so far from the Salford Lads Club – is the Crescent pub where Marx and Engels may once have met. Across the street is the site of the art school where Lowry attended evening classes for thirteen years; perfecting his painting after working during the day as a rent collector. Next door is Joule House, the former home of Salford-born physicist James Prescott Joule, who gave his name to the 'joule' unit of energy and who developed important early laws relating to energy and heat. And in the centre of this triangle of art, politics and science stands the Working Class Movement Library.

After my 'upper-class' Sunday night in the fancy Lowry Hotel flicking through *Luxury Review* magazine and drinking Bombay Sapphire gin and tonics – you can understand why the millionaire-likes of the Rooneys and the Beckhams feel at home there – I'm about to find out about the history of how the other half live. The library, which is more like a museum, is in a Victorian red-brick building that was originally built as a nurses' home, not far from a depressing row of housing blocks that wouldn't look out of place in Eastern Europe. It's another bright day and Anne has gone for a morning run along a path by the river Irwell (she's a running addict), so I walk up to the front door on my own and press a buzzer next to another that says: 'Intercom for Hazel Blears, MP, Tuesday–Friday.' The MP, who is embroiled in the Westminster expenses scandal not long after our visit (and has her car vandalised in Salford by angry constituents), shares the building.

I'm met by Veronica Trick, a small, cheerful woman with thick-framed glasses, a gold coin hanging from a necklace and a stripy top. 'Lovely to meet you, lovely,' she says warmly, as though there are not too many visitors to the Working Class Movement Library. She's a volunteer, and she's going to show me round the most extensive collection of material relating to the working classes anywhere in the world. We stand in a tiled hall with a big curving staircase and walls covered in colourful banners that say: 'SALFORD AGAINST THE MISSILES' and 'EAST BRADFORD SOCIALIST SUNDAY SCHOOL: KNOWLEDGE, PEACE, HAPPPINESS, TRUTH, PLENTY'. Around us are cabinets with black-and-white photographs from marches, old trade union posters, cardboard boxes of pamphlets and a pile of *Morning Star* newspapers.

First though, we talk about tourism in Salford. 'Too much of Salford is passed by. Everyone thinks it's just about *Coronation Street*: that annoys me,' she says.

I tell Veronica about our trip to the Lowry Centre and she says: 'When something is achieved in Salford, like the Lowry, it's always perceived as being in Manchester. But when there's a horrible murder, then it's always in Salford. I do think we've developed a slight complex about our bigger and more successful neighbour.'

She tells me about the library. It was set up by Ruth and Eddie Frow. Eddie, who died in 1997, was involved in a march highlighting the plight of the unemployed in the early 1930s, during which he was arrested and beaten by police, leaving him with a scar on his nose. A character from Walter Greenwood's *Love on the Dole*, is based on Eddie, 'a finely featured young man... heaping invective upon all with whom he disassociated himself on a social scale.' He trained as a toolmaker and was a life-long member of the Communist Party. Ruth was a teacher, a founder of Manchester's CND group. She died in 2008.

'So Ruth and Eddie must have shared a love of books?' I venture.

'Well, they realised that an area of history was being neglected – the history of the working class,' she explains. 'They became passionate collectors of books, anything they could pick up about the working class, the labour movement, radical history and politics. They did it for the history. The collection grew by word of mouth: people would go to see them and leave something.' Their semi-detached house was soon overflowing with left-wing literature; everywhere except the bathroom and kitchen was full. So they decided to make the collection into a charitable trust, says Veronica, as it was becoming valuable and they did not want death duties to split it up. In the 1980s, Salford Council provided the current venue for the library, which feels like a mini museum tucked away in a nice old building.

We enter a reading room with pictures of Tony Benn and Nelson Mandela on the wall. Beside a bust of Lenin, a bookshelf is stacked with socialist tracts and a copy of *The Communist Manifesto*.

'It almost feels like a time capsule, as though communism is a possibility, and one day soon workers will be marching on Salford Town Hall,' I comment. 'But isn't the library a little outdated – is there really all that much interest?'

Veronica replies: 'Yes, there's interest, but we don't get a huge number of visitors.' She pauses, and adds: 'We're all about working-class people's struggles and making a better life for them, particularly through self-improvement. We're not political with a capital "P" but we are political collectors.'

Most of the books are upstairs, room after room of them. Union posters from the nineteenth century, with slogans such as 'BE UNITED AND INDUSTRIOUS', cover the walls. Many have pictures that show the union members at work. 'That was partly for education,' says Veronica. 'The posters are very visual because in those days people weren't very literate. Children could look at them and say: "That's what dad does at work." People who could afford them would often put the posters in pride of place in their homes. Trade unionists were so proud of their crafts. But that's gone away now I think, and that's very sad.'

Veronica talks about the 1819 Peterloo Massacre in Manchester, when cavalry charged to break up an 80,000-strong crowd demanding parliamentary representation, killing fifteen protesters. She shows me a poster dating from the Chartist

Movement in 1848, when a petition of six million signatures was taken to Parliament after a giant gathering on Kennington Common in London. Next to this, protected from sunlight by mini curtains, is a photograph of that gathering. 'It's believed to be the first photograph of a crowd ever taken,' says Veronica. 'The government was expecting a French-style revolution. Queen Victoria was sent to the Isle of Wight. Wellington was brought out of retirement and there were more troops in London than there were at Waterloo.'

We look at the picture. 'It's a shame that most of the peoples' backs are turned,' I comment, as she examines it. Many of the men wear bowler hats and are looking inwards, perhaps towards a speaker. In the background there's the smokestack of a factory. As I gaze at the scene I am struck by a sense of the enormous potential of the moment depicted. 'Had events turned out differently that day, might this have become the crowd that sparked revolution in Britain?'

'Yes. It gives me a bit of a hair-raising thing when I look at it,' agrees Veronica. 'It was a people's army.'

On the top floor, there is a room dedicated to the works of Thomas Paine. 'This is our pride and joy. Thomas Paine is as close as we come to having a patron saint,' says Veronica. 'He was a working-class person and he was the first working-class intellectual, if you like. That makes him very important. In the *Rights of Man* in 1791 he called for free education and pensions for the elderly. He was way ahead of his time.' She describes how Paine went to the US to take part in the American Revolution. 'In the US, he wrote pamphlets about the injustice of slavery. He was also against capital punishment. Later on, he ended up in prison in France: he was against the guillotine. He was not a politician really... he was an idealist.' Paine escaped the guillotine to return to America, where he died of old age. Veronica tells me she's re-reading *Rights of Man*. 'I've got a copy here,' she says, smiling and patting her handbag.

The tour is over and I leave with a feeling that it would be fitting if Salford made more of its Working Class Movement Library. I feel as though I have been given a tour of a hidden history. First, I've learned about the Russian Revolution in Salford, now I've found out about the British Revolution that almost was. Yes, the Lowry Centre and the Lowry Outlet Mall are flash, brash and doing well, but here is a collection unlike any other that gives an insight into industrial life just as important as Lowry's.

And not a lot of people know about it... which is a shame.

I head back to the hotel, and after a pleasant stroll along the river Irwell, Anne and I catch a taxi back to Piccadilly Station. On the platform waiting for our train, I get a call. It's Harold Riley, the well-regarded artist who was one of Lowry's few friends. He was born in 1934 and became friends with Lowry when he was an art student. He is best known for his portraits of Nelson Mandela, Pope Jean Paul II, George Best and Tiger Woods (he has an interest in sport, and was once so good at football he was selected for the Manchester United youth team). We chat about his recollections of Lowry, and he tells me how for many years he used to walk around Salford with the artist every Thursday to record what they saw: they were working together on a joint project on life in the city. He says: 'We'd go out all day, have lunch at the Salford Gallery and walk on afterwards, maybe stop for tea and scones and go to my studio afterwards.'

'That must have been quite a thing: walking around the city with such a legend. What was he like as a person?' I ask, as our train pulls in.

'He had a great sense of purpose to get on in life,' says Riley. 'He was very loyal to people he knew, yet he was actually a very independent person – that's the quality I liked most in him.'

He pauses, and then says softly: 'But he didn't lead the life he wanted to live. He was shadowed by the life he might have had.'

'Did Lowry consider the industrial scenes he painted to be beautiful?'

'No, I don't think that he ever found beauty,' Riley replies quickly. 'He found drama and a story in the industrial scenery.'

I thank him for the call, then we board the train (no first class this time, not after the working-class library). And as the industrial north flashes past, Anne and I look back at all the drama and stories that surround Salford: from Lowry's brilliant pictures and lonely life, to Engels and Mary Burns, to regeneration at Chimney Pot Park and all the derelict terraces, to youths with nothing to do and dead-eyed junkies, to MediaCity and the rivalry with Manchester, to the Salford Lads Club and Morrissey, to the struggle to move on from the industrial past that seems to overshadow everything.

'Have you enjoyed it?' I ask Anne. 'Be honest.'

She pauses and seems to be thinking back over the visit. 'Yes,' she replies, and pauses.

'It was definitely different. I did enjoy it. Really, I didn't think I would, but I did.' For her, it's Lowry's pictures, the hotel and her sunny jog along the river that have stood out. For me, it's the sense of regeneration and of being in a spot that was so historically important as a centre of industrialisation, and seeing how life moves on now. And both of us just liked the journey, the whole weekend away.

Next weekend I've got another adventure. I'm moving on from a dirty old town to a city many miles away across the Irish Sea.

5

DERRY: ON HOLIDAY
IN BOGSIDE

I'm getting a taste for travelling around Britain by train. It feels strangely liberating walking to my local station in South-West London with my holiday already begun, even though it would have been quicker to fly to Derry. No checking in, or fast (but actually slow) bag drops, security queues, crowded WHSmiths, delays in lounges, scrambles for seats, endless circling before landing or hold-ups for baggage. The holiday starts here! I'm finding it's rewarding getting a sense of the country along the way. Catching planes, you just don't get that feeling of journey – all airports seem to look the same these days (modern and quite nice when you're through security, but you could be just about anywhere in the world).

After a prompt train from Euston to Liverpool – sitting next to a voluptuous Russian woman whose only conversation is 'Iz thees Leevpool?' when we arrive in the early evening – I catch a taxi from the station to Birkenhead's ferry port with a cheery driver, who poetically tells me apropos of nothing: 'Don't be mistaken, don't be misled, they're not Scousers, they're from Birkenhead!' He also declares, as we pull up to the ferry depot: 'We call it the Dark Side over here – among a lot of things.' And when I pay my fare, he gives my change and parts with a flourish: 'Here you go, sausage!' You don't get that from many airport officials.

There's a brief wait in a lounge where a TV is showing a live Everton match. Then I catch a crammed minibus with a group of lads who seem to be on a jolly of some sort to the *Lagan Viking*, a huge ferry painted red and looking well past its prime. 'We're not exactly going on a Caribbean cruise are we?' cracks one of the group. Another gazes down into the swirling Mersey and says: 'It looks cold in there. I wouldn't like a ****ing swim in that.'

Neither would I. It's a nippy evening in mid November. But it's also beautifully clear. Across the Mersey, from the deck, I can see the orange glow of the clock on the face of the Liver Building amid the twinkle of street lights in Liverpool. You get a whole new perspective on the city from Birkenhead. It looks like a grand place of entry into the country: a bold metropolis to return to from a journey across the Atlantic or further afield.

You also get to meet people on the *Lagan Viking*. This is thanks to the dining arrangements in the restaurant (dinner is included in the ferry fare). An announcement comes that food is ready and I find myself sitting at a table with a plastic tablecloth with Tim Tring, who is in his thirties from Aylesbury. He has short hair, a red hooded top and glasses. I enquire if he's a lorry driver; the ferry seems to be packed with lorries. 'No, I'm a carpenter and I'm going camping for three days, near Belfast,' he replies. 'I love camping. I hate the way cities are converging in on one another. Everything in Britain seems to be closing in. There's so little space. I like to try and find the places where there's some space, where you can completely relax.' A different kind of Unsung Britain.

After having a drink at a bar with blackjack fruit machines where everyone is chortling at a television showing the stand-up comedian Peter Kay – 'I met a Dutch girl with inflatable shoes last week, phoned her up to arrange a date, but unfortunately she'd popped her clogs' – I collapse in my cabin. It's warm, with a bunk, and the faint sound of pop music and ghostly voices echoing through vents. I drop off quickly and wake to find the ferry arriving into Belfast, where the great yellow frame of the H&W crane in the shipyard where the *Titanic* was built is the first thing I see through my porthole.

The train journey from Belfast to Derry is one of the most picturesque I have ever taken. Belfast's factory stacks, barbed wire and satellite dishes are soon left behind and the train trundles through damp emerald-green countryside. We pass a funny loaf-shaped mountain. A rainbow appears: the most complete rainbow I've ever laid eyes on. You can see exactly where it begins and ends – so sharp it looks as though it has been painted on the sky. There are twiggy hedgerows, rolling hills and luminous snaking rivers. A sign says 'Jesus Christ Came into The World' in the run up to Ballymena. There's a solitary heron in a bog near Cullybackey. White horses trot about contentedly in fields. Sheep wander on a hillside covered in clumps of reeds. Then we reach black-stone hills in the lead-up to Bellarena. There's a peculiar porcelain bathtub in a field; almost as though it has been placed there for Salvador Dali to come and capture. We disappear into a tunnel. Then we emerge to see the coast of the Atlantic Ocean, with a long pale beach looking on to a wide grey seascape with thin streaks of whitecaps disappearing into the distance. Inland, there are mountains shaped like whales, some with dramatic waterfalls. Rain begins to pour down and it feels as though our little train is going through a giant carwash. Everything turns into a grey haze, through which I spot two black horses in a field with a tiny runway but no planes – reminding me of flying again and why I'm glad I've come by train and ferry. The rain stops and the ocean reappears, now a huge expanse of flat white enamel against the grey-black clouds.

And not long after, the train pulls into the small quaint station at Derry. I walk up a hill in the late morning in a drizzle and then the sun comes out, making the pavements dazzlingly bright. After passing through an archway into the famous city walls I realise I'm lost, so I go into a healing arts centre to ask for directions to the Tower Hotel. I enter a small shop that smells of herbs, with relaxing oriental-style music pinging in the background and a sense of calm. No one is about at first as I take in the rows of oils, candles and herbal medicines. A sign says: 'Angel Meditations Available: £10 a session.' Another advertises a form of healing involving light therapy, announcing that 'the ionising bulb provides natural vitamins'. Indian head massages are also on offer. I hadn't expected all this in Derry, I'm thinking, and just as I'm about to leave as I cannot see anyone, a short woman wearing a bomber jacket arrives.

She turns out to be one of the angel therapists, and she thinks I've come for a meditation. 'Angels work with me,' she is soon telling me, fixing her eyes on mine like a hypnotist. 'I get in touch with the archangel. The angels help you to relax a lot; they teach you how to cope with modern life.'

'That's great,' I say, somehow finding myself following her into a side-room with a picture of a dolphin on the wall and a colour therapy chart.

'The angels have guided you to this place,' she replies. 'They are embracing you now. Can you feel it?'

'Not right now,' I admit.

To this, she points to a sign that says: 'It is perfect that we are here. Perfection is the very life within you, and it is guiding you right now. Open your heart to the Golden Age.'

'Oh,' I say. 'Thanks.'

She repeats quietly: 'The angels work with me.'

And I thank her again: I might not have got the directions I was after, but she has been quite charming. Then I head off into the streets of Derry in search of my hotel.

Round the corner near a war memorial on a roundabout – wondering if my heart is soon to open to a Golden Age in Derry – I come across a shop devoted to selling Celtic Football Club paraphernalia. The Glaswegian team is extremely popular among locals with a nationalist leaning, as it seems to symbolise an independent Catholic position, says Keith, the manager, when I pop in to ask if he knows where to find my hotel. He does, it's just nearby, but then I ask him more about his shop. It's a sea of Celtic FC green with shirts signed by players, playing cards, pint glasses, caps, posters, team kits for kids, and even an outfit to keep a dog warm (£14.99), and a

Celtic FC dog lead (£4.99). Everything coloured green. 'Do people really buy the dog outfits?' I ask.

'Sure, we've shifted quite a few,' he replies, as a group of tourists enters.

Keith looks over at them. 'They're American. I can tell already,' he whispers conspiratorially. They have yet to speak, so we have not heard their accents. 'There's an eighty per cent chance they'll buy something. They usually just see the green and think: "Oh it's Irish." They tend to buy things for their grandchildren. It's funny: a lot of them ask: "What is this team called Carling?"'

Carling is the team sponsor, with the name in big letters on the front of the shirt. We watch as they pick up green baseball caps and come over to buy them. They are indeed Americans. After they leave, Keith says that tourist business like this is booming: 'We're doing brilliant.'

The Tower Hotel is on the other side of the roundabout with the war memorial – and it is the only hotel, at the time of my visit, within the city's seventeenth-century walls. The lobby is smart with gold sofas and purple decorations – it has recently been revamped, according to the friendly receptionist. I get the feeling Anne would have liked this. I look in the bar, where a group of American students are drinking coffees at wooden tables, and take a lift to a small neat room with a red colour scheme and a view of the grey and rather uninviting-looking river Foyle. I lie down for a bit and read an article I've brought with me from *The Irish News*, which says that the Northern Ireland Tourist Board aims to increase tourism revenue in the province by 40 per cent over the next three years. It says that cash from overseas and domestic visitors already accounts for 3.5 per cent of the local economy, providing jobs for more than 30,000 people. Nigel Dodds, the enterprise, trade and investment minister, is quoted saying he wants to make Northern Ireland a 'truly world-class destination', with people coming to see the Causeway Coast (which features the dramatic basalt columns of Giant's Causeway, close to where my train passed); the province's St Patrick and Christian heritage; Mourne National Park; and 'the walled city of Derry'. Another story in the *Belfast Telegraph* declares that 'the city is going through a renaissance with heritage placed firmly at the heart of its regeneration strategy'.

Then I go downstairs to find out about this renaissance, courtesy of Martin McCrossan, who runs a successful tour-guide company recommended by the tourist board. I meet him in the lobby, and soon discover that he seems to know just about everyone in Derry: 'You want to talk to Seamus Heaney? Let me see what I can do.' He gets on his phone... but the Nobel Prize-winning poet is not in town. 'John Hume: oh I know John very well; I'll give him a ring.' He gets on his phone again... the Nobel Prize-winning politician is.

Martin's disarming honesty wins over people. 'I've got no axe to grind,' he says almost as soon as we meet. 'I'm in a mixed marriage. My wife is from the Fountain Estate. That's one of the last enclaves of Protestantism in the city centre. And let me tell you, a Catholic marrying a Protestant wasn't very popular twenty-five years ago. I'm a product of the Troubles. I've been through the doldrums. I've been through some difficult times.' He's also a dapper dresser, wearing a well-pressed yellow shirt, striped tie and a blue blazer. He has sparkling blue eyes, balding ginger hair and a ready grin.

Within a couple of minutes, I realise I'm very lucky to have him show me round. 'I've been going fourteen years now,' he says. 'I started [offering tours] in 1995, when we had the first peace talks. They were a sign of hope.'

'What did you do before then?'

'I was in retail, newsagent, confectionery. For four years I owned a newsagent. I'm always selling something,' he says. 'This time it's the city.'

As we walk around the city centre, he fills me in on the days of emigration from Derry to 'Ellis Island, Quebec and Australia… Derry is a city of refuge: people would come here before they went anywhere else.' America and Canada were especially popular. 'There used to be two bars here,' says Martin, pointing to the city walls. 'There was an American and a Canadian bar. And at the back of each there was a de-licing centre. You had to be medically examined before boarding the ship. There were three sets of steps that you could be led down when you arrived in the US: one for those who were physically OK, another for those who were borderline, and another for those who had to go back. The ship owner would have to pay the fee if you came back, so you'd be checked over before you went.'

We pass graffiti on the city wall that asks: 'Who? What? Why? Where? When? And How?' and shows the outline of a body. Martin leads me on and begins to answer a few of those questions about the city wall's history. 'The English recognised that Derry had an important natural strategic position – because of its location at the edge of the Atlantic Ocean. So in 1600 a large number of boats arrived in the city. On these boats were the Londoners for the plantation of Ulster. In simple terms: they came to take over.'

He pauses, and adds: 'Even back then, not everyone was happy with their arrival.'

A wall was built under the command of Sir Henry Docwra, after James I conferred city status on Derry in 1604. The wall took five years to construct, and was completed in 1618.

'Was it during the English takeover that the decision was made to rename the city Londonderry?' I ask.

'Yes exactly. That was contentious then and it's contentious now,' says Martin, who likes to speak plainly. 'There's a lot of argy-bargy about it. The population is seventy-two per cent Roman Catholic and they want the London name to be dropped. Protestants don't. There have been rows at local government level. Petitions to judges.'

Martin calls it Derry – as does almost all the tourist literature.

We enter the shopping centre. This is full of fashion shops: River Island, Monsoon, Debenhams, Topshop and Next. It's another bit of Everywhere UK, with most brands on show. 'These are exciting times: the money and the wealth here,' says Martin. The shopping centre is now on all tours: a visible sign of better and changing social conditions.

Then we move on to one of the defining moments in Northern Irish history. 'James II was thrown off the throne in England,' Martin says. 'He was thrown off by William of Orange. But then James secured the help of the French and the Jacobites. Unfortunately for us, he stopped here in Ireland.' When he did, he assembled a Catholic army of 100,000, Martin explains. But in 1688: 'The gates of the city were closed to his forces by a group of thirteen apprentices. There would be no surrender to the Catholic king.' This defiance has famously become symbolic of Protestants holding out against Catholics in the province. It led to a 105-day siege of the city the following year, when as many as 15,000 people are said to have died of starvation and disease. The population was reduced to eating mice, rats and dogs – some of the latter are believed to have been fattened on human corpses, says Martin.

Yet the city held out, and the next year William of Orange (William III) sent a relief force to tackle James, who was finally defeated in the Battle of the Boyne in 1690. 'The defeat is celebrated [by Protestants] with marching, marching and more marching,' explains Martin. 'There's a lot of marching in Derry.'

We march on ourselves, to the city walls. 'This is one of the finest walls in Europe and the most complete in the island of Ireland,' says Martin. 'It is nine furlongs long exactly. But very sadly, as you can see, there are these big ugly gates put up to stop marches, demonstrations and violence.' The metal gates are up on the top of the old city walls, positioned at intervals around Derry, and are locked at certain times. They look like something out of a high-security prison. 'It will be fantastic when they come down one day.'

The population of Derry is 106,000, Martin tells me as we look out across the walls and the river Foyle to the east. He says that 97 per cent of the people living on the west side of the river, where we are now, are Catholic. 'The river divides the two communities.' We are next to the Fountain Estate with its red, white and blue pavements.

'Are people allowed to paint the streets like this?'

'No. That's illegal,' says Martin. 'But it's just the young children who paint things. The hope is that this territorial colouring will end.'

Until a couple of months ago there were army barriers by the gate leading to the estate, but they have come down, says Martin. A military base here was also shut recently – an important moment for Derry according to Martin, as it was the last outpost of the British army on the west side of the river. 'Sectarian trouble is down,' he says.

'What kind of trouble exactly?'

'Mainly people throwing stones. This used to be a flashpoint.'

But this is nothing. 'The place we are about to see used to be one of the most violent areas in the world,' he announces. We are visiting Bogside. We walk down the hill past the famous sign that says 'YOU ARE NOW ENTERING FREE DERRY'. This is the site of Bloody Sunday. 'Soldiers shot from up there,' says Martin, pointing to the hill with the Apprentice Boys Memorial Hall. 'Thirteen people died on the day and one later. Twenty-seven people were seriously injured. On the night of the shooting the British consulate in New York said that they were targeting gunmen, murderers and bombers.'

This is, of course, hotly disputed. The results of an inquiry published in 1972, eleven weeks after the shootings, found that while there was 'no proof that any of the deceased had been shot while handling a firearm or bomb, there was a strong suspicion that some had been firing weapons or handling bombs in the course of the afternoon'. After calling more than 900 witnesses – and spending more than £172 million – the follow-up inquiry has yet to publish its report, at the time of my visit.

Colourful murals on houses depict victims of the violence – the fourteen people who died after the Bloody Sunday attack, figures coughing as they run from tear-gas canisters, civil rights marchers being targeted by masked soldiers. By the road there is a grey memorial to the fourteen who died – their ages ranging from seventeen to fifty-nine. And opposite is the Museum of Free Derry. This explains the tensions from the run-up to the partition of Ireland in the 1920s to the present day, putting forwards the nationalist perspective.

After partition 'Derry felt abandoned, a very reluctant part of the north' says a display that explains that at one point there was one police officer for every two Catholic families in the north. In the late 1940s, unemployment was 20 per cent in Bogside yet the Northern Irish average was 8 per cent: 'Unionist politicians directed industries to Unionist areas... Derry was the starkest example of anti-Catholic discrimination in the northern state.' In the 1960s, there was a 'sixty-seven per cent nationalist majority under Unionist rule'. Local people began to identify with the civil rights struggles in the United States and South Africa.

Batons, rubber-bullet guns and gas masks are in cabinets near a display on the introduction of internment in 1971 during which '342 people were arrested in a massive raid across Northern Ireland'. 'IT WAS WILFUL MURDER, SAY PRIESTS' runs the headline in the Derry Journal on 1 February 1972, describing Bloody Sunday.

It is a brilliant museum that helps me understand local divisions – well worth at least an hour of your time. I get talking to Jean Hegarty, who runs the small shop selling postcards depicting MI5 security cameras dripping blood. There are pamphlets on the ineffectiveness of the Bloody Sunday inquiries, as well as T-shirts with Free Derry slogans. 'We've been open a year and we've had tourists from 126 different countries,' Jean says – making Derry by far the most mainstream of the 'unsung' spots I've visited so far. Jean pauses. Then she tells me that her brother died on Bloody Sunday: Kevin McElhinney, aged seventeen. She was twenty-three at the time, living in Canada. She says: 'What the news reports said after Bloody Sunday was that the soldiers killed gunmen and bombers. As it turned out, the news reports were wrong and worse: the British Army knew they were wrong. The Bloody Sunday inquiry has cost a fortune – but the truth doesn't cost that much. It is the British lies that have cost that much. What happened to my brother can't be changed, but the character assassination by the British can.'

John Kelly, an education officer at the museum, tells me his brother Michael also died, also aged seventeen. 'He was shot where the monument is, believe it or not,' he says. 'He was unlucky – he was shot in the stomach. I grabbed hold of him and carried him away. It totally reshaped my life.' He has since been involved in a Bloody Sunday justice campaign, but instead of sounding bitter he has a positive outlook. How can he be so upbeat? 'Things round here are fantastically improved,' he replies. 'It's a peaceful situation now and the future is in the hands of the politicians.' The biggest problem is not so much political as economic, he says: Derry is short of jobs. 'Both my sons work in cheap call centres for a telecommunications company: five-sixty an hour. They're getting paid buttons. We need an influx of money into the area.'

Martin, whose daughter also works for a call centre, believes there should be a peace dividend. 'All the money that's been saved by peace should go to the area,' he says. 'The sadness and the reality is that if our children want a decent wage they have to move away.' Martin's other daughter is studying at university, but 'she's not coming back to five-sixty an hour.' John tells me that Desmond's shirt factory, formerly a big local employer, has closed: 'Production has gone to the Far East. There used to be major shirt-making and engineering works. Now it's just taxis and tourism.'

One day in Derry and I have already learned a whole lot more about the politics of Northern Ireland than I imagined I would. That's the thing, I'm discovering, about visiting the province: you can't help but become immersed in the political goings-on, even as a tourist. At least, that's what I'm finding. Back at the Tower Hotel, I have a rest after a long day. But then my mobile rings. It is the ever-helpful, well-connected and friendly Martin, once again. 'Would you like to have a ride in a police car?' he surprises me by asking.

'What do you mean?' I reply, a little dozily, feeling half-asleep.

'A ride in a police car, so you can see how safe the city really is,' he continues, sounding upbeat and as though this is perfectly normal.

'But tourists don't usually ride about in police cars in Northern Ireland, are you sure they won't mind?'

'I know an officer. He'd love to show you round. If you can see how safe it is, you can spread the word,' Martin says. 'I really think you should do it. He can make it round in about half an hour."

'Make it round where?" I say, waking up completely now.

'To your hotel. Want me to say yes?'

Which is how I find myself standing outside the Tower Hotel on a rainy Saturday night in Derry, not far from the site of Bloody Sunday, close to one of Northern Ireland's famous centres of Unionism: the Apprentice Boys Memorial Hall. Groups of revellers are heading for the busy pubs on Waterloo Street. Inside the hotel, the American students are now drinking beers at the bar. Taxi drivers look hopefully at me as I wait by the hotel entrance.

Soon my carriage arrives: a Mitsubishi Shogun belonging to the Police Service of Northern Ireland. Sergeant Sam Young of the City Centre Neighbourhood Police Team grips my hand, smiling. 'Great to see you! Jump in!' he says. There are two part-time constables in the back seats, Leighanne and Aaron, who have come along for the ride. They too smile brightly and shake my hand.

'What are you looking for tonight?' I ask as I get in a back seat.

'Anti-social behaviour,' Sam replies cheerfully, as though it's part of a (very) unusual tourist trail. It feels more than a little bizarre seeing the city from a police Mitsubishi Shogun. 'That's what we're after.'

'Is there much?'

'It's mostly OK. There's only what we'd describe as normal anti-social behaviour, these days. We've hammered the area pretty hard. The worst of it has been knocked on the head.'

Sam is aged thirty-four and has been working for the police since 1993. Now he's in charge of the team covering Brandywell and Bogside. 'Things have changed massively in the last ten years,' he says, as we pull out into narrow streets. 'Ten years ago the security gates were almost always locked.

They're only locked occasionally now. They stop anti-social behaviour.'

What kind? 'Assaults, fights, criminal damage. Organised fights have cut down: sectarian behaviour. But it still goes on.'

My unconventional new tourist guide is keen to impress on me how much Derry has changed for the better – especially since the Good Friday Agreement, signed on 10 April 1998. This peace plan, I read before coming, set out to create 'devolved government in Northern Ireland on a stable and inclusive basis, providing for the creation of Human Rights and Equality commissions, the early release of terrorist prisoners, the decommissioning of paramilitary weapons and far-reaching reforms of criminal justice and policing' – so says the Northern Ireland Office. It is working well, according to Sam: 'Back then [in 1998] we would patrol with the army. We'd have thirty soldiers and twenty police officers to caution someone for a traffic offence. Now all we need are two officers.' In the 1990s, instead of Mitsubishi Shoguns, he would travel in Saxon armour-plated personnel carriers – which would have made for an even more unusual, and frightening, tour.

'I'd carry a rifle. I'd wear ballistic body armour,' says Sam, who seems to want to tell me all this to give me a broader perspective on life in Derry and Northern Ireland than you would get on a typical weekend break. 'You didn't hang around on calls. You went in and you went out quickly. That's the way we did policing then. It was a different job and a different city. I used to work inside an army camp next to a helipad.'

We turn into the Fountain Estate, a Loyalist area with terraced housing. Union Jacks hang from lamp posts. A military-style mural says: 'BRITISH UNIONIST ALLIANCE.

FOUR COUNTRIES. ONE NATION.' The streets are empty. Curtains are drawn. It's an otherworldly and quite menacing setting. It doesn't feel like Britain at all. Yet crime in Fountain Estate is down 61 per cent year on year, Sam tells me. There are, he adds, about forty to fifty assaults a month across Derry: 'I actually don't think this is too bad. We had just ten burglaries in the whole of February across the city. There were only two street robberies. We collected one weapon in the whole month. Outside Derry there's a perception that things are a lot worse. But people have not been reporting the changes.'

We pass the pubs near Waterloo Street, where it is quiet, perhaps because of the rain. He admits that officers continue to suffer from sectarian abuse, but there is greater respect due to changes in recruitment: 'We're eight per cent Catholic now, but we have a target of thirty per cent in the next two years across Northern Ireland. There has been a fifty–fifty recruitment policy between Protestants and Catholics since 2002. There is no stigma dealing with the police any more.'

Before coming I'd looked up the BBC's website file on Northern Ireland, which estimates that more than a thousand people have been forced into exile through intimidation by paramilitary groups since the Good Friday Agreement. Should anyone return – says the BBC – 'the beatings are vicious, some of the shootings have been fatal... Usually it is gangs that carry out the attacks. The motive can be a personal grudge or a real or imagined slight.' I ask Sam about these beatings.

Sam considers his answer carefully. 'They happen every now and then,' he replies. 'Not very often.'

We cruise through a 'sectarian interface' at the junction of Gobnascale Estate and Irish Street. This is definitely not tourist territory. Trouble can sometimes flare up here, Sam admits. During the marching season between Easter Monday and the end of September, when members of the Protestant Orange Order take to streets that often fall within Catholic-dominated areas, he has in the past been attacked with petrol bombs in these parts. 'Oh, quite a few times,' he says. 'I've been in vehicles that have been on fire so many times I can't even remember. Thankfully, all that's calmed down now.'

In Bogside, we pass the Bogside Inn – a tough-looking pub with window grills. A baby's pram is lying on its side on the concrete forecourt amid broken glass. CCTV cameras are attached to the pub walls. The green, gold and white of the Irish tricolour is painted on pedestrian bollards. A lamp post has a fake traffic sign with the letters RUC with a red cross running through it (the Royal Ulster Constabulary became the Police Service of Northern Ireland in 2001). Next to this sign there's a picture of a hooded man holding a gun and punching his fist. Murals showing the Palestinian flag next to the Irish tricolour are painted on the side of a Ladbrokes. Graffiti by a shuttered grocery shop says: 'Young Bogside Rioters' and 'PC O'Kane – Don't Cry'. Another piece of graffiti sprayed in white paint on a fence says: 'SF: MI5 OUT!' – a reference to Sinn Fein wanting the British security service to leave Bogside.

Welcome to the attractions, Bogside-style. Would an out-of-town visitor be OK walking around these parts at night? 'Yes,' replies Sam. 'Of course. There's nowhere in the city where tourists are not safe now.'

I look around at the graffiti-splattered walls. Yellow paint by the betting shop says 'RIRA: One Down, More 2 Go'. The Real Irish Republican Army is designated a terrorist organisation in the United Kingdom and is held responsible for the Omagh bombing in 1998 that killed twenty-nine people.

As we are driving, I begin to realise that although I've visited Belfast before, I've never grasped the full implications of the divisions in Northern Ireland. Seeing the painted neighbourhoods, the tribal graffiti and the desolate streets, is bringing home the enormity of the situation. 'Anyone visiting Ireland should come to Derry. The city has got to be seen,' Sam says, suddenly sounding as though he works for the tourist board. 'There are the walls for a start – and the two cathedrals.'

From the back of the car, Leighanne, who is becoming a full-time constable next week after working in administration for the police, adds: 'There's so much more to do in Derry. More shopping. More restaurants.' Aaron, who tells me he has worked as a traffic warden, says: 'There's a lot of history here. There's not just the history of the walls. There's the history of the disembarkation at the height of emigration.' He's referring to emigration to the New World in the eighteenth and nineteenth centuries.

We stop outside the Apprentice Boys Memorial Hall at the top of the hill. Sam and I get out of the car. It's still raining. Figures are lurking near an entrance to the hall: a damp, cream-stone Gothic building with French chateau-style turrets. They watch us as we walk to the city wall. Through an 'anti-lob screen' that prevents stones being thrown, we look down on Bogside. Youths have gathered outside the Bogside Inn. 'The kids on both sides,' he adds, looking down at the people below, 'are trying to defend their areas.'

Which does not perhaps suggest that tourists are safe absolutely everywhere... all the time.

We walk along the wall in the rain, and then Sam drops me back at the Tower Hotel. I comment that I hope the night stays quiet, and Sam quickly replies: 'Don't say that!' Apparently it's a jinx. And off they drive into the darkness of Derry, leaving me well away from any anti-social behaviour (not that we ever saw any) in the comfortable surroundings of the Tower Hotel.

But the next day I move on. I'd only been able to book a single night at the Tower Hotel as it was full over the weekend. As luck would have it, however, there's room at Serendipity House, a five-room B & B right in the heart of Bogside.

Serendipity is on a row of terraced houses. The front is neatly painted in black and white. Inside it is quirky and stylishly designed, with a jukebox in a lounge with an illuminated globe and leather sofas. A model of Pinocchio is in a corner and a computer terminal sits on a wooden desk. The smell of coffee comes from a back kitchen that overlooks decking with a view of Derry's walls. Bob Marley is playing on a stereo as Stephen Lyttle, the co-owner with his father Paul, brings me tea and a croissant.

Stephen is twenty-five, with cropped hair and a genial manner. For the past five years he has worked as a manager for Wetherspoon pubs. Soon he's telling me all about the B & B, which opened four months ago with rooms for £50 a night: 'My Dad always wanted to run a B & B. After being a taxi-man for twenty years, he'd had enough.' They renovated the building, which is close to their family home, themselves. To drum up business they have registered with several websites and distributed flyers to taxi drivers. 'We've had guests from Australia, New Zealand, Canada, Germany and Spain,' he says. His enthusiasm for Derry is infectious: 'It's an amazing place – lovely.' People are reflecting on the Troubles these days, he says, and 'seeing them as part of modern history and embracing that... there's a lot of good in our history as well as bad'.

'It's sad that people see the city in a bad light,' he adds, offering me another croissant. 'Yes, there used to be big police barracks and watchtowers. But when you're growing up, you just don't know any different. There was a lot of friction and tension. If you were in England and you saw paratroopers, you'd ask: "What's going on here?" We'd just say to them: "Come on, give us a look through your telescope."'

'Were you ever stopped and searched?' I ask, between bites of my croissant.

'Loads of times,' he answers, laughing that I should ask this question. '"What are you doing? Where are you going? Where do you live?" You got used to it.'

He insists Bogside is safe, and says the Museum of Free Derry, the murals and St Eugene's Cathedral, just round the corner, are the main sights. 'There is no trouble whatsoever. Everyone now is friendly. Nobody who's stayed has ever said they've had a bad time.' He pauses as if to find the best example of how the area has changed. 'It was funny. The other day I saw a policeman riding on his bicycle. In the old days he wouldn't have come out of Bogside in one piece. My mate and I saw him and said to each other: "They're getting brave these days aren't they?"'

My room is in the attic. It's small with neat decor and a double bed. In the distance, I can see the site of Bloody Sunday. I drop off my bag and take a stroll around the neighbourhood.

To the right I wander past The Don pub, where Martin McGuinness, the former IRA commander and leading voice in the Irish republican movement, apparently drinks. It's a pleasant day, the sun is shining on Bogside and I feel totally at ease. It seems much more laid-back and quiet here than in parts of Salford (with its hollow-eyed junkies and hoodies near the Salford Lads Club) and prettier than bits of Slough I walked about (especially the more run-down parts of Chalvey where Romanian immigrants have moved in). Down a hill, I come to the tall elegant structure of St Eugene's Cathedral. Inside, the pews are full and a sermon is under way. From the doorway I can see a man in red who is saying: 'So I ask you children, do you reject Satan and all his works?' There's a brief pause, then: 'I do.' The priest asks: 'Do you believe in the Holy Catholic Church and the forgiveness of sins?' They do. 'This is our faith, this is our faith of our church,' he continues. And the children say: 'Amen.'

From these peaceful scenes, I continue on down the hill, and find a tourist-style sign at a junction that says I'm at Aggro Corner. This is where 'clouds of CS gas and a hail of rubber bullets met stones and petrol bombs' in the past. Next to this there is a small memorial to three members of the Irish National Liberation Army who were 'killed in action' in 1977. Then I walk on past the murals and find myself outside the front of the Bogside Inn. It is early evening now, and I open a door with a grilled window and find myself by a long thin bar.

I think it's fair to say that, as a tourist, I'm in the minority here. I order a pint of Guinness, and drop a coin as I do so. I pick it up off the sticky floor. A couple of people look at me and make a comment I cannot understand because of the heavy Irish accent. Everyone seems to know everyone else. Teenagers are playing pool in the corner. On the walls around the pool table are black-and-white photographs of civil rights marchers. In another corner, there's a jockey's silk in a frame. I read a tourist brochure, feeling totally out of place and beginning to wonder how I have found myself drinking Guinness alone on a Sunday night in the Bogside Inn.

But the Guinness is very good and later, back at Serendipity House, I meet Paul Lyttle, Stephen's father. He has spiky hair and a tan from a recent holiday in Malaga. He tells me about his days as a taxi driver, when he used regularly to take John Hume ('he loves his catnaps') and has also had Sinéad O'Connor as a passenger ('She was lovely, but she just got so much publicity about her comments about the Pope.'). During the Troubles he would be stopped at least once a night by soldiers who would open the bonnet and the boot. 'Once I was hijacked,' he says, as though this is the most normal thing in the world. 'They were masked and they had a gun. They just took the car off me. It was found two hours later. It had been used to rob a petrol station. The IRA got the blame but whether it was or wasn't them nobody knows. That wasn't frightening. I felt safe.'

All that is well in the past, though. Now, Derry is 'magic… the peace: I love it'.

The next morning, I pop into the Tower Museum, close to the Tower Hotel, where there are audio-visual presentations covering the Siege of Derry, and lots of information about immigration to the New World. Apparently, during the Potato Famines of 1845 and 1846, when there was destitution and disease across Ireland, the port of Derry 'profited', arranging the passage of as many as 16,000 people across the Atlantic in one year. Many of those who departed had walked across the countryside shoeless so they would not wear out the soles of their only shoes; needed for their lives ahead. It's also intriguing to learn that during the US Civil War in the 1860s, local factories experienced a boom as they provided uniforms for both the Union and Confederate armies. It is a good museum with interactive displays, interesting films and documents supplying first-hand evidence of historical events. I amble around for about an hour and only see a couple of other visitors – which seems surprising for a Sunday.

Then I go to my final meeting in the city – with a man who played more than a small part in creating that 'magic' of peace that Paul Lyttle had been talking about: John Hume. He grew up in Derry and both he and Seamus Heaney attended St Columb's College – giving the school the rare and possibly unique honour of producing two Nobel Prize winners. He was leader of the moderate nationalist Social Democratic and Labour Party and campaigned for a 'yes' vote for the Good Friday Agreement, along with David Trimble of the Ulster Unionist party, who was a co-winner of the peace prize.

His health has suffered in recent years, he tells me, when we meet in the swish purple lobby of the Tower Hotel. Hume is wearing a navy suit, a matching cardigan and a checked blue tie. His wavy black hair is swept back as though he pushed it that way without too much thought. He is sitting on a lurid gold sofa. From behind his spectacles, his blue eyes have an owlish appearance.

After apologising about his health again, Hume tells me: 'The city has transformed completely now, you know. There's no tension of any description on the streets.'

He speaks slowly, with a heavy accent, keeping his eyes fixed on me. 'What do you think about life in Derry now?' I ask.

'I'm very pleased with things,' he says. 'I'm also very pleased with the agreement that has taken place in Northern Ireland. That agreement has transformed the situation because, for the first time in history, the people of Ireland as a whole – north and south – have voted on how they wish to live together: overwhelmingly voting for the Good Friday Agreement. Now what's happening is that the Good Friday Agreement has been implemented by all sections of the community.'

The streets are safe, he says, and the civil rights marchers of the 1960s and 1970s have achieved their aims – at least for now. 'The people of the city live together in total peace and harmony. They are also totally committed to the city,' he says in a dulcet, patient voice.

He's curious to know why I'm in the city and who I've met: he asks for names and says 'Oh yes I know him' or ruffles his brow when he hasn't heard of someone, as though he ought to know everyone. A soulful song with the refrain 'how am I supposed to live without you' is playing in the background, and it suddenly strikes me as slightly surreal that in a trendy hotel not far from the site of Bloody Sunday I'm talking to a person who has, through the long and winding process of political dialogue, helped end a conflict that some believe to have caused more than 3,500 deaths. Given that there are approximately 1.7 million people in Northern Ireland, the death toll represents about 2 per cent of the population. A similar percentage would have meant 100,000 deaths in other parts of the UK, or half a million in America.

Although the situation is transformed, Hume is concerned about unemployment. Tourism, he believes, could make a big difference: 'I hope tourism will deal very effectively with our employment situation and provide real hope to our young people. Given the historic nature of the city of Derry, it's a major tourist centre.'

Then he asks, as though he's keeping tags on who is in town: 'How did you get to Derry, and how are you leaving?'

I explain my journey by train and ferry, and he seems surprised. 'Why didn't you just take a plane?' he asks, making me wonder a little myself. The journey by train and boat from London took eighteen hours.

He talks about the shopping mall that Martin showed me earlier – this seems to be a local symbol of the changes in Derry. He discusses 'people working together with common interests'.

'Could you imagine the Tower Hotel in Derry being here during the Troubles?' I ask. The hotel opened in 2002.

He simply says: 'No.'

Hume mentions his health once more, as we walk towards the desk in the lobby. I'm about to catch a taxi to the train station and Hume is going home to his house on the edge of Bogside. He asks if he can go in my taxi, so we share a ride to his house on a modest terrace not far from the Bogside Inn. Then he says: 'Hold on a minute, would you?' And he disappears into his house. He comes back with a miniature bottle of Tyrconnell single malt whiskey that has a label that says: 'Specially bottled to honour John Hume MLA, MP,

MEP, Nobel Peace Prize, 10 December 1998.' He gives me this, shakes my hand, and says, 'If you're in need of any more information, just call.'

Hume's generosity and sense of interest in my visit – despite his obvious physical discomfort – are touching and I can understand how someone with his qualities helped smooth the way towards peace in Northern Ireland.

And then I leave Derry. I've learned a lot about a part of the UK that it is not possible to understand properly, I now believe, unless you go there. I highly recommend a visit. Will I feel the same after a trip to another often-overlooked corner of Britain... in Wales?

6

PORT TALBOT: 'ON YER BIKE, BOYO!'

When I asked a Welsh friend where he would be least likely to visit on a holiday in Wales, his answer came quickly. 'Port Talbot,' he replied, sounding very sure of himself. 'I don't think I'd go on holiday to Port Talbot.'

My next destination was decided.

And the journey from London is simple – a breeze compared to the trip to Derry a fortnight ago, as enjoyable as the overnight ferry adventure on the rusty old *Lagan Viking* had been. The train from Paddington speeds towards the West Country, passing dear Slough (with its must-be-celebrated trading estate and Wit's End guest house) and the general loveliness of well-sung Bath (with its Georgian crescents, American tourists and pricey five-star spa hotels), before diving into a tunnel under the river Severn and resurfacing in Wales, where the feeling of being in another country is immediate, in a way I don't think you get on a train journey up to Scotland. We pass close to the exotic sounding Llanfihangel Rogiet, Rhiwderin and Coedkernew. Newport is not just Newport any more, it's Casnewydd, Cardiff is has become Caerdydd, and Bridgend is Pen-y-Bont ar Ogwr – and try saying that after a few drinks. Two hours from Paddington and it feels like I'm in another (unspellable) world.

Little villages with terraces cling to hillsides. There are fields dotted with bales of hay wrapped in black plastic. We pass the shiny offices of Casnewydd, an old castle on a hill, and rusty train carriages in a siding. Then we pull into Caerdydd for a stop-off, where I admire the Millennium Stadium, with its great curves and vast triangular support columns. After passing through the Vale of Glamorgan, the train eventually nears my destination, Port Talbot (Welsh name, rather disappointingly, also Port Talbot). It's a mild Thursday morning at the end of November. I take in the mad metal tubes, cooling stacks, conveyor belts and flames of the Port Talbot steelworks – more on this later – and shortly afterwards we come to a halt. I am among a handful of passengers disembarking at the small station. No other tourists in sight.

In the car park, I just miss the only taxi in the rank, but take down the number on its side. As seagulls swirl above, I call this and an operator says a vehicle will be on its way soon. I've booked a room at the Best Western Aberavon Beach Hotel, for a reasonable forty pounds a night. This is on a sandy beach overlooking the Bristol Channel not far from the steelworks. The beach is popular with surfers and kite-boarders, the hotel website said when I'd booked. A small white car pulls up, and I am greeted by a driver with 'DAVE' tattooed on his knuckles.

Then I have the type of conversation that is not exactly going to win over the tourist masses to the welcoming charms of this part of South Wales.

It goes like this.

'Please could you take me to the Best Western?'

'I don't know that one,' he replies sullenly, gripping the wheel tighter with his DAVE hand.

'It's down by the beach,' I explain.

'Down by the beach?' he replies, as though this is totally puzzling, even though the beach is a short distance away.

'Yes, the Best Western by the beach,' I say. I'm having flashbacks to the driver in Slough who didn't know the church in Stoke Poges. 'I think there's only one hotel there.'

'Hmm, a Best Western,' he says.

'Yes!' I say.

'I think I may know the one,' he replies, mysteriously.

We drive in silence over a course of speed humps, passing rows of depressing grey council terraces. Then we arrive at a building that looks as though it could pass for a low-security prison: four storeys of brick punctured by cell-like windows, with more dreary council blocks just behind it. Next door is an empty-looking Aquadome, a Hollywood Park cinema complex, and Burger Knight, a 'new luxury fast-dining restaurant'. There are no surfers or kite-boarders on the beach. There are just a handful of cars in the Best Western's car park.

'I never knew this was a Best Western,' says DAVE.

'Didn't you see the big sign?' I reply.

'Yes, but I never knew this was a Best Western,' he responds.

I smile thinly, hand over my fare and hope DAVE is a one-off in this rarely visited spot just off the M4 – and almost directly under it in places – between Caerdydd (Cardiff) and Abertawe (Swansea).

Inside the hotel there are no other guests in reception. The place is totally dead. But there is a smiley receptionist, who seems a little shocked to see me and genuinely glad to have some company. I collect my key from her and take a small lift upstairs to find a plain, cramped room with a double bed and views of the steelworks and the beach. The Best Western Aberavon Beach is unlikely to feature in too many glossy travel magazine features (Anne had taken one look at the website and politely declined a jaunt into South Wales). Then I head straight from the hotel, using another taxi company recommended by the nice receptionist, to the Port Talbot steelworks for an afternoon tour.

This is how I've found myself in a room full of monitors, protected by a sheet of thick blue glass that looks onto a furnace where molten iron is mixed with scrap and oxygen to create steel. An orange glow emanates from a hole on the far side of a chamber. A man in blue overalls is fiddling with buttons next to a sign that says: 'WARNING: DAY TECHNICAL WORKING.' It is stuffy, and tinny music is playing on a hidden stereo. The catchy song is 'Nothing Sweet About Me' by the pop star Gabriella Cilmi. Its loopy tune and chilled beat ring out across the chamber as a 'torpedo' container, used to carry molten iron, is taken away.

We're at the Basic Oxygen Steelmaking plant, next to a disused beach overlooking the Bristol Channel – and I'm about to learn the intricacies of steel production. It's hard to beat that for an unusual weekend break (although you can,

I've heard, take tours of Chernobyl in the Ukraine). The plant is not open to the general public: I've been granted special permission to visit as a journalist.

The building is part of the giant Corus steelworks that stretches for four miles along the coast. I'm with Tom Johnson, the internal affairs officer for Corus, which employs 3,500 people here, making it the most important source of local work, even though the workforce is down from a peak of 12,600 in the 1970s; the steelworks began production in 1953. He's just introduced me to Mark who says he is a 'primary team member' at the plant. Tom and I are wearing white-plastic hard hats.

'So what's going on in the chamber?' I ask Mark.

'We basically make molten steel here,' he explains, matter-of-factly. 'It can be very dangerous, you've got to be totally aware of what's going on.' A sign on the outside of the building lists the number of days since the last accident (491, which seems pretty good). 'We take eighty tonnes of scrap and two-hundred-and-eighty tonnes of molten iron and we mix them with oxygen.' He points towards the chamber. 'Usually it's white hot in there, but we're shut down for a couple of hours.'

'The temperature can reach 1,600 degrees Celsius,' adds Tom, 'and workers entering the chamber must wear a helmet with a protective curtain that falls around the shoulders to prevent sparks falling on their necks. The helmets have gold-mirrored visors to protect against the intensity of the white heat. The steel made here goes towards producing cars, building cladding, machinery, microwaves, cans, beams, girders, rail tracks – a hundred and one applications; we have half the market share of this type of steel in the UK.'

There is usually a giant flame from the roof of the building we're in. This can be seen for miles around at night. Along with the sodium lights and spotlights covering the many miles of metal tubes, conveyor belts, cranes, towers and chimneys billowing steam, the Port Talbot steelworks is quite a sight.

'I think it's fantastic,' says Tom. 'When you drive past at night, you get a sense of being close to this large... thing.' Apparently, the film director Ridley Scott was so impressed by this 'thing' that it was one of the inspirations for the futuristic scenes he created in the 1982 film *Blade Runner*.

We stare at the orange furnace. Mark tells me about his shift pattern. At the end of every ten weeks he gets eighteen days off. This means he goes on holiday quite a bit. 'Florida this year,' he says.

'If you were not from these parts, would you go on a break round here?' I ask, as I'm beginning to have doubts that you would: it really is very industrial. On first impressions, my Welsh friend who recommended Port Talbot as a *very* unsung spot seems to have known what he was talking about. Or perhaps not...

'Actually, I think I would,' he replies. 'The mountain biking's good.'

'What? Is there mountain biking here?' I ask. 'I can't see any mountains.'

Mark explains that several trails were opened in the hills just inland from Port Talbot, and he's taken up the sport: 'I love it up there. People come from all over for the mountain biking.'

Still wondering about this, I walk down a corridor with Mark where a poster on a wall says: 'There is no such idea as a bad idea. Yet ideas are money.' We go to a car park passing three flag posts. One flies the Welsh flag, the next the Corus corporate flag and the third the orange, white and green tricolour of India. 'We were recently bought by Tata,' explains Tom – an Indian company. Corus had been British-Dutch-owned since 1999, when British Steel merged with a Dutch producer. Then we go to the Port Talbot steelworks beach. This is 'the largest privately owned beach in Europe', according to Corus. Apparently, a few members of staff go fishing and surfing here.

But that seems hard to believe.

The beach is a mess. Just past a 'Slag Granulation Plant', which Tom explains has something to do with the residue of smelted metallic ore, and not far from a sign that warns 'Risk of Carbon Monoxide Poisoning; Risk of Fire and Explosion', we reach the shoreline. The sands are filthy, with a dark hue that looks like oil. Litter is piled against the dunes: old tyres, pieces of rope, broken crates and plastic bottles. If people just gave up caring, this is probably how every beach around the world would eventually turn out. Tom, who looks a bit embarrassed about it, says that plans are afoot to make changes: 'Our new MD wants to take all the scrap he can find on the site and put it into the furnace. He believes there is too much scrap around. "I want a steelworks in a garden", he has said. We're spending money on-site.' This garden approach is coinciding with a green scheme to make use of the gasses released from the Basic Oxygen Steel section. At the moment, these gasses are burned, releasing carbon dioxide and creating the flame: 'That flame represents a massive potential. We're going to put a cap on it and turn it into steam – to create a steam-powered turbine.'

Some locals are upset about the smells that come out of the plant. I smelled sulphur on the drive in, and saw a sign in the front window of a terraced house that said: 'CLEAN AIR: A HUMAN RIGHT DENIED TO PORT TALBOT.' Capping the flame, however, ought to reduce the pong. On this subject, Tom says: 'There are certain smells associated with production. We recognise that this [Port Talbot] is where our future workforce comes from. We have a very good working relationship with the environment.'

I'm not entirely sure what that means, and when Tom senses my confusion, he says: 'People see big clouds coming from the plant and they say: "Oh, there's the steelworks belching out all that awful smoke." Actually it's not dirty smoke – it's just steam.'

We pass a red statue of a dragon that celebrates a century of steelmaking at the site. Steel production began in South Wales because of its coal pits, which provided the furnace fuel. But the pits are no more: a few months before my visit, the very last deep mine in Wales, Tower Colliery in Hirwuan, closed. Now coal is shipped in.

Then Tom drives out of the main entrance and down a side road. We are very quickly, and quite bizarrely, in a country lane leading to the Corus reservoir.

'Nice, eh?' says Tom.

'Yes, very nice... What is this place?' I reply.

'Well, we use the water here for steelmaking,' Tom says. 'But the reservoir also acts as a centre for our sailing and angling clubs.'

It's really very odd. Here we are a few hundred yards from one of the largest heavy-industry sites in Britain, not far from slag granulation plants and the wasteland of the beach, and there are figures hunched over fishing rods with flasks of tea. Moorhens bob on the water. A man on a mountain bike smiles at us and raises a hand to say 'hello' on his way to the sailing club. You can't even see the steelworks from here: trees block out the machinery at the plant. It's almost totally silent. Port Talbot, I'm already learning, has its surprises.

After thanking Tom for showing me round – he could easily have declined my request – I go for a coffee in a cafe round the corner, where I read an article in Cardiff's *Western Mail*. The story reports on the findings of a 'planning and management consultancy' which has declared that Port Talbot's 'collection of flaming, smoking stacks, pipework and huge blast furnaces... could be a tourist attraction... the steel mill, which has fascinated passing M4 motorists for decades, could pull in thousands'. There is beauty, it continues, in the 'flames, crisscrossing lights and eerie glow at night'. The *Western Mail* goes on to highlight several other local allures including Aberavon Beach, the Aquadome (a swimming pool with water slides), the birthplaces of the actors Richard Burton and Anthony Hopkins, mountain-biking trails, Margam Castle ('a Gothic mansion with impressive spires overlooking roaming deer, Cistercian Abbey remains and a museum of important early Christian memorial stones'), waterfalls and canals. More than 1.7 million people, the article says, come to see the sights spending an amazing £74 million a year, according to latest council statistics.

I put down the paper, feeling flabbergasted. So much to explore! Tourism is booming! Who needs low-cost flights to fancy European capitals? On the basis of all this, Port Talbot seems to be a veritable treasure trove of tourist opportunities. I finish my coffee and head off to my hotel with a spring in my step and a sense of expectation: I may have already seen the *Blade Runner* steelworks, but Port Talbot appears to have a whole lot more to offer.

I start with Margam Castle, with its 'impressive spires and roaming deer'. It's on a hill overlooking the M4; a large grey building with turrets, cupolas, mullioned windows, and grand sweeps of chipped steps leading to terraces where ivy overflows stone balustrades. It is very grand, slightly worn at the edges... and full of history about the origins of Port Talbot.

I meet Dave Duggan, one of the castle's managers and one of life's (good-natured) grumblers. 'We're so short-staffed round here. So short-staffed!' he says soon after we meet. He seems to have about ten things on the go and is constantly on his walkie-talkie. He is in his fifties, wearing a shirt with two pens sticking out of a pocket. He's worked at Margam for years, having started out in life as a policeman, but leaving 'after five years for financial reasons – that was in the 1970s, with the Labour Party and all that'. He grumbles for a while (good-naturedly) about the Labour Party in the 1970s.

'How did Port Talbot get its name?' I ask, as we walk around.

'From a former owner of the castle: Christopher Rice Mansel Talbot,' Dave replies in a flourish. 'He was an astute businessman who had invested in railways, iron and coal. A very successful man.'

He was also the MP for Glamorgan for sixty years starting in 1830, at around which time his name was given to a harbour development. This was when he built the castle, I learn, on land next to the remains of a Cistercian abbey that was one of the wealthiest in Wales in the eleventh century. We pass the old abbey walls in a pretty garden down a hill.

'It's a helluva job maintaining all this,' says Dave, as his walkie-talkie goes off and he gives advice to a member of staff with an emergency. 'So busy, so short-staffed!' he says, clicking off, and pointing out ancient redwoods and tall, strange-looking trees with flowing branches. I ask what they are.

'Tulip trees: some of the largest you're ever likely to find,' says Dave. We stop to look at a gnarled cork tree. 'Nice, isn't it?' We also take in a giant eighteenth-century orangery. 'It's the longest orangery in the UK,' says Dave.

'There can't be too many people aware of that,' I reflect.

'You're right, there aren't,' he chuckles in reply.

Dave tells me that the castle has several famous connections: William Henry Fox Talbot, a relative of Christopher and the inventor of the negative–positive photographic process, often visited to take pictures. 'He liked the castle, as it stayed still,' says Dave. 'Nelson called by at the orangery in 1803 on a tour of Wales, and Dwight Eisenhower visited troops stationed here prior to the D-Day invasions,' he adds.

By the time of Christopher's death, his port was a success, his railway investments were valued at £3 million and he owned 14,000 hectares of land. The name Port Talbot was secure. But the future of his castle wasn't. It became derelict after the war, and it was only when the council took over in the 1970s that restoration began. The interior of the castle is now given over to rooms for teaching children about local history. Dave thinks more should be done to protect the estate. 'This area lets a lot of things go. English Heritage is a lot better than Cadw,' he says. Cadw, which means 'to keep' in Welsh, is the heritage arm of the Welsh Assembly. Dave grumbles about Cadw: 'In England they look after ancient buildings a lot better than in Wales.'

We look down the hill from a terrace. Beyond the M4 we can see the Corus steelworks, where I was just a couple of hours ago. The huge orange flame is back on and it is looking quite splendid down there. Steam suddenly bursts from one of steelworks' funnels, looking for a moment as though it has been struck by a missile. Lorries are turning out of the Slag Granulation Plant. No matter where you are around here, the steelworks seems to lurk in the background. Dave gazes towards the motorway. Cars and heavy goods vehicles are tearing past. 'That motorway has opened up the whole country,' he says, looking with displeasure at the traffic. 'It wasn't there when I was in the police in the 1970s. Now look at it. Wales was a different country then.'

As he says this, his walkie-talkie goes off. A visitor has been stung by a bee. 'We're so short-staffed! So short-staffed!' he says, as he dashes off to collect a first-aid kit.

I return to my hire car. After seeing the steelworks, having realised that I was probably going to need an awful lot of taxis during my time in Port Talbot, I had hired a Skoda from a small rental-car company near the Best Western. It's handy having your own wheels around here: the town is spread out and not so easy to get about on foot, although there is a centre with shops. I drive down the hill from the castle to take a look around, parking by a row of terraced houses that would not have looked out of place in Salford. At the end of the street is a beautiful art deco cinema that's derelict and covered in fly-posters advertising 'Hard trance, hard style'. I walk past a shiny statue of a man holding steel girders and a South Wales Police office. A bar called The Bank is holding a foam party. There's a body piercing and tattoo parlour. Groups of lads are hanging about by the Jobcentre Plus. I walk to a shopping mall with a Poundland and a half-price sale at Burtons. A ramshackle shop is offering one-pound jeans. There is a Cash Generator centre with a notice that reads: 'WE BUY ALMOST ANYTHING FOR INSTANT CASH! BUY-BACK AVAILABLE. RAISE CASH TODAY.' It is not the most salubrious town centre I've visited in Unsung Britain.

I keep on strolling in the direction of the steelworks, passing Jimmy's Bar Cuban Club. According to Dave, there are no 'pubs' in Port Talbot. This, he had explained, dates from a decree passed by Lady Talbot in the eighteenth century. She only allowed her name to be associated with the town if there were no pubs. The result is a lot of bars, clubs, taverns and inns. Whether this is a myth or not, no one is sure, but some quiz nights held in Welsh pubs, Dave had said, still ask the question: 'Which major Welsh town does not have a single pub within its boundaries?'

Down the street, I reach an old red-brick building housing Taibach Rugby Club's headquarters. This looks to me to be another pub avoiding Lady Talbot's posthumous wrath. Inside, it definitely feels like one. I go to the bar and order a pint of lime and soda. The barman, a young chap with floppy dark hair, says: 'What?' as though this is the oddest request he's ever heard. I ask again and he looks at me dubiously. Behind me, groups of men are drinking lunchtime beer, sitting at benches along a wall decorated with rugby shirts, trophies and banners. Some are chatting, but many are silent.

'Would I be able to have a word with the landlord to talk about the club?' I ask. 'I'm here visiting the area for the weekend and...'

Before I get a chance to say any more, the barman cuts in: 'Oh that's nice.' He smirks at me.

I explain again that it would be good to chat to the landlord. The barman looks at me again, and smirks once more, before wordlessly disappearing into a back room. I don't think the barman with the floppy hair particularly likes lime-and-soda drinkers. Welsh rugby club bars do not, I suspect, have a great deal of demand for lime and soda.

But a couple of minutes later I'm chatting with Hayley Williams, twenty-one, and Rhiannon Davies, twenty, the barmaids. They're in charge of the club as the landlord is on holiday. They're also very welcoming.

We fall into talking about famous Welsh players that have come from the area. 'There's Richard Hibbard. He plays for Wales. Hooker, he is. And he's a regular here – he lives nearby in Baglan,' says Hayley, who is blonde, chirpy and knows her rugby inside out. 'James Hook, outside half. He used to play for Taibach. Then there's Billy Mainwaring. You've got to mention Billy Mainwaring. He played for Wales in the 1960s. Billy James. Oh yes, Billy James. 1983. Hooker. Played for the Barbarians.'

She seems incredibly knowledgeable about the game. 'Do you go to all the matches?' I ask.

'Oh no! Well, sometimes. My dad was a rugby ref,' she explains. 'I know all the rules. I've been brought up with it.'

The club is, I learn, in division four of the South-West Wales league at the time I visit – and rugby is by far the most popular local sport. Hayley asks where I'm staying and then says: 'Oh, the beach is up and coming. When the weather's nice, I take my bikini and go down there.' She pauses. 'The only problem is: South Wales is the wettest region in the UK,' she says. 'It's just so wet!'

Almost all the regulars, she tells me, work or once worked at the steelworks, but a lot of younger people are moving away as there have been many job cuts at the plant over the years: 'They go to England. And most don't come back.'

'Do you think a lot of people worry about pollution? I couldn't help notice the strong smell of sulphur outside,' I say.

'Yes, that's from the steelworks,' says Hayley. 'The air quality's very poor. There are loads of asthmatics round here.'

Rhiannon perks up. 'I think it's disgusting,' she says.

'What about the appearance of the steelworks though – is it daft to consider it a tourist attraction?'

'Actually, when the lights are on at night, it's quite nice-looking,' answers Hayley.

'When I've been away, in London or wherever, and I see it again – I feel at home,' says Rhiannon.

They want to show me the building and they take me to the upstairs lounge, passing a fruit machine and a picture of the Welsh 2005 Six Nations championship winning team. A bald-headed bouncer leers at me. 'We pay them to be like that. They're intimidating on purpose: it keeps out the troublemakers,' says Hayley, who tells me that it is common for rugby players to drink as many as twenty pints in an evening. Players drink at the club on Saturday nights. 'If you're one of the players, there are free beer barrels on Saturdays. It's the way they're paid.' A pint of lager is usually £1.80.

'It gets super-rough in town on a Saturday night,' Rhiannon adds.

Have they ever seen a tourist in Port Talbot? 'Not in here. You get other rugby clubs coming sometimes,' says Hayley, after pausing to try and recall ever seeing a holidaymaker about. 'People should come here if they want to get a feel for real Welsh life. It's a close-knit community. Everyone around here knows just about everyone else.'

Then I go back to the hotel. After dropping off to sleep for a while – I must have been tired from travelling – I go downstairs. Time has slipped by and it's quite late. Nobody is around at all, not even the receptionist. The bar is open with a long line of shiny beer taps, with no bar staff in sight. The decor is swanky: stripy sofas with blue velvet covers, red velvet armchairs, spotlights, and a stained-glass window featuring a dragon. I wait for a few minutes, listening to 'What's Love Got to Do with It' by Tina Turner.

A large barman appears, nods 'hello', takes my order, and serves a pint of lager. I ask about food, and he says that it is past the usual food ordering time and that: 'Sandwiches are available from the porter.' I ask for a ham sandwich. He looks at me as though I must be mad, and goes off to find the porter. I sit at one of the stripy sofas. And wait.

An elderly bald man eventually appears with my sandwich. 'Is this for you?' he asks. I'm still the only person here. He hands over the sandwich and apologises: 'I cut it in quarters, but I think the bread was too chunky for that.' He disappears and I'm on my own again. The sandwich is on a small plate with greasy crisps and some browning lettuce. The music stops playing. Another guest (there is another) comes down, looks around, decides he doesn't like what he sees, and retreats. 'Crazy in Love' by Beyoncé comes on, echoing round the empty lounge. I stare at the empty chairs, the empty bar and the empty lobby and begin to feel a bit depressed.

Maybe, I'm hoping, the Best Western Aberavon Beach will liven up a bit tomorrow.

It does. But first I've got a Friday full of tourist activities in Port Talbot. This begins with a morning swim. Not many people, it has to be said, swim on the Port Talbot beach, especially not at this time of year (even if it is unusually mild). For a start, as Hayley pointed out at the rugby club, it's usually raining. Then there's the sand. The beach has a Blue Flag award for cleanliness. But on my visit there are lines of green-black slime near the water's edge. It does not, at first, look particularly nice. But I've (possibly madly) decided I'll do it, even if it is just a dip for a few moments, and when I go down to the beach I find I am not alone. Several other people are there in wetsuits, sprinting into the water, splashing through the slime, and diving into the waves. I approach a man near them and ask what's going on. He introduces himself as Martin and explains that they are lifeguards in training.

'Where does all that slime come from?' I ask.

'It's from the Bristol Channel. It's an industrial channel. You get fungi in it – and all sorts. But it's not always like this, and it's not harmful,' he replies.

His friend Dave joins us. 'The surfing here is good', he says. 'But the beach is usually quiet. It's a big change from the 1960s and 1970s, before tour operators to Spain took over. It used to be packed back then. Before mass-market travel boomed and when the mines were still open, the beach was extremely popular with miners.'

And before I know what's happening, I'm joining the swimmers. It begins to pour as I go up to my knees and then flop into a wave. It is very cold. My feet feel the slime. The rain pelts down even harder. I don't stay very long, but I've done it: I've gone on holiday in Port Talbot and I've swum in the Bristol Channel. I've even got the slime between my toes to prove it.

I dry off and get dressed. Then I sit on a bench looking across the bay towards Swansea. Enormous seagulls are circling and sunlight breaks out on the Bristol Channel, transforming the seascape. Suddenly Aberavon Beach looks very pleasant indeed. Anne may not have liked the idea of Port Talbot, but if I'd been going to Swansea it would have been a different matter, as she was born on the same day as its most famous son, Dylan Thomas, and has long been a devotee. His poem about his thirtieth birthday, 'Poem in October', which Anne knows by heart, seems to fit the scene as I stare across at the poet's birthplace and the curve of the coast that leads to the fishing village of Mumbles, at the entrance of the Gower Peninsular.

'It was my thirtieth year to heaven
Woke to my hearing from harbour and neighbour wood
And the mussel pooled and the heron
Priested shore
The morning beckon

With the water praying and the call of seagull and rook
And the knock of sailing boats on the net webbed wall
Myself to set foot
That second
In the still sleeping town and set forth.'

OK, Port Talbot is up and awake and I can't spot any herons or
rooks, but it is nice to imagine Thomas looking over this way
from the other side of the bay. And the sensation of morning
beckoning 'with water praying and the call of seagull' seems
just right on an early start in Port Talbot.

After experiencing the great British seaside, Unsung Britain-
style, I meet the masterminds behind the area's attempts to
shrug off preconceptions and attract tourists to Port Talbot.
Before coming, I'd been in touch with Karleigh Davies, 'Acting
Tourism Development Officer, Economic Development and
Valleys Programme, Neath Port Talbot County Borough
Council'. I'd marvelled at her fifteen-word title. Then I'd
arranged a meeting. This is how I find myself at the local
council headquarters on the Baglan Energy Park, a short drive
from the beach. Karleigh arrives with Sylvia Griffiths, the
eleven-word 'Strategic Marketing Manager, Environmental
Directorate, Neath Port Talbot County Borough Council'.
Sylvia is blonde and, I soon discover, originally from Bavaria.
She married a local in the early 1990s, when she moved to the
area.

'There is a long history of metal-bashing in this area,' she says
in a strong Bavarian-Welsh accent (can't be too many people
with one of those). 'And you're in the right place here.' She
points out of a window to a wasteland of muddy water and

146

overgrown weeds near the M4. 'Over there you've got Brunel's docks,' she says. 'We've created a package to rejuvenate it. The docks are buried there.' The plan is to create a focal point of shops, businesses and apartments around the docks, she says. I look out of the window at the wasteland. Traffic is roaring along the M4. I try (hard) to imagine the rejuvenation required.

The Baglan Energy Park is part of the sprucing-up job. It employs 1,700 people – Port Talbot's population is 49,000 – in companies including General Electric, Inter Tissue (an Italian company producing kitchens and bathrooms), and a company that makes beauty products. 'The fact is that we are moving away from chasing smokestacks, like we did in the 1970s and 1980s,' Sylvia says. The hope is: 'To create Silicon Valley – but we know that's not on the cards as yet.'

'But what about tourism – what do you think of the image created by the town's steelworks?'

Sylvia says: 'It's a perception people have of Port Talbot. But it's changing. We have made a big effort with regeneration on the beach.' This has included a new promenade and better lighting, she explains.

Karleigh, who is in her twenties, adds: 'It was packed there in the 1960s, with people from the valleys. There was a big fairground. My mother used to talk about it.'

Then Sylvia begins the Port Talbot tourist pitch. The area has, she says: 'The largest urban forest in Europe. That is a fact.' She is referring to Afan Forest Park, more than 9,000 acres of woodland that touches the back of the town. 'Our prime tourist target is the outdoor enthusiast: the high-adrenaline seeker. We have walking and cycling. Our mountain biking is massive! *Mountain Biking* magazine put us in the top ten destinations in the world... the whole world! We see this as a way of attracting people.' A series of tracks has been developed over the past decade in Afan, with centres opened near trails, and B & Bs for bikers.

'It's like little Austria up there,' says Sylvia, before telling me that a total of 922 people (precisely) are employed in tourism, according to the council, helping to improve unemployment statistics and shift the area away from manufacturing. At the time of my visit, 29 per cent of the workforce is employed in manufacturing compared to 13 per cent in Great Britain as a whole.

Tourism is regarded by Sylvia and Karleigh as 'a small factory in its own right'. Karleigh says: 'There has been a huge increase in quality graded accommodation. The B & Bs have bike wash facilities and places to lock up bikes.' She stresses this particularly as there has been a problem with mountain bike theft. The headline of the *Port Talbot Guardian* this morning reads: 'THREAT TO TOURISTS: POLICE HUNT BIKE THIEVES AMID FEARS THAT CRIMEWAVE COULD DETER AFAN VALLEY HOLIDAYMAKERS.'

Afterwards, I head for Port Talbot's hills. These begin almost immediately on the other side of the M4, and steadily roll upwards to a height of 370 feet, planted mainly with pine trees. Sylvia and Karleigh's mountain biking talk has made me curious. I've never really gone mountain biking before – I've been on a mountain bike, just not on a mountain. All this is suddenly and dramatically about to change. It doesn't take long to leave the M4 and the steelworks behind. As I drive up a valley in my pea-green Skoda, I'm soon immersed in 'Europe's largest urban forest', passing villages with yet more unpronounceable names (at least to a non-Welsh-speaker) like Cwmafan, Pontrhydyfen, Tonmawr and Blaengwynfi. Wales definitely wins hands down when it comes to tongue-twisting town names.

I arrive at Glyncorrwg, about ten miles inland, where I find Paul Peet working in a garage on a small business park. He runs Afan Valley Bike Hire and is one of the 992 locals who make a living from the booming mountain bike industry. 'It's been very successful. I've got twelve guides on my books. Business doubles every year. I'm more than content with how things are going,' he says, clasping a spanner. There are about a hundred bikes in racks along the walls. Paul is in his fifties, wearing an orange T-shirt and jeans. He owns a red Land Rover with a trailer on which he delivers bikes to riders using a network of trails developed over the past five years.

'We're getting swamped with full-on mountain bikers. It's a serious sport. People with their own bikes spend thousands on them,' he says. The average price is about £2,500. 'You get people coming from the likes of Morgan Stanley, down from the city. From London, Reading, Bristol.'

Paul got into mountain biking when he lived in Spain. 'I was talking to a group of lads from New Zealand in a bar in Malaga,' he tells me. 'They were mountain bikers and I was telling them how beautiful it was in the Atlas Mountains in Morocco. Two days later I was taking them in my Land Rover. We got the ferry across. I'd never been on a mountain bike before.' That was in the early 1990s. When his wife's sister fell ill, they moved back to Wales – and he was surprised to find he could offer similar trips here. 'They'd just opened a trail called The Wall in Afan Forest Park and I thought: "Hold on, what's going on here?" The trails round here are as good as anything you'll find in the UK, and better than you'll get just about anywhere. You can go to Paraguay, South America or wherever – all over the bloody place – and you won't get better.' The sport appeals to outsiders more than locals, Paul says, as the cost of bikes is high: 'Some of the younger lads are into it but most people are into rugby. Rugby's the thing round here. That's why you get so many chunky lads round these parts.'

Mountain biking is also a dangerous pastime, and I'm made to sign an accident disclaimer: 'So if you fall off it's not my fault – no it bloody well isn't.'

I get the sense that Paul thinks I may bloody well fall off. 'I had a husband and wife who hired a bike last weekend,' he says. 'They called from the hospital in the afternoon. 'Can you come and get the bikes,' they said. The wife had broken a bone. I went to the hospital and there were fourteen people waiting: all of them mountain bikers with various cuts and abrasions. Last Sunday the air ambulance was up here twice. The regular injury is collarbones, as well as legs and arms and wrists. When you come off, the first thing that goes down is your hand.'

He pauses for a moment. 'Do you see those bloody green things?' he asks me, pointing towards the pine trees up the hill. I do see the bloody green things. 'When you come off the trail that's what you'll be introduced to.' As he explains the gears (there are twenty-seven) and how to use the front break more often than the rear, Paul says he thinks I may well 'bottle it' and come down on an easy track.

He's not doing my confidence much good. I cycle tentatively round the corner to the Glyncorrwg Ponds Mountain Bike Centre. This is a new building with a campsite for bikers at the back. A shop sells £2,000 bikes and helmets for £100. A couple passes wearing heavy-duty shin guards. In the cafe, a handful of people are drinking coffees while reading *Dirt* and *Mountain Biking* magazines. Soon I'm driving up the mountain in a Land Rover with Dave Williams, a ranger working for the Forestry Commission, which maintains the trails. Dave, also in his fifties, grins a lot as he too tells me about the dangers of mountain biking.

'You've not been before?' he asks incredulously. 'You're wearing those?' he asks, pointing at my jeans. He's wearing Lycra shorts.

Normally people cycle to the top and then come down, but Dave's making it easy for me. 'Biking is breathing fresh life into the villages round here,' he says as we head through the trees. 'It's all about regeneration. This village,' he points down to Glyncorrwg, 'had its troubles. But it's starting to do something about them. The mines closed in Maggie's days – all of them. There hasn't been a lot going on round here, but this [the biking] is much better. About twenty B & Bs have opened on the strength of mountain biking. The Welsh Assembly made the decision to invest [by opening the biking centres and paying for maintenance of the routes] as they could see the benefits: all the spin-offs.' I mention the article about theft. 'There's been a little bit of that but the police are on top of it now. They got them.' He says that more people should know about the mountain biking opportunities – 'even some people in the centre of

Port Talbot don't know all this woodland is right on their doorstep.'

Then we hit the trails. It is steep, fast, exhilarating, peaceful, beautiful and a lot of fun. The trails are about a metre wide, curving through the forest. At the start they have a gentle decline, but in parts it's like riding down a roof. There are boulders to negotiate, narrow bridges across streams and a jumps section. Other riders come hurtling past – part of the skill is getting out of the way. The air is crisp and clean; no sulphur fumes here. Dave explains the process of clearing trees and building the paths. 'People don't appreciate the engineering that goes into them,' he says.

'I notice there is very little litter,' I say.

'That is frowned upon, so it's self-policing, really.' We avoid black routes and keep on the red, intermediate tracks named Darkside, Energy, Goodwood and Windy Point. It's mostly downhill with a bit of uphill from time to time. There are dozens of bikers about. One of the trails is fifty kilometres long and takes riders a whole day.

As we reach the bottom, it begins to rain. I am soaked, exhausted, in one piece, and happy: mountain biking seems to do that to you.

I stop at the Drop Off cafe, where lots of other happy mountain-bikers are cheerfully talking about their day on Port Talbot's hidden hills. And I chat to John Gregg, a forty-two-year-old architect from Sheffield. He's a mountain bike tourist staying at a local guest house. 'I think it's fantastic here,' he says, before describing the trails as 'technical with good solid uphill climbing'. He tells me he broke his collarbone in eight places on a trip one time in the Peak District. 'I've broken all sorts, all over the place,' he says. 'Round here doesn't get the recognition it deserves. It's phenomenal. Definitely one of the best places in the world.'

With that endorsement from a mountain biker who knows his stuff, I drive back down the valley, parking at the small, hilly village of Pontrhydyfen, the birthplace of Richard Burton. I have a look around the tiny rows of houses and enter the Miners Arms pub. 'Did you know Burton?' I ask a local. Keith, a retired steelworker replies smartly: 'I met him and all his wives. Susan Hunt and Elizabeth Taylor were my favourites.'

He sips his pint after mentioning Taylor. 'It's hard not to remember her,' he says, his eyes going a bit misty. Then he grabs my arm and shows me into a lounge beyond the small bar. There are framed pictures of Burton and his wives on a wall. One shows him leaning against the bar in the pub. 'He'd come by – come in here for a drink,' says Keith. 'He'd buy a round, but he tended to drink tonic water himself because he was on the wagon or else he'd drop dead.'

Keith believes that the area has done well when it comes to entertainers: 'There's Rebecca Evans, the soprano – sings all over the world. Then there's Burton, Anthony Hopkins, Catherine Zeta Jones and Michael Sheen.' He's keen to talk. The pub name is part of the past, he says: 'The mines have been gone a long time now. People work for the steelworks and for the council. There have been tremendous changes. In the old days, everyone in this village spoke Welsh. It was predominant. I speak Welsh. But now you've got people from England buying houses, because it's so cheap. They're going for £90,000. But it's diluting the language. Every word that was spoken in that chapel,' he says, pointing to a church up the hill. 'Every word was Welsh,' he continues. 'Not a word of English. If it wasn't for the Welsh education system, children wouldn't speak Welsh at all. It would all be English.'

He asks where I'm from. 'London, eh?' he replies, and says: 'That's *Llundain*.' He writes it down in Welsh so I get the spelling right.

Afterwards I take in the nearby Aberdulais Falls, a National Trust-run former copper smelting and tin-plate works that was once painted by Turner. It is tucked away in a gorge and explains the old production processes. There is also 'Europe's largest generating waterfall' (I never expected to stumble upon that) harnessing the energy from the falls and cleverly covering all the energy needs of the attraction as well as topping up the national grid. I buy a postcard of Turner's 1795 painting, after reflecting on how odd it is to think of the master painter in this out-of-the-way spot. Then I arrive at Port Talbot's number one unofficial attraction and my final port of call: the Baked Bean Museum of Excellence. This is located in a council block near the hotel, and it is run by a man who used to be called Barry Kirk. Now he is named Captain Beany – it even says so on his passport, which he shows me after greeting me with: 'Welcome humble earthling!' Captain Beany is dressed in an orange cape and has covered his face and bald head in orange paint. He describes himself as a 'self-employed superhero'. In 1986, Barry, as he was then called, sat in a tub of baked beans for a hundred hours to raise money for charity. At the time he worked in the BP chemical plant. He explains what happened next: 'Well the boys at work used to say: "Why don't you change your name to Beany?" I called their bluff. I changed it by deed poll.' His flat has become a museum dedicated to baked beans. There are endless piles of cans, posters, a plastic Heinz chair and a signed photograph of Mr Bean, played by Rowan Atkinson. On one wall there is a framed front cover of the *Independent on Sunday*'s magazine. The headline says: 'BLAIR BEWARE: IT ISN'T OVER TILL THE MAN IN TIGHTS LOSES HIS DEPOSIT.'

He says he is frustrated not to be sponsored by a baked bean company, and then he tells me a story about when he visited the United States: 'The immigration officers took me into a back room. They said "Would you come with me. We'd just like to verify your passport, Captain Beany."' He pauses, looking particularly orange. 'But they had to!' he says proudly. 'They were brassed off about it. But they had to let me in!' I look around the room and take in Captain Beany, who almost seems to be glowing orange now. Of all my stop-offs in Unsung Britain so far, this has got to be the most bizarre.

As I leave Port Talbot the next day, I reflect that visiting the town as a tourist is, perhaps, as unlikely as meeting a man wearing orange tights and answering to the name of Beany. In other words: extremely unlikely indeed. I have also got to admit that the Best Western did get me down at times, and to be totally honest, I cannot see myself rushing back to see all the Cash Generators and Poundlands in the town centre. But the mountain biking is truly excellent and I will definitely give that a go again. There are Gothic castles and hidden abbeys; there is a positive spirit and the strong sense of the close-knit community that Hayley mentioned at the rugby club (with only the occasional DAVE); the villages in the hills are charming; and there is, of course, the steelworks. All the metal tubes, flames, lights and steam are 'quite nice-looking', as Hayley also said, and I can understand how they might have caught Ridley Scott's *Blade Runner* eye. They also inspired a recent poem by Gillian Clarke, the National Poet for Wales, entitled 'A Heron at Port Talbot', which seems to encapsulate the coming together of heavy industry and nature in the town, describing snowfall on the plant's cooling tower, with sulphur billowing 'like dirty washing' and the sky stained 'with steely inks and fires' as a lonely heron flies above.

Poetry never seems far away in this part of South Wales. And tourism is always close at hand, too. Learning about all the latest strategies to attract visitors from Karleigh, the Acting Tourism Development Officer, Economic Development and Valleys Programme, Neath Port Talbot County Borough Council, I found it intriguing to see how 'tourism', in whatever unusual forms it may take, is almost everywhere now. There doesn't seem to be a corner of the country where council officials have not got holidaymaking plans in place.

With that in mind, for my next trip I will be heading east to visit a place without slimy sands or steelworks, and where tourism is going strong (despite all the jokes).

7

NORWICH: MUSTARD FACTORIES, CHE GUEVARA AND DELIA

There are no motorways to Norwich. Aside from the odd helicopter owner, few people (I'm guessing) fly there from London either. The way to go on a quick weekend break is by train. The problem is that you have to leave from Liverpool Street Station. I hate Liverpool Street Station. Most of the time it seems to be full of harassed folk with laptop bags in a terrible hurry either because the 8.23 a.m. from King's Lynn is running half an hour late (and they're afraid their bosses will be enraged and they'll get the sack), or those who have been caught on delayed Tubes on the way home (and they're afraid their partners will be enraged and they won't get dinner). Add to that all the tourists and stag/hen parties heading off for the low-cost wonderlands offered by Ryanair and easyJet from Stansted, the odd vagrant or two, people blocking the way because they're waiting to meet friends, yet more travellers queuing for slow-working machines, and large parties of Italians attempting to buy tickets to Cambridge using hundred-euro notes... and it can be quite a busy, frustrating and tense place.

I give myself twenty minutes to collect my ticket, locate the platform, buy an overpriced sandwich and then get to the train. And I only just make it, with just a few briefcase bruises, and moments of almost getting into fisticuffs with Essex lads with gelled angular haircuts thrown in. Yes, train travel to places in Unsung Britain is a generally brilliant thing, and I've been having a great time with it so far, but that doesn't count when you're at Liverpool Street station.

On the train, however, all is calm. We roll away leaving behind the briefcases and low-cost passenger mayhem at the station, with the stark silhouettes of the Gherkin and City skyscrapers in the background as the train curls onwards. It is a crisp December day. To the right is the glistening tower of Canary Wharf, steam trailing from its peak into a clear blue mid November sky, and the huge frisbee of the O2 Arena – the first making me wonder what people do in there all day, cooped up with their calculators and spreadsheets while the world economy goes into freefall; the second reminding me of a forlorn morning in the run up to Millennium Eve when I reported on the merits of the various educational 'zones' in the quickly dumped Millennium Dome. All I seem to recall is walking into a giant plastic version of a human body and seeing lots of adverts for the type of multinational companies that tear down Brazilian rainforests. The Dome may not exactly have been 'unsung' at the time, but there weren't many people singing its praises.

Soon the train is passing the likes of Colchester (Britain's oldest recorded town), Manning Tree, Ipswich, Stowmarket and Diss (which looks quite nice). As we move into flat countryside, I think back to a conversation I'd had over the phone with the local tourist office before my visit. I had talked to Clare Packer, the tourist board's marketing manager, who had discussed the city's 'image problem' – that the city is often seen as 'a rural backwater' in a difficult-to-reach spot. The TV character Alan Partridge (Steve Coogan's infamous hapless local radio DJ character from his popular comedy show, *Knowing Me, Knowing You... with Alan Partridge,* set in Norwich) has not helped much either, she said. 'We've got a job on our hands,' she'd admitted. 'You've got to make a special journey to get to Norwich. People think we're closer to Holland than to London.' This is not actually true, I'd later checked, by a matter of not so many miles, although until the London–Norwich railway track was completed in 1845, it was quicker to journey by boat to the Netherlands than to cross the countryside to the English capital.

When I arrive, I catch a bus to the city centre, and try to find my hotel. This is not as easy as I'd thought. St Giles House is a peculiar place close to the main market that I manage to walk past twice without noticing. Perhaps that's because it looks so grand, with sandstone neo-classical columns, a great archway entrance and decorative stone urns on the roof. At first, I'd assumed it was some kind of museum. Inside, a small, tight-lipped woman in a reception with a black-and-white tiled floor and gilded mirrors, gives me the key to room ten. I say 'thanks', she smiles enigmatically, saying nothing, and I walk through an airy bar with sofas with faux animal-skin covers and art deco pictures of ocean liners. An oriental man in a suit is sitting on one of the sofas with two young people listening attentively. He appears to be in recruitment, and he's saying to his companions: 'Smile. Eye contact. Excitement. "Have S.E.X. with your customer." That's our motto.' Apparently, 'excitement' is the 'x'. 'Yes, have S.E.X. with your customer,' he continues. 'Those are the first five words of business.'

I take the lift to room ten, which has 'Revolution' written on it; each room has its own name. The room is furnished with art deco-style cabinets and wardrobes. There's a shower room, a decent bed and a view out of the back window overlooking furniture workshops and the gold clock-face of the City Hall. I've stayed at a lot worse.

After leaving my bag, I walk down a hill passing a couple of shifty characters drinking cider outside a YMCA, an oyster bar, and a member of the Jehovah's Witnesses who tries to give me a magazine. At the bottom is the marketplace. It's a pleasing warren selling just about everything you can imagine from boxer shorts and fish 'n' chips, to belly-dancer outfits, 'Super Value Bags £3.99' and lamb chops. Light filters through multicoloured awnings into narrow alleys, where stallholders cry out the bargains. There has been a market here since Norman times; said to be the longest continuously trading market in England. The tenor of the cries and calls of the latest deals cannot have changed all that much over the years, I'm thinking, as I pass by.

I'm soon at my destination, about a twenty-minute walk from the market, parts of it along the pretty river Wensum: Carrow Road football stadium. I'm here to watch the Canaries

(Norwich City Football Club) play the Blues (Birmingham City). But before the game starts, I'm meeting the club's press relations department in the hope of getting a behind-the-scenes look, and also to meet the chair of Norwich City and unofficial spokeswoman for the city in general: Delia Smith. This is how I find myself in a back-room office with framed copies of cup final programmes talking to a man with slicked back hair and a yellow tie. He is the club's director of sales and marketing, Andrew Cullen.

After working for the brewers Bass and an advertising agency, Andrew moved to Norwich eleven years ago, he tells me. Since then, the number of season ticket holders has risen from 7,000 to 20,000, he says. Andrew, I very quickly discover, loves his figures… and soon they are coming thick and fast.

Of the last 150 games, 120 have been sold out, he informs me in his rapid-fire delivery. The club has a higher attendance than six of the Premier League clubs; Norwich, when I visit, is in the Coca-Cola Championship. There are 7,000 seats in a 'family area'. The capacity is 26,014. A season ticket costs £370–£450, for which an interest-free payment scheme has recently been introduced. Of the 20,000 season ticket holders, 11,000 are part of the payment scheme, which allows them to spread the cost over the year. More than a million people across Norfolk are considered within the club's catchment area, including 125,000 in Norwich.

'It sounds like the club is doing well: I suppose the players are paid a fortune?'

'Not really,' he replies. 'The total annual wage bill for the thirty players is eight million on a turnover of nineteen million.'

This, Andrew says, is 'tiny' compared to the Premier League: 'It's extremely difficult for clubs in the Championship to compete with the big boys.'

Which sounds like a fair comment, especially when you consider that Manchester United's Wayne Rooney is said to earn more than £6 million a year.

Cash is a constant concern at Norwich City, Andrew says, and as we walk around the stadium, he shows me what is being done to help boost income. There are corporate boxes that cost £20,000 a season to hire. There's a room called 'The Business' with ten tables each seating ten people. Here, local movers and shakers, 'solicitors, property people, members of the chamber of commerce and local players' dine together on match days, sitting at different tables each week so they can network. Such a ticket costs £1,800 for a season.

We pass an excellent wheelchair-friendly box. There's a Study Centre, which is open during the week and 'addresses kids with potential issues. We had a group of Congolese children in recently, to help them with their English.' There are courses for the over-fifties struggling with the Internet. Andrew tells me that 'community' is very important to the club. Players make trips to support local hospitals. Training grounds are open to members of the public. 'People who live in Norwich and Norfolk have a fierce sense of local identity,' says Andrew, standing by a cabinet full of silverware. 'In these parts, people talk about being in a county. In a lot of the rest of the country, the concept of the "county" is dead.'

We go to get some food before the match starts – lots of people do before matches here, with the Delia connection being a big draw. First we try Delia's Restaurant and Bar.

It's absolutely packed, with tables full and people waiting on cream-leather horseshoe armchairs next to a long chrome bar. Orange flowers bloom in vases. Jazz plays. There's a picture of Delia on the far wall, but no real Delia to be found – and no seats free for us. I take a look at the menu: Thai marinated-chicken with honey and ginger served with mango and sultana salsa, saffron pilau rice and oriental beans with chilli and toasted sesame, followed by fresh peach baked in marsala with mascarpone cream comes to £32. It's a (very) long way from pies and cups of Bovril on terraces of old.

Outside near the main ticket office, there is a Norwich City travel agency, a face-painting stall and a group of samba dancers. 'Even if it's a nil–nil draw, we want people to come back for the entertainment,' says Andrew. Next to the samba dancers there is Yellows, another Delia restaurant/bar. Here it is £10 for a burger and a beer in a breezy room with a US-theme and more jazz music. There's no seat free here, either – and again, no Delia in sight.

But finally we find her. She's in the Gun Club, yet another restaurant. This is a big room with a low ceiling and a lot of laughter. Delia is at a table on the far side, with her back to us. Before we get to her, though, we eat a very good meal (well, I suppose it would be) of chicken, new potatoes and veg, sitting at a table with Ronnie Brooks, a genial ex-Norwich player whose short career ended after a knee injury in 1947. 'How have things changed at Norwich City over the years?' I ask as we eat. 'Beyond recognition,' he replies. 'Back in those days, it wasn't like now. When I was injured I had a bad knee operation with a knife and a fork... and that was it.'

The operation ruined his knee and ended his career.

'I guess it is pretty hard for small clubs to break into the Premier League and stay at the top,' I comment. Brooks nods in agreement. He is bullish about what he believes is 'widespread hypocrisy' in English football. 'Big clubs like Manchester United and Chelsea are millions in debt,' he says passionately. 'Yet there are players getting £120,000 a week. It's abhorrent. If all those clubs had to pay off their debt now, it would be like a pack of cards. They'd all be in demise.'

I nod in agreement. 'I support lowly Gillingham FC,' I tell him.

'And I thought I had it bad,' he says, laughing and sounding sympathetic.

The next thing I know, I'm chatting to a former home secretary. Charles Clarke, MP for Norwich South (when I meet him), ex-Labour Party chairman and one-time possible candidate for prime minister, is wearing jeans, a blue shirt and white trainers: looking like most other supporters. And he's keen to set the record straight about the perception some people have of Norwich.

'People have this impression that Norwich is a rural backwater filled with country bumpkins far removed from the rest of the country,' I say.

'They may do, but that's completely wrong,' he says, sounding rather put out by my line of questioning. 'Just wrong.'

'Why?'

'Well, for a long time, until the industrial revolution, Norwich was the second city in Britain,' he answers. 'It has some of the best medieval remains in the country. Prague and Kraków are newer than Norwich.'

'And yet the backwater perception persists…'

'We're at fault for not making enough of what we have,' he replies, after a pause. He believes the city does not shout about itself enough.

Then the former home secretary and I talk about the match.

'Which team is your money on today?' I ask.

'Norwich, 1–0,' he says with a red-faced grin.

Next I'm introduced to Delia, who is cheerful and seems full of energy: wearing a neat white jacket and a green-and-yellow Norwich scarf. She tries to grab my notebook and pen (she thinks I'm an autograph hunter). 'Oh sorry,' she laughs, and when I put the same question to her as to Clarke, she replies: 'The fact that not many people come through Norwich makes it an exclusive area: a unique place. Norwich people are proud of living where we are living… out here in the 'Far East'. In the north of Norfolk there are not so many people about, but Norwich is wonderful: steeped in history.'

'What do you think of Alan Partridge?' I ask.

'That's just a joke,' she replies quickly, obviously not wanting to say any more.

I ask if she has any tips for my weekend break.

She pauses for a moment and then surprises me by telling me about a medieval anchoress who lived in Norwich from around 1342 to 1416, withdrawing from normal life to devote herself to her prayers and religious studies in a tiny cell. The anchoress is known as Julian of Norwich, Delia says, as she lived at St Julian's Church: nobody's sure of her real name. She is the first writer of the English language who can certainly be identified as female, a contemporary of Chaucer, Delia adds. Julian of Norwich completed her meditations on God entitled *Revelations of Divine Love* on her deathbed.

'She's one of my favourite writers,' says Delia, clearly a big fan. She is completely carried away by her enthusiasm for the anchoress, oblivious to all the goals from recent games flashing up on TV screens in the background and fans in the Gun Club laughing noisily over pints. 'She said that whatever happens to you in your life and whatever happens to humankind: "All shall be well, and all shall be well, and all manner of thing shall be well."' Delia pauses thoughtfully, then adds: 'And I really like that.'

I look at the great celebrity cook in a new light: I hadn't expected quotations from medieval anchoresses at a football match. Delia is, after all, famous for raucously telling fans to make more noise during half-time at one match. 'Let's be having you!' she'd cried, prompting the *Daily Mail* to write a story with the cheeky headline: 'HAD A TAD TOO MUCH COOKING SHERRY, HAVE WE, DELIA?' But that seems to have been a one-off, heat-of-the-moment thing. When she's finished telling me about Julian of Norwich, she gives me a big smile and asks: 'Is that OK? You must go to St Julian's Church.' And on this note of optimism, I head to the stands... where another unexpected episode awaits.

I find my seat and take in the impressive view: probably the most interesting one I've ever had at a football match. Beyond a bright yellow roof with two bright yellow flags, a Union Jack and a St George's Cross, a huge stone building sits on a hill in the distance – like a giant, damp cardboard box. This is Norwich Castle, one of the finest Norman buildings in Europe, constructed from limestone shipped from Normandy between 1067 and 1121. The immense project was begun by William the Conqueror, I'd read in my guidebook (Norwich, unlike so many of the places I've been, is in my Lonely Planet guidebook), to stamp his mark on the region. After many years as a prison, the building is now a museum and gallery housing an extensive collection of works by the Norwich School of Artists. Henry I, the fourth son of William, once spent Christmas at the castle. Parts of the interior were re-designed in the eighteenth century by Sir John Soane, architect of the Bank of England.

To the right of the castle, solid red-brick Victorian buildings frame the grey skyline, leading down a slope to the spire of an impressive cathedral. This is Norwich Cathedral, a Romanesque masterpiece and one of two in the city (there is also a Roman Catholic cathedral). It is also built from Normandy stone, and was completed in 1145. For many years it was a Benedictine monastery, housing up to 260 monks. The monastic cloisters are the largest of their kind in Britain, I've read. The stone spire, at ninety-six metres, is the second tallest in England, after the spire at Salisbury Cathedral.

It's a beautiful view. But the man sitting behind me is not reflecting on the historic horizon. 'Your support is ****ing ****!' he's screaming at the top of his lungs – over and over. He switches tack: 'Stop playing that fancy triangle ****!' A Norwich City player collides with an opponent in the Birmingham City penalty box. 'Ah **** off, referee! Penalty!' He turns to the Birmingham supporters once again. 'Town full of yardies!' he yells. 'You're just a town full of yardies!' The referee awards a free kick to a Birmingham player. '****er! ****er! ****er!' Birmingham City scores just before half-time. The man behind me – bald, tattooed and snarling – swiftly and wordlessly departs with his mates.

The tension in the seats around us lifts as they depart. An elderly couple looks visibly shocked. 'I would hate to have to sit next to someone like that the whole time,' says the woman. Her companion quietly replies: 'It's a disgrace.'

In the second half, the effing and blinding starts again. Eventually, with ten minutes to go, a steward comes over. 'Excuse me sir, can I have a word?' he asks. The steward talks to the man in the aisle. He is silent for a few minutes when he returns. But then he's off: 'You're support is ****ing ****! Go back to Birmingham you ****!' The steward is nowhere to be seen. The game ends 1–1, but for most people around us, the score line hardly seems important. For us, the bald man behind us has been the main player.

The next day after a good night's sleep at St Giles House, I learn a whole lot more about the 'rural backwater' of Norwich. Near the market, I meet Michael Loveday, chief executive of Norwich Heart, a heritage trust that aims to highlight the historic buildings in the city and restore old properties. I find him in the forecourt of The Forum, a huge glass structure with a bread loaf-shaped roof next to the City Hall. He is full of enthusiasm about Norwich... seriously full of enthusiasm for the town. 'Barcelona! Prague! Budapest! San Francisco!' Michael says, as we shake hands. 'That's who we should be competing with!' Michael, in his fifties, is wearing an olive suit and has a bushy mop of curly hair, a grey beard and a rosy complexion. He's soon energetically striding onwards on a tour of his favourite city centre sites. As I hurry to keep up, he tells me: 'Apart from London, no city in the UK has so many buildings spanning a thousand years!'

We pause at the Assembly House, a distinguished red-brick building built in the eighteenth century, where the composer and pianist Franz Liszt once performed, and where there was a huge 1805 celebration of Nelson's 'Glorious Victory of Cape Trafalgar', Michael says.

'Was Nelson a local?' I ask.

'Yes, he attended Norwich School before enlisting in the Royal Navy aged twelve,' says Michael, striding onwards, quickly leaving behind Assembly House, which is tucked behind The Forum at the top of a hill leading downwards past a busy shopping centre and several pretty churches.

'Norwich has thirty-two churches,' he says, pointing at one that appears to have been turned into some kind of community centre. 'But if you think that for a congregation for a church you might need about two hundred people, that's a big ask,' he adds, explaining why some of the buildings no longer actually act as churches.

We march past another former place of worship. 'There are more medieval churches in the city than anywhere else in Northern Europe,' says Michael, mentioning an old saying: 'There used to be a church in Norwich for every Sunday and a pub for every day of the week.'

We arrive briskly (everything about Michael is brisk and to the point) at Surrey House. This is the headquarters of Aviva, formerly Norwich Union insurance company, a major local employer. It looks strangely familiar, and I'm soon learning why. The architect for this impressive building – lots of neo-classical columns and embellishments – is George Skipper, the designer of my hotel. Norwich Union commissioned Skipper, who began work in 1900, to make a bold statement about the company. 'This building lets people know: "Your money is safe in our pockets." For a few years they were on the cusp of whether to keep it [as a headquarters], but they felt it showed that they are a reliable insurance company,' says Michael, as we climb the steps and enter an extraordinary reception.

I've never seen so much marble. For a moment I'm reminded of a fancy lobby at a hotel in Dubai, but it's far grander than that. In the high-ceilinged hall there are marbles in pinks, purples, turquoises, greens, creamy caramels and silky whites. Columns are one colour, panels in the walls another. There are decorative marble hoops near the ceiling concealing marble caskets festooned with marble flowers. The floor is marble, black-and-white checked tiles. It's almost as though the entrance to Aviva's headquarters is an extremely elaborate tomb; designed for the Chancellor of the Exchequer during a rare economic boom, perhaps.

'How did all this come about?' I ask. 'It looks incredibly expensive.'

'Originally the marble was for Westminster Cathedral, which had ordered three consignments from Greece and Italy,' Michael replies. 'But they realised they could only afford the first consignment, so Norwich Union got the second for a knock-down deal.' He looks admiringly around the room: 'You can't make places like this any more. The quarries in Sienna have been worked out.'

Norwich Union, I learn, began in 1797 as a society for the 'insuring of buildings, goods, merchandises and effect from loss by fire' with twenty-seven backers each investing £1 – during its first seven years there luckily never was a claim for more than £27.

And then we zoom onwards once more, past the enormous Norman castle. As we do, Michael mentions that he is chairman of Living Streets, formerly the National Pedestrian Association, a group that aims to 'improve the conditions for walking and make public spaces great'. The group was established in 1929 and has over the years lobbied for the 30 mph speed limit, zebra crossings and the introduction of driving tests. This anti-car bent led to the creation of Norwich Lanes, a partly pedestrianised area in the centre of the city with 300 historic buildings occupied by small scale retailers. 'We've invested £500,000 in interpretive signs and plaques to knit together all the shops in the area. It's reckoned that we've created £17 million in new jobs and start-ups.'

A blue plaque on a wall in the Lanes 'remembers Jem Mace [1831–1910]. He's the father of modern boxing. Apparently he floored an immense American and took the heavyweight title,' according to Michael. Further on, past a *Big Issue* seller and a trendy trainers store, Michael explains that back in the seventeenth century Reverend Johannes Elison was a senior minister of the Dutch congregation at Blackfriars' Hall – and that he and his wife were the only English residents to be painted by Rembrandt (in 1634). There was a big Dutch, Flemish and Huguenot population in Norwich from around the 1560s onwards, when large numbers of refugees fled persecution on the Continent – 'as many as forty per cent'.

Then I'm taken to the main magistrates' court and shown an excavated Norman house below its floors. 'Not every court has a Norman house underneath it,' says Michael, matter-of-factly. We pass the Adam & Eve pub: 'The oldest pub in Norwich.' Moving on, we arrive at the Great Hospital, which has a 'chancel ceiling decorated with more than 250 black eagles painted in honour of Anne of Bohemia who visited with her husband Richard II in 1383'. This hospital is still used as an old people's home and is 'one of the longest remaining structures still doing what it was set up to do'.

Michael once showed the travel writer Bill Bryson, who lives in a village not far from Norwich, around the city centre. As we leave the hospital, he says: 'Bill Bryson was suitably impressed. He said: "I'm really fascinated by all this heritage. I'm from Des Moines in Iowa. There are only eleven old things in Des Moines, and one of them's my mum."'

There's plenty more than that in Norwich. Our final stop is the Guildhall, back near my hotel. We climb steps into a lobby with a cafe, and then descend a narrow passage into an undercroft dating from the 1200s. It is in this dingy space that Thomas Bilney, a Protestant martyr, spent his final night in 1531. 'He was the first to be burned by the Catholics. Queen Mary stuck him in here. The story is that he held his hand over a candle in this room to feel what it would be like to be burned alive,' says Michael, who really should enter *Mastermind* with Norwich as his specialist subject. It was also in here that Robert Kett, leader of a 1549 proletarian revolution demanding land and fishing rights spent his final night, says Michael.

'I have to admit that I haven't heard of him before,' I say sheepishly.

'Oh but you should have!' Michael replies. 'Kett led a popular revolt of 20,000 to 30,000 people. They took over Norwich, so the king sent in the army and the rebels beat the army. Then another force was sent in and they slaughtered the peasants. Kett was captured. He was taken to the battlements of the castle, killed and left to rot.'

Michael pauses, then adds: 'Pleasant, eh? He was a champion of the common people. A Che Guevara of the English people. Here in Norwich!'

Back in the daylight, Michael summarises his grand plans for the city: 'I've been to the bosses at English Heritage and I've said to them: "We are the best heritage city in Europe: we've got undercrofts, thirty-two churches, two cathedrals, monuments." They said to me: "You've got a point there."'

He's on a roll: 'York is fantastic, but it's half the size and hasn't got thirty-two churches. Bath's nice but it's all the same. Chester's pleasant: interesting cathedral and some shops. Stratford-upon-Avon has a ridiculous high street of tourism: people just go to see Shakespeare's house. Ludlow's beautiful but tiny.'

He pauses again for a very brief moment, and stares at his beloved Guildhall, where his offices are based and the Che Guevara of the English people was held. 'Outsiders think we're a small insignificant market town up the largest cul-de-sac in England. Actually, and I'm nothing if not ambitious, we're like Sienna. Come to Norwich, the Sienna of the east of England.

'Now we're up and running!' he cries, shaking a fist in the direction of the Norwich Lanes, and echoing so many others I've met in Unsung Britain. 'No matter what anyone else thinks!'

Back at my hotel in the afternoon, I take a break from my everything-you-need-to-know-about-Norwich lesson. At the bar, two men with highlights in their hair are drinking green cocktails and making flamboyant gestures. A cackling group of women on a hen party is drinking white wine in the courtyard. A glass smashes behind the bar, and a sleepy waiter sweeps up the pieces. No one else is about.

I catch a taxi to the Sainsbury Centre. 'You mean the art gallery, not the supermarket?' asks the driver. And soon we are on the campus of the University of East Anglia, driving to a rectangular building that could be an aircraft hangar. This is the Sainsbury Centre for Visual Arts, the first major public building designed by Sir Norman Foster (opened in 1978) on a commission by Sir Robert and Lady Sainsbury, who collected hundreds of artworks donated to the university in 1973 and gradually added to them over the years; Sir Robert died in 2000. Before coming to Norwich, I had no idea this enormous gallery existed.

It's fantastic. Inside, there's a vast open space with skylights and spotlights. To the right is the main gallery with Francis Bacons, Henry Moores and Picassos mounted on panels in between plinths with rare objects from primitive societies. To the left is an exhibition focusing on modernism, with brightly coloured, angular modern art and chairs designed by the architect Le Corbusier. Straight ahead is a circular reception desk, manned by a woman wearing a checked red dress and a man with floppy hair, lots of tattoos and a ginger beard. They both have a nonchalant air: cool, arty types.

The cool woman tells me admission is free. Her name is Ellie.

'How did the Sainburys come to choose this location?' I ask her.

'Apparently they tried Oxford, but Oxford didn't want it, or couldn't have it,' she answers. 'But because one of the Sainsburys' daughters attended UEA and the university had room for the collection, they decided on here.' The cool man with the tattoos, Duncan, wants to show me the outside of the building. He exits the circular reception wearing flip-flops and a pair of trousers with one leg rolled up to the knee, seemingly for style reasons. His tattoos depict skulls and marijuana leaves. 'I'm the hardest working member of staff,' he tells me apropos of nothing. 'You can quote me on that.'

Duncan takes me to one side of the building where he wants to show me something: the university's famous pyramid-like accommodation blocks, known as the 'ziggurats'. 'This used to be a golf course,' says Duncan, pointing at parkland leading up to the strange buildings. He tells me he is doing a MA in history and working part-time at the gallery. 'Do you like living in Norwich?' I ask.

'I like being on the campus,' he replies. 'It's a great life in Norwich, but racially it's a very white city. Here at the uni you get more multiculturalism and different ethnicities: Japanese, African, everywhere. So many different people to meet.'

Looking back in the direction of the gallery, he points to a walkway connecting several of the concrete buildings housing the faculties, and switches tack. 'See those elevated walkways,' he says. 'The idea behind those was that students and academics could walk around while all the maintenance and supplies and all that went on below them, out of eyesight. In a strange way, it's elitist: head in the clouds studying at the university, with real life happening below and not impinging.'

He pauses, thinking about what he just said: 'But it isn't really.'

The gallery is eclectic, extremely good value (being free), totally empty except for me on a Saturday afternoon – and all in all quite fantastic. Within a few minutes I've seen a Francis Bacon portrait, a 'mother and child' by Henry Moore, a Japanese Buddha from the eighth century, an Indian charcoal of an eighteenth-century 'enraged elephant', a Jacob Epstein and a Picasso. The scattered plinths and panels have a labyrinthine effect, like an ancient Egyptian temple. I pause by *Woman Combing Her Hair* by Picasso wondering: why don't more people come here?

While I've been going round, Duncan has dug out an audio guide to the campus architecture and he is insisting I take a look around the elevated walkways of UEA, which has been dubbed a 'plate-glass university' (founded in 1963). 'People studying architecture come from all over the world to see the buildings,' he says, holding out a small audio device with earphones. And I'm soon standing amid molehills on the former golf course looking at the ziggurats and being informed: 'The wedge-shape design means the rooms all have a nice view of the countryside.' The campus displays the height of British modernism, I'm told, though some regard the look as brutalism. I kind of like it: the way you can wander around all the elevated walkways between the big modern buildings. I follow more directions, getting lost near the Islamic Centre, and trying to imagine Kazuo Ishiguro, Ian McEwan and the many other writers who have attended the university's well-known creative writing course following these paths. 'Real' life does feel a long way away... Port Talbot's steelworks,

Bogside's murals, docks full of second-hand caravans, and Salfordian council estates included.

As do mustard factories. I never imagined I'd visit a mustard factory. But here I am at Colman's mustard factory on the south-east of the city, just across the river Yare from Norwich City's football stadium. I'm surprised to find it's on the site of an old Benedictine priory; which is how I've found myself sitting in an empty canteen looking onto ancient stone remains that border a pretty garden and a fine old house made from flint. I could be at an English Heritage venue or a country house hotel. It's just about the least likely setting for industry you could imagine.

Andy Watts, the marketing manager at Colman's mustard, has worked at the factory for seventeen years. He's proud of the history of a company that has an 85 per cent share of the English mustard market and a 50 per cent share of the overall mustard market in the UK. Mint sauce, horseradish, tartar sauce and several 'dry sauce mixes' such as Colman's 'Sauce for Swedish Meatballs' and 'Luxury Peppercorn Sauce' are also produced by the site's 160 workers, who are employed by Unilever, the multinational packaged food producer, which owns Colman's.

'We were founded in 1814 by Jeremiah Colman,' says Andy, another evangelist for all things Norwich – locals seem particularly proud of the city, more so perhaps than in any place I've visited so far. 'He outgrew his original site at Stoke Mill, just south of Norwich, and he moved here in 1856.'

Jeremiah was a cut-throat businessman and whenever competitors became a threat he would buy them out, a policy that was continued by his son, who purchased Keen & Son mustard-makers in 1903, Andy says. 'You know the expression "as keen as mustard"?' he asks. 'Well that's where it came from. That was their advertising slogan. It's a phrase that just seemed to stick.'

'Now that's a good pub quiz fact, if ever I heard one,' I say, smiling.

The Colman's factory site was once home to the second biggest church in Norwich, says Andy, showing me a history cabinet next to the canteen that explains that Henry VIII destroyed the church and the priory in 1539, but spared the Prioress House, now known as Carrow Abbey, which he gave to a relative of Anne Boleyn (members of the public can request to be shown round). We go inside the grade one listed building, now used by Colman's executives for meetings and hired out for weddings: the site is that picturesque. 'I love it here,' says Andy, who is in his forties and in charge of maintaining the abbey. 'Elgar used to visit one of the Colmans. This factory had the first occupational health nurse in the UK, as well as a school for the children of staff.'

Next, we head out towards the factory silos and put on paper overalls, hats and plastic shoe protectors. I'm made to take off my watch for 'health and safety reasons'. We enter a large building where men in blue overalls are listening to the radio and bagging yellow powder in plastic bags. There's a fine dusting of yellow on the floor, and a musty, but pleasant, smell. Andy explains the production process: 'We take the seed off the field. Then it's dried and stored in silos. We turn it to make sure there is the right level of moisture. We then mill the seed into flour – either white or brown seed. Then it goes into tote bins and we make slurry to add to the mustard, or just sell it as powder.' Winter is the boom time for condiments: 'September to January is our peak season. Half of our volume is produced in the last third of the year. Roast meats and hot meals in winter: people want some mustard.' Regarding the mysteries of mint sauce production, he adds: 'We get a thousand tonnes of fresh garden mint a year and when it comes in we've got to mill it within an hour, otherwise it turns into compost, like anything else.'

Afterwards, Andy gives me a lift in his silver Porsche back to the centre of Norwich. As the car surges away, he tells me that he had a choice after a bad motor-biking injury: 'Either to feel sorry for myself, or get on with life'. And he certainly seems to have done the latter.

Everywhere you go in Norwich, history seems to seep out... even under its mustard factories. There's plenty at the Adam & Eve pub, which dates from the thirteenth century and 'witnessed bitter battles' during Robert Kett's 1549 rebellion (so says its website). These battles included the killing of Lord Sheffield, who was 'hacked to death nearby on August 1 by rebels'. His ghost is said to haunt the pub.

After a lazy Sunday morning looking around the market, I enter completely soaked after getting caught in a downpour that started while I was walking through the grounds of the cathedral. 'You're soaked,' says a cheerful local standing by the bar. I thank him for his observation and order a pint of orange juice and a steak and ale pie. 'Steak and ale pie is off,' says a barmaid with reddish-blonde hair. She stares at me with a doubtful expression – perhaps because it looks as though I have just had a swim in the river Yare. I order 'Elizabethan pork with vegetables'. It's a nice-looking pub, with nooks and crannies and side rooms. I settle steamily in a small room at the front with old black-and-white pictures of Norwich Cathedral. I eat my Elizabethan pork and vegetables (very good), while listening to two people discussing a friend who is going out with a 'nutter... he's not even got a job... he's scrounging her money'.

Then I go for an afternoon stroll around the city centre. On these weekends I'm finding that part of the fun is simply pottering about and seeing what you stumble into. And there is no better place to potter than Norwich. Soon, not far from St Giles House, I find myself at the Roman Catholic cathedral. This is just outside a ring road, and looks imposing, Gothic and damp. Inside there are sturdy columns and prayer boards: 'Write your prayer intentions on a slip and your prayer intentions will be included at Mass during the coming week.' I sit in one of the pews and marvel at the sheer size of this huge Gothic space.

Next door, as if I'd prayed for a corner of paradise, I stumble across the Plantation Garden. I didn't know this place existed, but down a gravel path, past a donations box, and through a wooden gate next to a hotel, I find an extraordinary hollow with trees and shrubs on every side, seeming to keep out prying eyes. It feels totally cut off from the rest of the city. The air smells fresh and oxygenated. There are banana plants and great banks of lilac, yellow and pink flowers. A stone wall with a trellis on one side of the hollow looks as though it should belong in an Italian villa. There is a little carp pond. A short walk from the ring-road traffic near the cathedral, I seem to have entered another, tranquil, world.

The site is about 150 metres long and 50 metres wide with steep sides bordered by chestnuts and beeches. A sign says the hollow is an old chalk quarry that was converted into a garden by a wealthy nineteenth-century cabinetmaker named Henry Trevor. There used to be glasshouses holding exotic tropical plants, but those disappeared over the years as various owners converted the main lawn into a tennis court and later, during World War Two, into a vegetable patch. In 1980, by which time the garden was totally overgrown, a group was formed to restore Trevor's pride and joy, and it has since been listed. I climb up steep steps at the far end, where there's a small 'rustic summerhouse' at the top. I'm the only person in the garden and I haven't spotted a soul since turning off the street by the cathedral. This is a secretive, contemplative corner.

As is my final stop in the city. I walk past the Roman Catholic cathedral, traverse the market and walk down a hill below the Norman castle. 'Good old Delia, she often sends people down here,' says Felicity Maton, honorary secretary of Friends of Julian of Norwich, whom I meet at the Julian Centre, a small stone building connected to the church. 'But people do have a terrible job finding us. There ought to be better signs.'

I mention the 'all shall be well' saying that Delia quoted to me back at the football match. 'Oh yes. Counselling people are always taking up her sayings; she was a medieval counsellor, you see. She could have written in Latin, but she chose to write in English,' says Felicity, who is softly spoken and wearing beads. 'She was an anchoress,' Felicity continues. 'She was in a cell attached to the church for quite a long time. She had a near-death experience just over the age of thirty, and when she was at death's door, she had revelations, but it took her quite a while to make sense of them, and to start her text. Unfortunately the cell isn't there any more, it's a reconstruction.'

'What happened to it?' I wonder.

'Apparently a Nazi bomb did for the original building,' she replies, sounding a bit sad.

Friends of Julian has more than 700 members, says Felicity, who sells me a copy of Julian's sayings entitled *Enfolded in Love*. 'All we know of her is from her writings,' she says, as I flick through to the page with the 'all shall be well' text. 'I hope you enjoy it.'

I go to see the reconstruction of the small white-walled cell. Then I walk up the hill towards the castle. As I stroll along, I reflect that of all the places I've been to so far, Norwich has definitely had the most to see and do as a typical 'tourist'. It's a great medieval city that few people – as Michael and Clare lamented – consider visiting. I feel as though I have seen an 'important' place, somewhere that does indeed stand alongside the likes of Bath and York. It may not be, as Michael hopes, quite a 'Barcelona! Prague! Budapest! San Francisco!' But it's got castles. It's got history. It's got bustling markets. It's got quirky hotels.

And it's got Delia. 'Oh she's God, she is,' says my taxi driver to the station, summing up the general local feeling during my stay. Being stuck out in the east, Norwich may feel isolated (a bit like Hull) but there is also a great sense of relaxation, of a place that is at ease with itself, that is slightly outside the rat race of the rest of Britain: with secret gardens to explore, fine art galleries, architectural wonders, cathedrals, mustard factories, and hidden stories of Protestant martyrs, anchoress scribes, peasant uprisings and 'Che Guevaras of England'.

There are only forty-odd years of history to explore in my next port of call. Julian of Norwich's 'all shall be well' worked in her home city, but will all be well at a little-visited town just off the M1, not far north of Luton?

8

MILTON KEYNES: FEELING GREEN IN THE CITY OF DREAMS

This is bizarre. I'm in a picturesque village with lovely ivy-clad cottages and distinguished red-brick houses. There's a grey stone church with a castellated roof on a hillock. Neat hedgerows and stone walls separate properties. A hedge-cutter buzzes nearby, momentarily disturbing the birdsong. Ancient trees cast dancing shadows on tiny winding lanes that smell of leaves. I pass a field with a chestnut horse and a man walking a Labrador. Blackberry bushes are ripe with fruit. Apples have fallen on the road at the end of Church Lane.

It's a classic English countryside scene – real H. E. Bates land. Yet I'm two minutes (by bike) from Milton Keynes Central train station, just across a walkway over the A5 heading west. What's going on? Isn't Milton Keynes meant to be all about concrete cows, roundabouts, grid road systems and shopping malls?

I look at my map. I'm in Loughton, one of fifteen villages, along with three towns (Bletchley, Stony Stratford and Wolverton) that make up the new town of Milton Keynes – created in 1967 to help cope with a shortage of housing in the south-east, particularly the overspill from London's East End. I've just come out of a meeting with John Lewis, chief executive of the Milton Keynes Partnership, the local planning authority in charge of developing the town as it grows over the next few years. He had told me that the population is expected to rise from 230,000 to 350,000 by 2031 and that Milton Keynes is a 'city of dreams'. He had also asked how I intended to get about during my weekend. When I'd said I'd walk, catch buses or take taxis, he'd interjected. 'Everyone thinks this is a town for the car,' he said. 'Get a bike!' His assistant, Nadir, joined in: 'You can have my husband's bike if you like.' Are you sure? 'Absolutely no problem,' she'd replied nicely.

Which is how I find myself on two wheels once again (without Port Talbot's hills) in a pretty countrified lane next to Loughton's church on a lovely Saturday with a clear blue sky in early December, the weekend after Norwich. As I gaze across the strangely bucolic scene in the heart of Milton Keynes, I think back to my conversation with John. He had told me all about the many miles of cycle-ways around the town, designed with passages under roads so you almost never need to stop for traffic. He had also given me a map that is coloured purple to show 'areas of employment', yellow for residential zones and orange for shopping districts. 'You'll notice there's no one place that everyone goes to work. There's no cluster. It's phenomenal when you think about it: the incredible foresight,' he said, sounding evangelical about the original 1960s planners, whom he went on to describe as being 'like hippies' in their laid-back approach to creating a 'perfect' society. 'There are some fabulous places to live. Some fabulous houses... as well as some not-so-fabulous. And look at all the green,' John had continued. The map does indeed show large areas of green.

There is certainly a lot of it from what I've seen so far in Loughton. And there are a lot of trees, too. 'There are more than twenty-two million trees in Milton Keynes,' John had announced. 'Certain people will have the view that Milton Keynes is a concrete jungle full of roundabouts until they die. They're mainly people aged over fifty now.' Impressions of the town, he told me, are changing. 'People used to laugh or say "Oh dear" when I told them I lived here. Not any more.'

I lock my bike against a fence next to Loughton's twelfth-century church, not that it really feels as though I need to, the place seems so law-abiding and quiet: a charming neighbourhood that does, I suppose, have the feel of a 'perfect society'. I make my way up a path towards the entrance, where I find a bespectacled woman with a walking frame sitting on a wooden bench reading a magazine. We say hello, and are soon chatting away.

Her name is Audrey Pountney, a former pub landlady from Hertfordshire. Like John, she is a Milton Keynes convert. 'I retired five years ago and when I said I was moving here, people said: "What for?"' she tells me. 'The reputation of the town is very unfair.'

'I hear you can get some incredible deals on property in Milton Keynes,' I say.

'Yes – so many people are simply put off by the town's associations with roundabouts and endless shopping malls,' she explains. 'But they shouldn't be.'

While we're discussing this, a man wearing a smart blue suit exits a church side door. He comes over and introduces himself as Derek Martin. He's a lay minister and is soon giving me an estate agent-style spiel on local life.

'I think it's fantastic,' he says. 'The grids work [he's talking about the grid road system, around which all the roundabouts are set]. There's a lot of green space. You step out and there are huge trees everywhere. You really don't feel like you're in a town of 230,000.'

The people of Milton Keynes, I'm quickly learning, love to talk up the town, though both Derek and Audrey seem genuinely shocked that I'm a tourist. 'You're spending a whole weekend here?' asks Audrey.

'Er, yes,' I reply hesitantly, wondering if I've made a bit of a mistake. Even if it is rather nice around Loughton, perhaps there's not all that much to do. But after a pause, Audrey continues: 'Oh, you'll have a good time. It's wonderful in Milton Keynes.' As she says this, she smiles, realising that this statement may sound odd to an outsider. It seems as though locals have a sense of humour about the town – as though they don't mind the jokes as they enjoy living here so much.

I cycle onwards, not really knowing where I'm going; the joy of pottering in Norwich seems to have rubbed off in Milton Keynes. There are thatched cottages, chestnut trees, joggers and dog walkers. Front doors are open in a peaceful cul-de-sac of mock Tudor buildings, where children are playing. I pass a gurgling stream and find myself at Two Mile Ash Farm, where a small wooden stall is selling free-range eggs and pots of honey. A farm in the middle of Milton Keynes! However, I soon discover that Two Mile Ash is to be the site of one of the latest phases of the Milton Keynes town plan. I know this because, as I'm putting coins into a metal box to buy some honey, I'm approached by a teenager in wellington boots. Robert Harrison, seventeen, who is about to go to agricultural college, tells me: 'All this is going to be built on soon. The expansion is coming this way. We've sold the land already.' Homes are to be built to house the growing population.

But Robert does not sound concerned about losing the farm, which used to have cattle, but now just keeps sheep and chicken on its 110 acres. This is despite the fact that this morning's *Milton Keynes Citizen* ran a story headlined 'HOW MANY MORE HISTORIC FARMS WILL GO TO RUIN?' with locals expressing regret at the speed of the expansion. 'We've got another farm in Calverton, so we'll be OK,' he explains. 'I come from a family of farmers going back hundreds of years. This one here has never been particularly profitable. But we get European Union subsidies so we struggle through.'

We say goodbye and not far on, I come to a Sikh temple just off a main road. It is housed in a barn-like building with a terracotta-tiled roof and a tall pole in front wrapped in pale orange fabric and topped with a crescent-shaped symbol. In the gravel car park, I meet Jag Panesar. He's twenty-eight and an NHS customer service advisor who moved here from Birmingham ten years ago; yet another friendly person in Milton Keynes.

Jag seems pleased that I'm cycling.

'Assuming you have no disability, you can get anywhere on your bike, it's a good way to get round,' he says, explaining that the temple has been here more than twenty years and has a congregation of about fifty.

He invites me inside. In a room with an orange canopy and a red carpet I'm introduced to the priest, and we have a chat about Sikhism, during which I learn all about the gurus of the religion. Then Jag tells me, sounding conspiratorial, that he eats meat: 'To be honest, I do, but I'm not supposed to.'

He pauses, and adds: 'I gave up drinking five years ago. I just thought it's an expensive, silly game. You're not supposed to drink or smoke in Sikhism.'

He gives me some advice.

'Come here on a Sunday,' he whispers secretively. 'It's free curry, you don't have to believe, or anything like that.' And with that traveller's tip for Milton Keynes, I get back on my bike and head into Stony Stratford, heading along cute lanes lined with big houses, before travelling on a cycle track beside the larger V4 road (part of the numbering for the city's grid road system).

During the age of coach travel, Stony Stratford was an important resting point on the way between the north and south of England, known for its coaching inns. These included two adjacent establishments on the High Street, the Cock and the Bull, and it is from these two inns that the phrase 'cock-and-bull story' is said to derive. The phrase came about as travellers who stopped for refreshment in one pub would pass on tales that would often get exaggerated or confused when re-told later at the other (usually after an ale or two). I stop at the Bull, opposite a damp-looking church. I lean my bike against a lamp post and look at the elaborate wrought-iron sign that curls like a fancy signature above the street. Folk guitar music emanates from inside the red-brick building, which advertises rooms from £29 a night. I look through the front window. In a cramped, crowded bar, a man is strumming an acoustic guitar and melodically singing the lyrics: 'Slow down, slow down, it's strange when you don't.'

But as I stand there with my bike thinking how jolly the Bull seems, a large man with a red face steps out of a side passage next to the pub. Everyone I've met so far in Milton Keynes has been polite and well-mannered. The man with the red face possesses neither of those qualities.

He is smoking a cigarette and he immediately turns to me, staring with a look of intense disgust. He stares intensely right at me. I decide to stare back. Not realising that the words are coming out, I ask, a little abruptly perhaps: 'Can I help you?'

He squares up to me, his face getting redder. He's obviously had a few. And without quite realising what I'm doing, maybe I'm feeling light-headed from all the cycling, I suddenly hear myself laughing at him.

'Are you having a pop?' he asks, looking as though he may soon explode in redness. 'Don't have a pop at me!' he bellows.

He is, I now realise, wearing a rugby top and his hands have shaped into fists that look as though they could hammer heavy wooden stakes into the ground. At this moment, a friend of his arrives and, slurring, coaxes him back into the Bull's side passage.

The friend returns a moment later and says: 'Don't worry about him.'

Not always so lovely in Milton Keynes. I move on to the Cock Inn, just down the street. It's much quieter here than in the Bull, with neither guitarists nor violent locals. I order a chunky ham and cheese sandwich with a side salad (all very tasty) and read a sign by the front entrance. It says that the property dates from 1450 when John Cok was the landlord; the inn is named after him, not the cockerel. The venue was once the official stopping point for the Manchester Flyer coach service from London to Manchester, departing from London at 8.30 a.m. one day and arriving at 5.10 a.m. the next, with a pause for food and drink at the Cock along the way. The arrival of trains connecting London to the north in the 1800s brought an end to this arrangement (my train from Euston had taken just thirty minutes). I look around the bar, and try to imagine the good old days, when cock-and-bull stories echoed round these walls. It's nice to think of all the bedlam there must have been back then (some of which seems to have survived down the road at the Bull). Then I jump on my bike and pedal onwards, wondering what this city of dreams will throw up next.

Back in the lively lounge bar at my hotel, I settle into a burgundy sofa. I'm staying at the comfortable Jurys Inn hotel, in a tower block in the town centre overlooking modern restaurants and glass-fronted apartments filled with young professionals, who I see tapping on laptops from the window of my £62-a-night room. I call Anne and tell her about the cycling.

'Oh, that sounds nice,' she says, seeming a little jealous about this stop-off in Unsung Britain (it's the first time I've had such a reaction from her).

Then I tell her about the local who turned on me this afternoon.

'Oh, really?' she replies, brightening up and sounding better about things, even having a bit of a chuckle.

'Yes, if it wasn't for his mate, I think we would have come to blows,' I reply. And she has another chuckle. (*Schadenfreude* and my offbeat travels definitely seem to be natural bedfellows, I've increasingly noticed.)

After our chat, I drink a coffee and begin reading *A Social History of Milton Keynes: Middle England/Edge City* by the historian Mark Clapson. Though the title may sound a touch heavy, if not downright daunting, the book turns out to be a light read, succinctly describing the town's background. Clapson explains that in the Domesday Book of 1086, a village of Middletone was recorded, but that during the medieval period this became Middletone Kaynes. This was 'a bastardisation of the Norman "de Cahaignes", a family that settled in North Bucks during the twelfth century'. Within the wider area of Milton Keynes today there is a 'Milton Keynes village' that dates from these medieval connections. Back in the MK Partnership offices, John had confirmed this: 'We are not named after the economists [Milton Friedman and John Maynard Keynes]. People believed it could have been named after them, after all that would fit: all this was dreamed up in the sixties. But it's just not true.'

Clapson feels that many writers have succumbed to the 'temptation of easy journalism or knocking-copy' when making fun of the town's concrete cow sculptures (more on these later) and the roundabouts. He also believes that, rather than being a joke, Milton Keynes 'tells us more about the nature of both urban and social change in late-twentieth century England than almost any other provincial city… It has been a Buckinghamshire test-bed for the "new" economic, technological and social forces shaping England.' To highlight the symbolic importance of Milton Keynes, Clapson points out that New Labour under Tony Blair began its American-style general election campaign of 1997 in the town – appealing to Middle England literally from the middle of England. Several writers have since said that if Tony Blair were a city, he'd be Milton Keynes. And now that I think about it, it does feel as though the town is a good place to take the temperature of the country. Even from what I've seen so far, it seems like a progressive part of Britain – that there is indeed an 'edge city' side to Milton Keynes.

I head off on my bike the next morning along the American-style Midsummer Boulevard towards the number one tourist attraction in Milton Keynes. It is also, as some argue, one of the most important tourist attractions of any in recent British history.

The ride takes longer than expected. Cycling along 'red route' paths, I travel through parks, passing a succession of lakes, before pedalling up to the Milton Keynes Bowl. This is a huge outdoor venue that can hold 65,000 spectators and has seen performances from the likes of David Bowie, the Rolling Stones and Michael Jackson. It opened in 1979, with gigs performed by Desmond Dekker and Geno Washington. It's surreal being the only person there, imagining all the superstar acts and the thousands of screaming fans. It's also strange to consider that Milton Keynes has, from time to time, been so 'cool': who would have thought that?

Half an hour's cycle further on, I make it to Bletchley Park, the headquarters of Britain's World War Two code-breakers, where I soon find myself in Hut 8, a small temporary-looking building with a room packed full of tourists on fold-up chairs. There is a scattering of huts like this, some looking distinctly run-down, on a sprawling site set around a Victorian house with bay windows. Before us, a woman with neat blonde-brown hair and red lipstick is standing with her hands neatly folded before her.

It transpires that Ruth Bourne, our guide for the tour, joined the Wrens, the Women's Royal Naval Service, aged eighteen in 1944. She was one of the operators of the Bombe machines at Bletchley who helped read Germany's Enigma code, and was at the top secret location during the run up to D-Day when the world's first semi-programmable computer, Colossus, was used to break Hitler's even more complicated Lorenz code. The code-breaking by some of Britain's foremost mathematical minds at what is now the southern tip of Milton Keynes, surrounded by housing estates, helped shorten the war by around two years, according to some historians.

'You won't see anything magnificent by way of buildings here,' Ruth says, standing before us like a school teacher. 'Two or three times we've just avoided having this site pulled down. BT used to own it and they wanted to pull it down and sell the land. But the trustees went to the Milton Keynes council after they'd talked to a tree specialist. They put a preservation order on the trees. So we're very pleased about our trees here.'

Bletchley Park's history dates from the 1880s when it was a 'Victorian gentleman's place', says Ruth. It was used as a shooting estate until 1938, when MI5 and MI6 were looking for a base outside London with good transport links. Being near a railway station, Bletchley fit the bill: 'So Captain Ridley came saying he wanted a place for a small shooting party for six months.' To outsiders, they might have appeared to be toffs on a jolly; they even brought a Savoy Hotel chef with them. But they were in fact members of the Government Code and Cipher School.

In 1939, there were 250 code-breakers at the site, and to give an indication of how important they became and how big their task was, by the end of the war there were 8,000 code-breakers with 8,000 support staff working at sites around the country. Ruth tells us that Enigma machines had been available to buy from 1924, when 'they were used by stock exchanges, bankers, people who wanted to keep things secret'. For security, the machines had 17,576 different settings. By the early 1930s, the Poles had worked out how to intercept and decode messages sent by Enigma machines used by the German government, which had created its own, tweaked version of them: 'In 1938 the Poles realised they were going to be invaded, but in 1939 the Germans added a further two wheels.'

These wheels – cogs within the Enigma machine – meant the permutations increased and the Poles could no longer understand the German messages. 'They came to the Bletchley people and said: "Look we can't read these any more." By bringing their machines to us, it gave us a six-month start.' By the beginning of the war, the number of settings the Germans could use on the Enigma machines was 150 million million million.

Our group files outside. Bletchley has almost become a victim of its own success of late, following the film *Enigma*, based on the Robert Harris novel. As many as 4,000 people come each day, creating great weekend crowds, though not many realise they are actually taking a day trip in Milton Keynes. Close to Hut 8, there's another hut with peeling paint and buckling wood. Beyond is a stable yard where Alan Turing, the brilliant code-breaker and pioneer of computers, worked in a cottage. 'In February 1940 Turing broke into the Luftwaffe code. So he knew what Goring had in mind: we were going to be invaded and that it would be as easy as falling off a log. Understanding the code helped the airmen in the Battle of Britain to know where to be at the right time.' It was an exciting moment, but also an anxious one: 'Security here was terrific. People working in one hut would not know what went on in the next. As soon as the Enigma code was broken, the people involved were put into quarantine for several months.'

We are shown a replica of the Bombe machine that Ruth operated. The machine consists of red, yellow and brown wheels with plug-boards and connection wires. 'We had to have one hundred per cent accuracy or it wouldn't work,' says Ruth, looking at the wheels as though she's about to decipher a new German code. 'While Montgomery was having his eggs for breakfast, he needed to know what Rommel was up to.'

Alan Turing, we learn, was an eccentric genius. 'He was a very withdrawn gentleman and very strange,' says Ruth, who is one of only two guides at Bletchley who worked here during the war. 'He used to chain his cup to the radiator. Everything was rationed then and you couldn't get another one unless you knew somebody with their own supply. In the summer, as he had asthma, he used to wear a gas mask when he was cycling around. He looked very odd. Because of that, people used to tell their children round here: "If you're naughty we'll send you to the Park." He used to do things like count the number of revolutions that he had pedalled on his bicycle, so he could predict when the chain might snap.'

She pauses for a moment and says softly: 'Poor chap, he eventually committed suicide. Homosexuality in those days was criminal. He even had his security pass taken away when it came out.' Turing died in 1954, not long after being prosecuted for homosexuality.

After the war, Churchill ordered the Bombe machines to be dismantled for national security reasons, but two were rebuilt in the 1960s. We pass a memorial commemorating the part the Poles played by offering their Enigmas to Britain, and arrive at a building containing the rebuild of the Colossus machine. Ruth explains that it was a German teleprinter operator's mistake in 1941 that helped the Bletchley team crack the Lorenz code: 'A long message was sent, but the person who was meant to receive it had not noticed it had arrived. So it was sent again. By having two messages sent with the same information, British intelligence could see that there was a certain amount of logic. After four months, they found the logic.'

We're led into a room with the new Colossus machine, where an engineer introduced to us as Tony Sale is wearing a beige cardigan, an olive tie and black-framed glasses, standing before his beloved contraption. It seems incredible that a version of this giant computer, bigger than the average living room, with red valves, wires, yellow switches and ticker tape, helped turn the war. But it did. Tony, for whom computing has always been a passion, has recreated the working machine 'as a memorial to the work done here', he says. The project began in 1994, he tells us, and he and his wife Margaret provided money from their savings to help towards the high cost of parts. Recently, he says, 'a message was sent by radio signals from Paderborn in Germany as a test. We intercepted the signals and punched it onto a tape. After three and a half hours I found the setting and was able to decipher.'

Hitler knew that the British could break Enigma but not that they could break Lorenz: 'That was the big secret. In the build-up to D-Day as many as three hundred messages a week were being deciphered, fifty-three million characters of high grade text.' The semi-programmable computer was 'a British first... and that put out a number of the Americans'.

After the fascinating tour – more than enough of a reason on its own to visit Milton Keynes – I have a chat with Ruth in the staff canteen. As she eats her sandwiches, she's candid about life as a Wren operating a Bombe decoder. 'What was it like working at Bletchley Park?' I ask, feeling privileged to talk to someone who lived through such an historic period in a place that was so important to the outcome of World War Two.

'The work itself was dull and boring,' Ruth replies candidly. 'They never told you what was in the messages, you see.'

She pauses and considers her words. 'But it nevertheless gave you a strong feeling of immense satisfaction,' she continues. 'Apart from anything else if you were told "job up" [that the work on the machine had produced a result] that meant you had been accurate. And that our troops' lives may have been saved. It's terrible, but you wanted dead enemies. If you could do something to lessen the enemies' likelihood of invading this wonderful little island, then you'd achieved something.'

She pauses again, then adds simply: 'We loved Britain.'

Ruth is Jewish, she tells me, and many other workers at Bletchley were Jews who had fled Germany: 'Lots and lots of relations of mine were murdered. I had an extra reason to be pleased with our work.' Hitler's persecution of the Jews had a knock-on effect at Bletchley, Ruth says: 'One of the reasons we had such great German speakers here was that they were all refugees, and a large percentage of them were Jewish.'

'My next destination is Coventry – being here I can't help but be reminded of the terrible bombing that town experienced during the war,' I say.

'We couldn't evacuate Coventry without giving the game away,' she tells me plainly, not that she had a say in this decision, of course, or knew about it at the time. 'You'd feel cross [if you lived in Coventry], but that's surely the fortunes of war.'

Before leaving, Ruth introduces me to Jerry Roberts, one of the last surviving code-breakers. He's a flamboyant character wearing a leather cowboy-style hat, a bright red jumper under a tweed jacket, and a cravat. A pair of sunglasses hangs around his neck and he is accompanied by a much younger Asian female companion.

'I'm strong as an ox,' he tells me soon after meeting. 'An eighty-eight-year-old ox.'

Jerry used to work with Bill Tutte, who first constructed Colossus and who died in 2002: 'One commentator said breaking Lorenz was the greatest mathematical achievement of the twentieth century. I would agree with that. Turing broke Enigma, but he had the machines [from the Poles]. Tutte had to make his own.'

He explains that knowing the Lorenz code was crucial to knowing where German troops were during D-Day. Then Jerry shakes my hand firmly and says with a proud look from beneath his leather hat: 'Bletchley decrypts shortened the war by at least two years. People were dying at a rate of eleven million a year.'

He waves an arm towards the buildings I've just visited: 'At least twenty-two million lives were saved here.'

People don't save lives in Milton Keynes any more... they go shopping. Jurys Inn hotel is a five-minute walk from the main shops. I leave my bike at the hotel in the afternoon and do what most people seem to do in Milton Keynes: I go to thecentre:mk, as the main shopping centre likes to call itself. This walk takes me past a sushi lounge bar, with a Porsche and a Jaguar parked outside. Next I come to a Thames Valley Police Station connected to the shopping centre. The place seems to be so big it needs its own police. And then I find them: the concrete cows.

The cows are in a pit in a circular enclosure surrounding what appears to be a living oak tree that's been pruned to create a skeletal look. There are three large cows and two calves. I read a small purple sign that tells me they are the creation of the Canadian artist Liz Leyh, finished in 1978. She was an artist in residence during the early days of the new town. The sign goes on to say that the cows were 'once cynically said to symbolise a new town consisting entirely of concrete. The reality of course is very different: twenty per cent of the city is parkland.'

After reflecting on the fuss and controversy surrounding the famous cows, I stroll on through the American-style mall. It is vast. The shops seem to stretch forever along corridors lined with tropical plants. Just about every brand name you can imagine is here. A security man glides by on an electric buggy. Jazz floats across the walkways. A display near a jewellery store gives an indication of the size of the mall, saying that it attracts 31 million people a year, with 305 shops and 114 restaurants and bars. An information panel informs me: 'There are 59,000 lighting units in thecentre:mk – this is the same magnitude as the whole of Cambridgeshire.' The area of Central Milton Keynes, says the display, covers 845 acres, and there are 20,880 parking spaces. The attractions, including shops, a theatre, an art gallery, an indoor ski-slope and ten-pin bowling alleys, brought in 53,696,692 visitors last year. More than twenty million people, 35.5 per cent of the UK's population, live within a two-hour drive.

It's almost scarily big and busy. I step into a Waterstone's bookshop, where things are quieter, to look for local books. I ask an assistant if he has any recommendations, explaining why I'm here, and soon Matt and his co-worker Sherry are telling me all about places to visit in the town.

Matt recommends Willen Lake: 'It's an oasis of calm.' Sherry says: 'Get off the beaten track: there are loads of nice villages.' Matt mentions a windmill.

Sherry says: 'Go to Peace Park to see the Buddhists [apparently there is a Buddhist temple]. I sometimes go there. It's so lovely. The monks are so lovely.'

Then Matt says: 'Come and look at this.'

I walk behind the desk where he's on the Internet looking up the website www.balconyshirts.co.uk. The site sells T-shirts with amusing slogans relating to British cities. The slogan for

Milton Keynes is 'City of Dreams' – just as John back at the MK Partnership had said. The joke seeming to be that most people think the town is dull and full of concrete cows and roundabouts (definitely not dreams).

'Yeah, I had one of those shirts, but when the council started using the phrase, I had to stop wearing it 'cos it wasn't cool any more,' says Matt.

We flick through the website. Hull's slogan is 'A Taste of Paradise'. For Norwich, the T-shirt shows a hotdog covered with mustard: 'Norwich: It's the Mustard.' Salford's slightly puzzling slogan is 'Like Paris without the Tower', with a picture of the Eiffel Tower. The slogans for Hull and Norwich, if not perhaps Salford, seem just about spot on.

Afterwards, I cross a vast car park, enter a huge semi-circular building called Xscape and find myself at an indoor skydiving centre called Airkix, one of the most popular new tourist attractions in town. The tourist office side of MK Partnership has arranged for me to leap into a 110 mph air flow in a vertical air tunnel. I wait anxiously with my fellow diver, an Asian man named Depak, who is celebrating his fiftieth birthday. The skydive is a present from his children. We read information on a board that says the 'flight chamber' has 1,000 horsepower fans and 1.2 million cubic feet of air moves through the chamber each minute. The Beckhams, Frank Bruno and Frankie Dettori have all given it a go.

Trevor, our instructor, takes us to a briefing room. 'Keep it nice and still and stay relaxed,' he says. He tells us that this is the best indoor skydiving unit in Europe. The beauty of indoor skydiving, he says, is that you can make several jumps to perfect your technique without having to spend huge amounts of cash on taking flights to do skydiving for real. 'An outdoor skydive from twelve thousand feet will have about forty-five seconds of freefall,' he says, but here Depak and I are having four minutes.

We're kitted out in jumpsuits, goggles and helmets, and led up stairs to the flight chamber. The previous group has just finished. Depak and I look at each other a little greenly. And moments later I'm being blown upwards in winds of 110 mph, hovering ten feet in the air and grinning inanely. It's impossible not to grin inanely with all the air coming at you. Trevor is there to hang on to you, floating on one side, should anything go wrong, and towards the end of each two-minute burst, he grabs hold of me and we perform a crazy spin.

Depak and I pat each other on the back, tell each other how well we've done, and then I go for a beer in a bar kitted out like a mountain lounge with fake fireplaces overlooking 'the UK's premier indoor real snow slopes'. Through big windows, a 170 metre snow slope rises upwards covered with 1,500 tonnes of snow. The barmaid tells me that there will be a 'freestyle' night with jumps later on. The jump is being prepared and looks enormous – all the snow is created by artificial machines that somehow manage to turn Middle England into the Alps. I settle into a sofa to watch the skiers and snowboarders, and dip into a little more of *A Social History of Milton Keynes*. The grid road system, I read as the artificial snow machines spurt snow and as a snowboarder flips up in the air clutching his board, 'reveals an aspiration for movement and for meaningful connection with the social, cultural and economic life of the city'. Milton Keynes, it continues, is 'a city of our time'.

Pondering this, I take a look around the rest of Xscape. It's the first of three such complexes in the UK, the others being in West Yorkshire and Scotland. There are climbing walls, a multi-screen cinema, shops selling ski gear, fast-food restaurants, and a section called City Limits, with a tenpin bowling alley. I enter the bowling alley, where I count twenty-four lanes. All are full. There's a bar at the end with a purple-and-lime-green carpet. There are neon lights. As I'm about to leave, I've only been here a minute or two, a short pugnacious woman comes up to me.

'Excuse me sir, what are you doing?' she asks.

'I'm just visiting, having a look around,' I explain politely.

She looks at me doubtfully.

Then I tell her about Unsung Britain.

She says: 'Have you got permission to be here?'

'No, do I need it?' I reply, admittedly in a slightly annoying manner, though I can't see why what I'm doing is wrong.

She shuts up and talks into a walkie-talkie. 'Manager and security,' she says.

I tell her I'm going, and walk towards the exit.

She follows me.

Along the way a man wearing a stripy blue shirt is with an enormous bald bouncer dressed in black. They block my way. The bouncer looks like he could play rugby for any international team of his choosing. He is huge.

I explain myself again.

The manager looks at me dubiously, and I get the impression he believes I'm causing trouble.

'I'm not exactly enjoying the welcome that I'm getting at City Limits,' I say.

The man in the blue shirt does not like this. He mentions that there are some strange types who sometimes come in and might be trying to take pictures of youngsters.

I point out that I don't have a camera and I ask for his name.

He replies: 'I'm not prepared to give you that.'

Then he says: 'Don't roll your eyes at me.'

I wasn't aware that I had, and I point out that it's not an offence to roll one's eyes.

And so I leave Xscape, with a bitter taste in my mouth. I think the place is fantastic with its indoor skydiving, climbing walls and skiing. But some bits involving managers and security guards aren't so great at all. As I walk back towards Jurys Inn, I'm reminded of a book I've just finished by the recently deceased J. G. Ballard. In *Kingdom Come*, the novelist describes an undercurrent of violence, emptiness and nihilism centred round a fictional Metro-Centre shopping mall. OK, this is not close to what I've found in thecentre:mk, but my encounter with the manager and security man has made me think of it. In Ballard's nightmare vision of consumerism and shopping, the desire to spend seems to wipe out all reason and any sense of right and wrong.

He writes: 'The human race sleepwalked to oblivion, thinking only about the corporate logos on its shroud... At the sales counter, the human race's greatest confrontation with existence, there were no yesterdays, no history to be relived, only an intense transactional present.'

There are definitely ghosts of Ballard at thecentre:mk.

People are free to write whatever they like at my next stop-off: the headquarters of the Open University. The OU, established in 1969, is the biggest employer in Milton Keynes with a staff of 4,000. The campus is in Walton Hall, an area to the east of the shopping mall, where you are met in the modern, open-plan reception by a bronze head depicting Betty Boothroyd, the university's chancellor until 2006. It is much smaller than the UEA campus in Norwich and, as you might expect, there are no students running around. I sit on a leather sofa and admire a piece of modern art that looks like a giant red and yellow kite, hanging above an atrium with a cafe below.

Soon I'm meeting Louis de la Foret, the ebullient university spokesman. He's grey-haired with specs concealing sparkling eyes. 'I'm from New Orleans,' he says, almost immediately, as we take a stroll around the campus. He moved here fourteen years ago with his wife. When he was in New Orleans he was a news reporter: 'I covered five hurricanes.' He pauses as we go down some steps, then wistfully says: 'I sure miss the jazz.'

Louis tells me about the Labour Party origins of the OU, which was begun under the prime ministership of Harold Wilson, although it was Jennie Lee, the wife of Nye Bevan, architect of the National Health Service, who was the 'mover and shaker who got it going'. The student body is 180,000, making it the largest university in the UK. 'The great thing about OU is that you don't need any qualifications,' Louis says, as we inspect St Michael's Church, a fourteenth-century church in the grounds. 'You get people who dropped out at school or at university. You get people like nurses seeking further qualifications. But to be an OU student you've got to be motivated. It's not: "Oh, mummy and daddy wanted me to go to university." You've got to want it for real.'

It's also cheap. While a recent NatWest student survey found that the usual student leaves university with £33,000 debt, the average OU course costs £4,000 over six years. The students are getting 'younger and younger, twelve per cent are under twenty-five and the average age is now thirty-two'. We go inside Walton Hall itself. There has been a hall here since the twelfth century, but the current structure dates from the 1830s (this may be a new town but there are some very old buildings). A poster on a wall says: 'Ability not age. Ageism matters.'

Louis, who is one of life's nice guys, reminisces about his New Orleans days. 'I used to live in the French Quarter,' he tells me. 'There were so many characters: Ruthie the duck lady, she skated about on roller-skates followed by a duck. Wherever she went the barmen gave her free drinks. Clay Shaw used to be my next-door neighbour. He's the only man who was ever tried for the assassination of JFK.'

Louis returns to the subject of music: 'Yes, I remember the jazz festivals. Where else can you drink beer, smoke a cigarette and listen to gospel?'

He pauses, and whispers: 'I sure do miss the jazz.'

On a final cycle ride, after seeing real cows in fields near the river Great Ouse, I meet the Buddhists of Peace Park. Before coming, I hadn't expected to find a Buddhist temple in Milton Keynes. But there it is, complete with a Zen garden, overlooking Willen Lake. The Milton Keynes monks are away visiting temples in Japan, I discover. But there are Buddhists about. I ask one whether she likes living in the city.

Samantha, thirty-nine, a 'mental health advocate', smiles and says: 'We've got a very good town plan: very clean and convenient. Everything's so young though. There's no rootsy subculture. It's quite one-dimensional.' Glen, aged fifty and who also describes himself as a 'mental health advocate', has lived here all his life and helped build the main shopping centre in 1979. 'I worked on the footings of the centre, putting drainage in when they cleared the fields and there were still farmers working the fields,' he says. 'I don't see it as bizarre. I like it here.'

The monks, they tell me, were given their land by the 'hippy' town planners in return for planting a cherry tree each year. 'We may be in debt with that,' admits Glen, grinning. 'We may owe a few trees.'

After I drop off the bike to Nadir at the Milton Keynes Partnership's office, I think back over my unusual weekend. Samantha's 'one-dimensional' comment, the odd J. G. Ballard feeling I got after my tenpin bowling jaunt, and even Louis' yearning for jazz, all point to a lack of something in Milton Keynes. A lack of a soul in the town? A lack of Ballard's history and yesterdays? Or maybe all this is just amateur psychology. After all, the new town has a lot going for it. There is one of the most important historical sites in Britain in the form of the excellent Bletchley Park. There are beautiful villages straight out of the pages of H. E. Bates. There are plenty of well-priced housing estates, with bigger than average houses and a standard of living that generally seems a cut above most parts of Britain (the middle of Middle England seems to be doing pretty well for itself). There are Buddhist and Sikh temples. There is skydiving, skiing and bowling. There are amazing shopping centres and a well-considered theatre and gallery. There are lots of friendly people who are proud of where they live. And there are origins of well-known phrases (as well as red-faced men who want to have a 'pop').

Bill Bryson once wryly quipped in his travel book *Notes from a Small Island* that the best thing about Milton Keynes is that he did not hate it on first impression – the implication being that the longer he stayed, the more he disliked the town. But I think that's unfair.

Milton Keynes is fun... especially if you see it by bike. It's not so far to my next destination, where it's cars not bicycles that rule the roost.

9

COVENTRY: CAPPUCCINO WITH LADY GODIVA

If you send yourself to Coventry, I suppose you get what you deserve, I'm thinking on my first morning, after catching a crowded train (that passes back through Milton Keynes) to a rather dreary station near a ring road. The journey followed a motorway for large sections of the way and in the run-up to Coventry there were warehouses, council houses and a 'Waste to Energy Plant'. Not perhaps the most promising of arrivals: my heart isn't exactly racing at the sight of the ring road. But never mind about all that, I'm thinking. I'm visiting the biggest city I've been to yet and I'm about to see one of its most interesting tourist attractions. First impressions may not have blown me away, but I've got a packed weekend full of the hidden gems of this West Midlands city that most people do not have at the top of their weekend-break list.

They are – as I have been up to now – missing out on a lot.

I'm on the outskirts of town, where I've just been dropped by a taxi at the entrance to the old Jaguar factory on Browns Lane. A large man in a fluorescent jacket on the security gate is eyeing me suspiciously. Beyond the security barrier stands a decrepit warehouse with peeling paint and damp patches. Next to the security hut, and a pile of broken paving stones, is an unmanned mechanical digger. There's no one else in sight.

Surely this is not a tourist attraction?

But it is – and it is one that almost feels as though it gives a special insight into life in Coventry, and how things have changed in the city over recent years. The insight comes from seeing with your own eyes a place, now falling into disrepair, which used to be a hive of money-making activity that helped bolster the UK economy. Beyond the security gate, I get an eerie feeling walking into the plant. This plot of land has its place in British industrial history: it's the spiritual home of one of the pride and joys of British motoring. Thousands upon thousands of top-of-the-range Jags were once produced here by a workforce that peaked at around 5,000 in the 1970s. The road I'm walking along would have hummed with motors being tested and lorries carrying away the finished product. A faded sign on a red-brick wall says: 'Strictly no walking on the test track.' I look at the test track, trying to imagine the gleaming XJ6s, sparkling E-types, and dazzling coupés that once raced along here. It all feels quite sad. Before coming, I'd read up about Jaguar, learning how super-cheap competition from the Far East and Central and Eastern Europe had hit the business, as it has so many other manufacturers in the Midlands. During the past few years Ford has closed its Dagenham plant, Vauxhall has shut up shop in Luton, MG

Rover has collapsed with the loss of 6,000 regional jobs, and Peugeot Citroën ceased production in Ryton, a village to the south-east of Coventry.

At Browns Lane, car production came to an end in 2004, with 1,150 redundancies. All that remains, though I can't quite see where on this huge site, is a 'wood veneer' plant. Somewhere nearby there are 500 people making wood panels for the luxurious interiors of the 80,000-odd Jaguars still sold across the world each year. Most of these are produced at a plant at Castle Bromwich in Birmingham. Some have blamed Ford, Jaguar's owners, for the closure of the Browns Lane factory. Ford bought Jaguar in 1989 imagining there would be little trouble turning round the fortunes of an internationally recognised marque. But a misguided decision to stick with the traditional 'fuddy-duddy "heritage" styling' of the cars (as *The Observer* put it) as well as being 'blighted by ruinously poor productivity and miserable reliability' (*The Daily Telegraph*) accelerated the company's decline. The closure means that there are now no mass-market cars produced in Coventry.

It's not the greatest time for Jaguar, I reflect, as I walk on, avoiding a piece of corrugated metal hanging precariously from a shed wall. Rusty tubes snake along the side of buildings. It is grey and cold. I turn right at the phone box and am soon at the headquarters of the Jaguar Daimler Heritage Trust.

It is a wonderful place that gets very few visitors – in a building with row upon row of gleaming motors in a shiny showroom. There are sleek racing-green sports cars polished to perfection, futuristic silvery vehicles, a Formula One racing car and lovely old models from the 1930s. On the walls black-and-white pictures show comedians and football stars standing proudly in front of their Jags. George Best is lounging on a bonnet looking particularly happy with life, a beautiful model by his side. Soon I'm talking to Anders Clausager, the archivist, and Steve Meakin, finance controller of JDHT. They seem glad to see me. 'Ah yes, welcome welcome!' says Anders, who is German, in his forties and has cropped grey hair. 'Not so many people come here you know!'

Anders explains that the museum is open one Sunday a month. There are about 150 cars, some of which, I learn, are worth a small fortune. I'm shown a low-slung sports car with big drooping headlights. 'The XJ13 from 1966,' Anders says. 'It is the only one in the world.' Jaguar has recently turned down a £7 million offer to buy the car, he tells me: 'We will not sell!' While Anders fetches a brochure, Steve, who is wearing a blazer and has a bushy moustache, says: 'We were all very upset when it closed here. People were terribly disappointed. This was the home of Jaguar. It is a bit of an odd feeling now really. Outside in the car park –' he says, pointing to a vast empty car park – 'that used to be buzzing. You couldn't find a space.'

Anders returns with *The Jaguar Story*, full of pictures of cars from Jaguar's better days. The company, he tells me, is in the process of being sold. When it is, the museum will probably move to Jaguar's research and development site at Whitley, on the other side of Coventry. Preserving the museum is crucial, Anders says: 'Our main reason for being here is to keep a record of the history. If we don't, who will?'

We walk around, admiring the vehicles. 'How do you find time to keep them so polished?' I enquire. 'Volunteers,' explains Steve. 'Some of them used to work at the factory. There's a lot of local pride.'

Sir William Lyons, the displays inform me, founded Jaguar in the 1920s. His motto was 'grace, pace and space' and I can definitely see the 'grace' coming through in the cars from the 1930s. The museum explains how the first cars were branded 'SS'. This came from an amalgamation of two previous brands: the Swallow and the Standard. Anders says: 'Well, after the war people obviously didn't like that.' So the company went for Jaguar, a name suggested by their advertising agency. This was 'an ideal choice: feline grace and elegance, combining docility with remarkable power and agility', says an information panel. The local nickname for Jaguar is, they tell me, the Coventry Cat.

The cars are wonderful. There's an emerald-green Jag from the James Bond film *Die Another Day*, with a fake machine gun fixed to its back. 'Bond of course always drove an Aston Martin,' says Anders. We take a closer look at the F1 car, which is surprisingly small. Jaguar, Anders says, was a sponsor of Formula One from 2000 to 2004, when it sold its interest to the energy drink company Red Bull. Steve says that some of the vehicles on show are vastly expensive 'supercars' of which only tiny numbers were ever produced.

'Who can afford them?' I ask.

'The Sultan of Brunei and Elton John,' says Anders. 'People like that.'

'What do you drive?'

Anders looks embarrassed. 'A Ford Focus,' he replies.

But Steve has an X-type estate. 'Mine really is superb,' he says. 'It's top of the range: CD, cruise control, satnav, electronic windows, heated seats, automatic wipers and lights. It's a Sovereign two-point-two diesel with cream seats. It does forty-three miles to the gallon. I love it, I really do.'

Before leaving I have a chat with a man in blue overalls, whose name I don't catch. He is rueful about Jaguar's future. 'My next job could be in Delhi,' he says, referring to rumours that Jaguar will be sold soon to an Indian motor company [which it soon is]. Not so good then? 'Well it would be warmer than here, I suppose,' he answers. 'We just don't know what's going to happen. It's in limbo. Things have to change in life sometimes.' Then he shrugs and smiles: the smile seeming to suggest that deep down he is confident about the company's future, despite all the troubles of late.

And on that positive note – despite the not so positive surroundings of the old plant – I catch a taxi on to my B & B, passing a shopping centre and a McDonald's, and soon arriving at my digs.

In hindsight, I shouldn't have been *quite* so cheap when I picked a place to stay in Coventry. Before visiting I'd read a report that said the average price of its hotel rooms is £54. This makes it the cheapest city for hotels in Britain, at the time of my visit. The national average room rate is £72, with the highest prices unsurprisingly in London, where rooms are £128. So I'd reasoned that, if I got a very cheap room in Coventry, I'd be getting just about the best deal possible in the whole of Britain.

My B & B, which I won't name as maybe I just had an unlucky stay, costs £25 a night and is just to the south of the ring road. This is even cheaper than Wit's End in Slough. The bargain-hunter in me makes me feel very pleased about this as I ring the doorbell while taking in a sign that says 'WELCOME TO EXCELLENCE'. But I soon discover that the website description of 'distinctive budget accommodation in the heart of Coventry' is not wrong. As I look about my room, which is about the size of a double mattress, with a slim single bed on one side, I'm thinking: 'Yes, very distinctive indeed.'

The colour scheme is ruby red and orange. There's a tiny television on a bracket above a small sink, and a pint-sized kettle on a sideboard with two digestive biscuits and a packet of coffee that says it is 'Good to the last drop!' The dirty walls have an odd lumpy woodchip surface that makes them look as though they've caught smallpox. A small picture of the Eiffel Tower hangs above a radiator. The radiator gurgles, and sometimes sounds as though a woodpecker is trapped inside. Through the prison-style window I can hear traffic growling past. A police siren shrills by. I hear a toilet flush in the next door bathroom. A door slams. There are footsteps in the hall. A fire door creaks shut. I close my eyes and for a moment or two I consider heading for the station: what on earth am I doing here?

I'm not the first to ask. When J. B. Priestley visited the city while writing his travel book *English Journey* in 1933, he had an uncannily similar experience. I've brought along a copy, and it makes almost spooky reading in my new abode. For example, Priestley's description of his hotel room is of an 'inhuman little box lined with stained wallpaper, and containing no running water. The window looked out on to a blank brick wall.' OK, I've got running water in a tiny sink, and a view of a busy street, but the 'inhuman little box lined with stained wallpaper' is spot on. Priestley's reaction to his surroundings is to ponder whether 'to dodge the town, to say not a word about having been there'. Exactly how I'm feeling right now.

But like Priestley, who goes on to visit a production plant where cars are still actually being made, I don't run away. Instead, I go for a stroll with a copy of *The Premier Visitors' Guide: Everything You Need to Know While Staying in the Coventry Area* that I find in reception. My first stop on a getting-my-bearings walk is a mini supermarket with graffiti on its pebble-dash walls on a corner near the B & B. Outside, a man wearing a baseball cap and attending to a pit bull terrier is looking shifty. He eyes me as I enter to buy a bottle of water. People carrying cameras and looking like tourists are, I can already tell, pretty thin on the ground in these parts.

Inside, there's a queue for the counter. The man in front of me, a tall elderly chap with a lumberjack shirt covering broad shoulders, but with strangely thin legs, is fidgety and anxious. He's also tottering slightly. The queue moves along and when he reaches the front he picks up an eight-pack of large cans of Stella Artois beer. He places these gently, almost lovingly, on the counter and hands over £7. The polite Asian assistant points out that the offer for £7 is for the smaller cans of the beer and that the giant ones are £1.49 each.

'No, no, you've got that wrong,' says the man in the lumberjack shirt, in a tone that suggests he is an innocent victim of injustice and is simply asserting his rights in our consumer society.

The assistant will not back down. He recommends that the man in the lumberjack shirt tries a cheaper brand such as Carlsberg.

'No, no, I won't drink that rubbish,' is the reply. He doesn't raise his voice; he just maintains his I-know-my-rights expression.

It's a stand-off. The queue is going nowhere fast. After further discussion, however, the customer reluctantly buys the smaller cans saying: 'I'll be back! Oh yes, I'll be coming back tomorrow to talk to the manager. I'll talk to him about this. I'll be back!'

What a classy neighbourhood, I'm thinking, as I pay for my water and head for the centre of Coventry. Along the way, I pass a £4 car wash, an industrial cleaners' with a sign saying 'no job to big or to small for a quote' [sic], and a residential care home where elderly folk stare glumly through a bay window. Soon I'm at the infamous ring road, listening to the roar of traffic. This road was built in a tight circle around the city centre in the 1950s by 'modern planners' who wanted to relieve traffic congestion, I have read. I look about in either direction. Even though it's noisy, the road seems to be doing its job: not a traffic jam in sight.

I crunch along a concrete path sprinkled with broken glass. A hunched man approaches wearing a bomber jacket, glances my way, spits, and hurries on. I pass mounds of rubble and a ramshackle barbed wire fence. Then I cross two roads and walk beneath the underpass. Beyond is the Lamb Street Community Mental Health Team and a Salvation Army office. Two youths with hooded tops look up. A woman clutching plastic bags, sitting at a bus stop, says loudly to a friend: 'I fancy getting pissed tonight.'

It's a big weekend in Coventry. An IKEA superstore is opening, which the *Coventry Evening Telegraph* describes as 'IKEA's first city centre store in the UK' under the headline 'RETAIL STAMPEDE: NEVER A SHOPPING WEEKEND LIKE IT!' More than 30,000 shoppers are expected to go through its doors during the weekend. The Lord Mayor of Coventry, Dave Batten, is quoted saying: 'The atmosphere's fantastic. IKEA is going to make a real difference to the footfall in Coventry – it's going to be a big attraction for shoppers.'

Past the Salvation Army office, I come to a giant, seven-storey, yellow and blue cube-like building next to the city's Belgrade Theatre (showing a panto). It's the new IKEA. There's a short queue and 'opening party' celebrations are in full flow outside. Yellow and blue pieces of celebratory confetti cover the pavements. On a platform an enthusiastic woman dressed in yellow and blue is talking into a microphone. 'I think it's time to learn some Swedish!' she says brightly. 'How about we learn some Swedish?' Nobody in the queue says a word. Meanwhile, figures on stilts are juggling yellow and blue balls. 'OK now, "yes" is "*ja*". Have you got that? Shall we give it a try? What is "yes"?' Nobody says a word again. The woman with the microphone looks exasperated. 'OK, OK, maybe that wasn't such a good one.' She tries again. '"Good morning" in Swedish is "*god morgon*"! What is good morning everyone?' Yet again, nobody pipes up. I feel a little sorry for her.

Further on, I enter a labyrinth of concrete buildings in a seemingly endless shopping precinct. Most of these buildings, I'd read in a guidebook on the train from London, were built after World War Two, during which a Luftwaffe attack on 14 November 1940 destroyed much of the city centre including the old cathedral. How much did Churchill really know in advance about the attack, I wonder, thinking back to the code-breakers at Bletchley Park?

I get thoroughly lost amid all the concrete walkways. Gangs of youths wearing baseball caps hold court on corners, swearing loudly and causing shoppers to walk in arcs to avoid them. Sales posters say '50 PER CENT OFF!' and 'LAST CHANCE DISCOUNTS!' A shop wants: 'Scrap gold. Best prices paid.' A homeless woman sitting on a bench mutters worriedly to herself. I walk past and along some shadowy streets near Trinity Church, the modern cathedral, and the shell of the old cathedral destroyed in 1940. There's hardly anyone around. The only people I see are a couple of hooded figures furtively smoking cigarettes in the garden by the ruins of the Benedictine priory. I walk on and head back to the subway under the ring road. Everyone seems to pick up their pace here, seemingly avoiding eye contact with others. In the centre of the subway, a busker with scraggly grey hair is strumming the song 'That's Entertainment' by The Jam. The lyrics about screaming police sirens, pneumatic drills, screeching brakes and ripped up concrete seem spot on for the location. It feels a long way from pottering about the unexpectedly pretty villages of Milton Keynes, or the fine medieval centre of Norwich.

It's early evening now and near the guest house I go to a big corner pub, where The Police is playing on the stereo and the lyrics 'Sending out an SOS' are being repeated over and over. Wondering whether the music in Coventry is beginning to talk to me, I look around the busy bar where people are eating 'spudtastic' baked potatoes and 'two steaks and a bottle of wine for £9.99.' Pints of lager are £1.49. A group of lads in baseball caps is at a nearby table. They take off their caps, however, when their food arrives, as though this is the done thing.

I order a pint of Bank's bitter and a 'right royal feast' of lemon-and-pepper haddock. The landlady recommends that I go to the 'car museum', apparently there is another one that has nothing to do with Jaguar, though she 'doesn't really know the area because we've only been here two weeks'. A twenty-something barmaid with big brown eyes is surprised I've come to Coventry. Why, I ask?

'It's pretty rough round here,' she replies. 'I don't really like being in the city. There's too much hustle and bustle.' She suggests going to Warwick or Kenilworth. She even tells me which buses to catch to go there.

'There are some nice boutique shops in Warwick. A better atmosphere,' she says, sounding as though she works for the Warwick tourist board. The problem with going out at night in Coventry is, she adds, that 'people are raring for a fight. They want to fight all the time.'

'Why?' I ask again. She pauses and simply says: 'They just can't handle their beer.'

With a pint of Bank's bitter before me, I turn to *English Journey*. When Priestley came to Coventry, he asked his hotel porter what to do on a night out. The porter, who was not a local, 'answered my questions about a possible evening's amusement with the most sardonic negatives. It was the wrong night (it always is) to see them enjoying themselves; and anyhow they didn't enjoy themselves much.' Now, according to the barmaid I've just spoken to, they enjoy themselves too much.

I take a look around. A couple near me are complaining to each other about their steaks, which they are poking with their knives in a sniffy fashion. The lads seem happier with their meals, which they finish quickly and then promptly replace their baseball caps. My haddock arrives. It's not bad at all. But then a Christmas song comes on the stereo with the refrain: 'Ding a-ling a-ding dong ding.' This is repeated over and over. Sitting in a pub by a ring road in the West Midlands watching people in baseball caps take them off and on and listening to 'ding a-ling' music is beginning to get to me. I have, I suddenly realise, hit an Unsung Britain low. I walk back to the B & B... my smallpox room awaits.

Coventry is throwing me surprises, whether I like them or not, and the next morning – a Saturday – I get the biggest surprise of all. I meet Lady Godiva.

Lady Godiva and I are at a cafe-bar, drinking cappuccinos and sitting on black leather sofas. There's a picture of skyscrapers in New York City on a wall, and a row of red swivel-stools by a bar with chrome beer taps. Lady Godiva gives me an enormous smile. She has long blonde hair flowing from a silver crown with a red stone in its centre. She's also wearing a blue cape over a white frock decorated with gold embroidery. She gives me another enormous smile. I had not expected the guide for my city centre tour to be kitted out quite like this.

In 1982 something happened to Pru Poretta, Coventry's real-life Lady Godiva, that changed her life forever, she says, by way of explaining her unusual outfit. Every year, there is a summer fair in Coventry, but by the late 1970s and early 1980s, the recession meant the fair had begun to slump, with fewer and fewer visitors, she says. So 'somebody in leisure services' at the council had an idea: 'To bring back Godiva to ride at the fair.' A competition was held to select a suitable candidate to appear on horseback in a procession. 'My mother said: "Oh you'll make a good Godiva." And I said: "Won't I have to go naked on the horse?" But she said: "Oh you won't have to do that. It'll be proper and everything."'

She won. And after being picked, she went to the library to mug up on her strange new identity: 'I went through the archives and I discovered lots of things about Godiva: that she was a real woman, a wife and a mother.' Pru had a costume made, consisting of a red, velvet cloak and a 'skin-coloured bikini'. Wearing this, she rode a white horse at the 1982 fair. It brought her national attention, and soon *The Sun* was offering her 'lots of money, it kept going up, they wanted to give me five hundred pounds for page three – that was a lot then'.

She turned down page three, but accepted supermarket openings and visits to schools – and has been in demand ever since, setting up a few years back as a tour guide who dresses up as Lady Godiva. As we sip our cappuccinos, Pru runs through the legend of Godiva.

In 1043 (Pru begins), Godiva defied her husband Leofric, a local earl who had imposed heavy new taxes on his tenants, by riding naked through the streets of Coventry as a form of protest on behalf of the people. 'She did it for the poverty of the children,' Pru says, sounding animated. 'The children had pleaded to her. She was touched by them. She took on their problems and pleaded to her husband for them. He said: "No way." She continued to plead. He set her a challenge: she had to become like them [like the poor children]. She had to lower herself to their level, by going naked on the horse. He didn't believe she'd do it. Anyway, she did it, after asking the friar to tell none of the locals to look at her naked on the horse. Apparently one person did: a "peeping Tom". Nobody's sure whether this bit is true, as the first mention of him came five hundred years later.'

Many academics believe Peeping Tom to be fictitious, I have already read in a guidebook. Even so, few doubt that the phrase came into the language from the legend, according to Pru.

Pru has an incredible scattergun style of speech. Everything she tells me seems to come at a hundred miles an hour: I've rarely met anyone who talks as fast as the modern day Lady Godiva. And she keeps going, rattling off facts about the city. Within minutes I learn that the name Coventry may have come from a combination of the Anglo-Saxon word 'treo', meaning tree, with a local character called Cofa. Over the years 'Cofa's Tree' evolved into its present form. I hear a dizzying array of stories about the barbaric King Canute (who laid waste to many Warwickshire towns, destroying and doing 'God knows what' to a nunnery in Coventry at which St Osburg was once abbess), the Battle of Hastings (apparently Harold was Godiva's grandson), and King Henry VIII (who destroyed the city's old cathedral). Then Pru is telling me that the first use of a Godiva at the annual city fair was in the seventeenth century, that Shakespeare, Dickens and Mary Queen of Scots (who was held captive) all visited St Mary's Guildhall, and that Godiva chocolates are so named because a Belgian chocolate-maker came to the city in 1951 and thought the name was 'rather catchy'.

Amid all of this, my attention wanders when a man wearing a baseball cap enters. Sales of baseball caps must be doing well in Coventry as I've seen people wearing them everywhere. He sits near us and orders a pint of lager, not taking off his cap.

He quickly drains his pint, paying no attention to Godiva in her medieval costume. There's not the slightest glance in our direction, although we're the only other customers and one of us is dressed as though it's the eleventh century.

Lady Godiva and I are soon strolling around the streets of Coventry. People say: 'Oh hello Pru, looking beautiful today!' Almost everyone seems to know her. She's a local star. We head past the concrete shopping precincts in the direction of the cathedrals: the shell of the one bombed in the war and the one designed by Basil Spence that was consecrated in 1962.

After a short walk, we reach the courtyard of the old cathedral, with its haunting red-stone remains. As we look about the open site, I try to imagine what the original cathedral must have looked like. It seems such a shame that the structure was wiped out, and standing here it's hard not to imagine what would have become of Coventry had Hitler not ordered the infamous bombing raid. Back at my B & B, I'd read that the *Evening Standard* described Coventry as 'the best medieval city in Europe' in 1921. Meanwhile, in his *English Journey*, Priestley is 'surprised to find how much of the past, in soaring stone and carved wood, still remained in the city' in 1933. He goes on to say that Coventry is 'genuinely old and picturesque'. Had it not been for the war, the city would almost certainly be swarming with tourists: one of the highlights of any tour of England.

On our visit though, the old cathedral is empty. We are the only people in a small tourist office. We look at the replica of the wooden beams that were found in the shape of a cross on the morning of 15 November 1940. These are now maintained as they were discovered that day in an alcove on one side of the courtyard as a form of remembrance. 'What do you think would have happened to Coventry had it avoided being bombed?' I ask Pru.

'That's hard to say, but what is sure is that nothing was ever the same again,' she replies, going on to explain what occurred on the ill-fated day. 'Almost one thousand people died and another thousand people were injured. The attack used incendiary bombs. The bombings went on from seven at night to seven in the morning. It was terribly bad luck. There was a high moon, so the city was all lit up and the Germans could see where they were bombing. The word "Coventrated" was invented: a whole new word to describe total devastation. The whole city was lit up like a fireball. There was this glow in the sky above Coventry that could be seen for miles around.'

We walk down some steps and enter the new cathedral. From the outside it looks big and bleak, but inside the giant Graham Sutherland tapestry of Christ above the altar, the huge stained-glass side windows, and the light filtering through the big window by the entrance are stunning. Basil Spence was among 600 architects to apply for the commission to build the cathedral, says Pru, and his creation is remarkable. She also tells me that the tapestry is made of merino wool and took 'ten ladies two years to create… the eyes of Christ never leave you'. We cross to the altar and gaze back towards the enormous window looking on to the old cathedral. From here, the stained-glass windows are lit up along the side walls in a tree-like corridor of multicoloured light.

'Some people say that the new cathedral is grey and dull,' Pru comments. 'But how can they think that? Spence did this on purpose. He wanted to create a surprise, so that when you got here to the altar you'd be amazed by the colours.' We pause and just let the beauty of the scene seep in for a while. 'Now Coventry has become a centre of peace and reconciliation,' says Pru quietly, after a minute or so. 'Whether that is about the war in Iraq or the trouble in Palestine.'

It's a very moving spot. And, just as Bletchley Park made my Milton Keynes trip, standing here near the altar of this fantastic cathedral, looking along the corridor of colours and considering the symbolism of this building has made me glad to come to Coventry.

Lady Godiva and I say goodbye. She's been a great guide. Then I catch a train to Nuneaton, eight miles to the north-east of Coventry, to find out about another female who has left an indelible mark on these parts.

On the train, I read up about Mary Ann Evans, who wrote under the name George Eliot, and who was born in 1819 at Arbury Farm, just outside Nuneaton. The great Victorian novelist went to school for three years in Coventry in a building that has now become an estate agent, next to the ring road and close to a statue of James Starley (1830–1881), a local who invented bicycle spokes. Later, in her early twenties after the death of her mother, Eliot lived in Coventry with her father, who had previously run an estate at Arbury. The local tourist board has created a George Eliot Trail for those interested in the author's local connections. While Eliot was in Coventry, the George Eliot Trail pamphlet tells me, she met 'radical thinkers... people with whom she could discuss every topic under the sun'. It is believed that this period had a liberating effect, says the pamphlet. After her father died,

Eliot moved to London where she worked as an editor on the *Westminster Review*. She is also believed to have had an affair with her publisher. She then met a married man named George Henry Lewes 'with whom she began to live "in sin", defying convention and shocking Victorian society'.

John Burton, chairman of the George Eliot Fellowship, is a huge fan, as you might expect. We meet in Nuneaton town hall, just around the corner from a shopping precinct that has a bronze statue of Eliot in the centre of a square surrounded by cafes and all the usual high-street shops. Burton is quietly spoken, wearing a blue raincoat and a multicoloured jumper. And he is full of enthusiasm for Eliot: Unsung Britain seems to be teeming with enthusiasts, one of the great pleasures of making the journey.

'What do locals make of Eliot?' I ask, after he arranges cups of tea.

'We have a huge sense of pride that she is a local girl,' he answers. 'Some argue that she was the greatest nineteenth-century writer: certainly in the top three of Victorian writers, immensely popular during her lifetime.'

'When I went to Hull I met someone from the Philip Larkin Society who thought the city should have a Larkin centre, to celebrate their local famous poet. Do you think there should be an Eliot museum here?'

'That would be nice,' he replies with a smile, although he points out that there are already displays about her at the Nuneaton Museum and Art Gallery. This is unfortunately closed today as it's a Monday, but includes a reconstruction of Eliot's London drawing room of 1870 that's well worth seeing, John tells me.

He believes that too little is made of Eliot, and that the local authorities should get together to promote George Eliot Country. 'Tourists should be told to go to the south of Warwickshire for Shakespeare Country, then go to the north for Eliot Country!' he exclaims.

He's soon explaining why he finds Eliot such an interesting figure. 'She was a woman with an independent mind,' he says. 'She was prepared to live with public disapproval of her actions to pursue what she believed in. When you read *Middlemarch*, her masterpiece, you are seeing her independent approach to life taking full flight.' *Middlemarch* describes life in a gossipy provincial town, and is partially based on Coventry, says John.

'I've been reading the book for the first time over the weekend and I am enjoying it immensely,' I tell him (it's been helping to keep my mind off my B & B in the evenings). 'Very good. Yes, you must read *Middlemarch*!' he says, sounding as though he is on a mission to spread the Eliot word.

After our teas, we walk to the bronze statue in the square. This was recently knocked over by a pub delivery lorry, John says. Bollards have since been erected to prevent another accident. 'Eliot would have been most amused by that,' he says, chuckling to himself. We walk on to the nearby St Nicolas Parish Church, which featured in her book *Scenes of Clerical Life*, passing a pub called the George Eliot Hotel, with boards advertising £0.79 teas and £1.79 pints. Stained-glass windows on the burgundy-tiled building are decorated with the letters 'GE'. The pub, I learn, appeared as The Bull in one of Eliot's novels.

In the churchyard, I say to John: 'What is it about Eliot's work that you enjoy so much?'

'There was a subtlety in her writing, in her humour, that makes Dickens appear a caricaturist,' he replies. 'She was so popular when she was alive. She really was. She was respected, and she knew she could hold her own with anyone in intellectual life.'

'Do you feel as though her work is neglected in Britain? I recently read in a magazine that the novelist Martin Amis considers her the "best writer in the English language ever", yet she is clearly not as well known as the likes of Dickens or Austen.'

'Perhaps in the past she was overlooked,' he answers carefully. 'Interest in her went into decline over many years but recently her works have been re-evaluated.' He pauses. 'I think there will always be an interest in George Eliot, always, always.' He pauses again, trying to find the right words. 'And I think that is because she is so intellectually challenging. That's what makes her work stand out.'

From nineteenth-century novelists who deserve a better following, I move on to less intellectually challenging pursuits in the form of elite league ice hockey. I catch a train back from Nuneaton, clutching a copy of *Scenes of Clerical Life* kindly given to me by John. And then I go to my first ice hockey match.

The Skydome arena is next to the ring road, not far from my B & B. Tonight it is the Coventry Blaze, the league leaders, versus the Belfast Giants. I take a seat overlooking the oval of ice, while rock music blasts from giant speakers: 'Girls, girls, girls!' goes the refrain. A slogan on a wall says: 'COVENTRY INSPIRES THE FUTURE!' A cheerful and chatty red-faced man sitting next to me says: 'They don't sell you a seat here, mate, they sell you the edge of it!'

He and his son, I soon discover, are regulars. His son, who is wearing an Adidas cap and knows his elite league ice hockey inside out, tells me: 'They've cut down on the rough stuff in this league. But every team has got what you'd call a fighter, or an enforcer as they're technically known.'

Play begins. I'm hoping to see the 'enforcers' in action, and lots of goals. But there are no fights, and very few goals. A large man behind us starts shouting: 'Moron! Come on! Come on! What's wrong with you tonight! Hey, hey, you muppet! You couldn't score in a brothel tonight! Stupid! Stupid! Stupid!' I agree: the game is pretty lacking in incident. Even the red-faced man next to me apologises: 'They're not usually this bad.' But then again, the whole event is quite a spectacle, with the packed-out stadium, the rock music, the hotdogs, the 'Pukka Pies: the very best pies', the concessions selling beers, the banter in the crowd, and the occasional clatter of players against the sidescreen. This bit of Coventry within the ring road at least seems alive at night – whereas so many of the other parts seem deserted after nightfall after the offices and shops shut (very few people appear to live within the ring road, it largely consists of commercial properties). It feels like a little bit of Canada or America, in a least-expected spot. 'We just like ice hockey in Coventry,' says the chatty man with the red face. 'We've taken to it. I couldn't say why.' The home team – which I've been told has a terrific record usually, often topping the league – on this occasion loses 2–0, and we trudge off into the reality of the cold Coventry night. If Lowry back in Salford is my unofficial artist for Unsung Britain, and Larkin in Hull its poet, perhaps ice hockey in Coventry is its unofficial sport, I'm thinking on the way back to my dreaded B & B.

At breakfast the next morning, before catching my train onwards, I think back over my weekend in Coventry. The phrase 'sent to Coventry' is believed to date from the Civil War when Royalists were imprisoned in the city and shunned by locals. But nobody knows for certain whether this is the origin. It might also have come from London traders who lost their licences in the capital many years ago and then went to work in the city: effectively 'sent' to the city. As I tuck into a tiny, greasy plate of sausages, eggs and bacon, I consider whether I'd send myself to Coventry again, or recommend anyone else to go. At first I'm not so sure, but despite the dreary ring road, my depressing B & B, all the concrete walkways and shops, and the feeling of decline now that car manufacturing, once so important in the city, has sadly gone, I would definitely return. The story of Lady Godiva, the cathedrals and the cars, including those in both the excellent Jaguar museum at Browns Lane and the equally fine Transport Museum in the city centre (which I popped into after seeing Lady Godiva, taking in Thrust 2, a sleek car that once held the official land speed record at 633.468 miles an hour), are good enough reasons for a weekend break. But for me it was the new cathedral that made the weekend. I loved the sense of reflection and peace in the vast, impressive building. Coventry's history of destruction at the hands of the Nazis really hit home when I was standing by the altar with Pru. The beauty of the cathedral and the feeling of hope it represents seems to shine out amid the concrete city centre, with its broken glass and baseball caps.

But not many tourists make it to Coventry. The landlord at my B & B tells me that 'about five to twenty per cent' of his guests are holidaymakers. Mind you, he includes 'Burnley supporters – they come to stay every time they play here' within this definition. But he is also getting more French guests: 'There are new flights to the local airport from Marseilles. We do get a few French folk.'

'What are the main attractions of the city?' I ask, just in case I've missed something. He scratches his head, thinking for a bit. Then he says: 'Coventry is just Coventry really,' and heads back to the kitchen.

And as I walk along the not-so-lovely ring road to the station, I decide I agree with the B & B owner: Coventry is just Coventry. That just about sums it up. When I next visit, I'll splash out on a better place to stay: I won't forget that B & B in a hurry.

Next I'll be catching a train north, hoping a bit of sea air will clear away any Coventry blues.

10

SOUTH SHIELDS: FISH 'N' CHIPS... AND ANCIENT HISTORY

My journey from London to South Shields – the furthest north I'm going in mainland Britain – is unusual... but fun. It starts with a ride on a Grand Central train from King's Cross. This is an eccentric four-train company that began in 2007 and operates between Sunderland and King's Cross and has pictures of Marilyn Monroe in its lilac-and-grey carriages, as well as tables with Cluedo, chess and Monopoly boards marked on them (you can buy the pieces for a fiver in the buffet car). I'd been confused about where to sit as the seats – which are much larger than on normal trains, making the whole carriage seem like first-class standard – do not have an ordered number system. This means on my journey that seat twenty-seven is next to seat thirty-three, which is next to seat fifteen. 'Just sit anywhere, mate,' a fellow passenger advises.

So I do. The ticket inspector has a distracted air, with grey hair swept haphazardly to one side and an untucked white shirt. He reminds me of Benny Hill. 'Tickets from wherever you've been to wherever you want to go!' he bellows, on entering the carriage as we pass the Emirates football stadium. Regarding the numbers, he merely says: 'Oh yes, it's a joke,' when I ask.

It's an enjoyable trip in a train with the best interior of any I've been on so far. A sign says: 'Grand Central is proud to be the first train operator in the UK to offer all its passengers free internet access.' The Benny Hill conductor comes past again and I hear him explaining to a fellow passenger that all the seats are designed so they have unblocked views. We pass a golf course on the way to Thirsk and the conductor cheerily tells us that anyone getting off at Thirsk station must 'go to the back of the train as the council won't let us use the main platform'. It feels like we're on some kind of rebel train, small guys taking on the giant, loss-making rail corporations – with their impersonal announcements, dirty seats, over-priced sandwiches and general sense of 'just put up with it'. A brochure at my table, with yet another picture of Marilyn Monroe staring out from the front page, says: 'This is the train you've been waiting for.' And it does kind of feel that way.

The North Sea appears, looking grey and moody – contrasting starkly with the bright sunlight on yellow-grass fields leading to the water. A man walking two spotted dogs stops to stare as we pass by. It is eye-catching, dramatic scenery. But not long afterwards we reach Sunderland's big warren-like station. Then I take a taxi to my hotel in Westoe, a suburb of South Shields, with one of the chattiest taxi drivers I've ever had. He has short hair, tattoos, ripped jeans, and gives his name in a grand flourish as 'Richard Mitchinson: Sunderland born and bred'. On hearing about my weekend ahead in South Shields, he comments: 'All them lot down south, they'll be saying: "Bloody South Shields? Where the ****'s that!"'

He's soon giving me a lesson in local dialect and nicknames. 'Mackem and tackem, that's Sunderland,' he says. 'Geordie in Newcastle. Sand-dancers: that's what you get in South Shields, sand-dancers. That's where they're from: all sand.'

I ask about the origin of 'mackem and takem'.

'Well, it means "would you like to *mak* a cup of tea?" That's the "mak" as in "make". Then there's: "I'm just going to *tak* the dog for a walk." That's the "tak" as in "take". Mak and tak, that's Sunderland. That's how we pronounce things.'

Richard pauses, briefly, with me feeling a bit perplexed. Then he says: 'You're not from up here, so I've got to speak English. That's not easy.'

He continues on accents: 'We've all got different accents: Newcastle, South Shields, Sunderland, Cleadon. Cleadon's just a mile down the road: a different accent. Very strange. Pitmatic. That's what you've got round here.' Pitmatic, Richard explains, is a dialect that covers Northumberland and Durham and is said to use terms that were created by mineworkers in coal pits. 'If you go eight miles in the other direction, in Seaham, they talk Biblic. They ask, how is thine? Or, how is thee? Is that thine pint there?' The local accents often cause confusion, he says: 'I was once taken for a Scotch... by a Welshman.'

'In Easington, people put an "o" at the end of everything,' Richard adds. 'As in: "I was out last night, o." Or, "I had a good drink last night, o". That really does my head in, that does.' He switches tack. 'The trouble is that a lot of people from down south, they think we're all skint, on the poverty line, pigeons and flat-caps,' he says. 'That's not true. I've got a four-bed house, a thirteen-grand motorbike and a caravan in the country. I only work thirty-three hours in a week: Thursday to Sunday. I ride my motorbike on my days off and take my grandbirns out.'

By grandbirns, he is referring to his grandchildren. 'When we get students coming up here from London for university, they absolutely love it,' he says. '"Why aye", they're soon saying. "Why aye" means "yes" in Geordie.' We stop in Westoe, where Richard asked road workers for directions: 'See they're all friendly here. You wouldn't get that in London.' And with a 'Cheers Bud!' he drives off.

I'm staying at the Sir William Fox Hotel. I drop off my bag and walk down a hill with a Simply Workwear shop selling overalls, a Catholic men's club, and two men (somewhat amazingly) wearing shorts and T-shirts even though it's freezing and the first week of January. Then I turn left onto a terraced street, not far from a 'Pawn It' shop and a row of curry houses. In these unlikely surroundings, I'm about to visit South Shields' World Heritage Site and one of the most important Roman locations in the north of England.

There are twenty-eight World Heritage Sites in Britain including Stonehenge, the Tower of London and Durham Cathedral (not so far away). The South Shields entry is part of the package that makes up 'Frontiers of the Roman Empire: Hadrian's Wall', even though it is not, strictly speaking, part of the wall ordered by Hadrian in AD 122.

The Arbeia Roman Fort is on the top of a hill overlooking the river Tyne, four miles from Wallsend, across the river, where Hadrian's Wall begins its twisting seventy-eight-mile journey over the mainland to the Solway Firth. It does not look like much from the front: an unimposing building that might pass as the changing rooms at a municipal sports field. But inside the ticket gate and beyond, I'm about to learn a lot about the Romans in this north-eastern town.

Sometimes you strike it lucky with a guide who brings a place to life (it happened with Lady Godiva in Coventry, and Martin in Derry), and that's how I'm soon feeling about Angus McDonald. He greets me with: 'You're *in situ*, exactly where they were! You're about to see a reconstructed Mediterranean-style commander's residence! It's the only Roman fort intact in an urban area!' Angus, a former British army soldier, loves Arbeia. He has a shaven head, sparkling blue eyes, a silver neck-chain and a fascination with what went on in these parts 1,900 years ago. 'Arbeia means "place of the Arabs",' he's soon telling me, almost conspiratorially. 'The last known unit to be stationed here, believe it or not, were Iraqi [or Persian] bargemen from Basra. The Romans used people from all over their empire. They would ferry them up and down, wherever they were needed. There were Syrians up the road at Wallsend.'

Arbeia was excavated in 1875, I learn, as we walk into a wide-open space with the foundation stones of the buildings that used to house granaries and infantry barracks. 'But local people always knew about its existence,' says Angus. It was, effectively, the first port of call for Romans coming to Hadrian's Wall, and was crucial as a supply store, he informs me. Now, the fort is surrounded by terraced houses, but at the time of the Romans there would have been sweeping views of the mouth of the river Tyne, a strategically important point in northern campaigns.

I'm shivering; it really is cold. Angus says: 'Oh yes, the north of England must have been a shock to them – the Iraqis. But I think it's the same the world over and has never changed: it's politics at the stroke of a pen. The Roman emperors decided to campaign in freezing Scotland and the soldiers just accepted it. Same as our soldiers accept decisions to go to Afghanistan and Iraq, same as all the grunts in Vietnam. I always feel sympathy for the soldier.'

We cross the foundation stones and enter the barracks next to the Mediterranean-style house, which is open to the public, though there is no one else about. The barracks are made of wattle and daub. 'It's authentic, like,' says Angus, who clearly takes great pride in showing visitors around Arbeia, and has a casual delivery that seems to make all the old stones and buildings come to life. I'm shown the Roman latrines. Then we enter the reconstructed house: 'Back in the old days, you wouldn't have got in here without an appointment – you'd have to go through aides and adjutants. There would have been heated water. There would have been servants. The commander would have drunk wine with his guests.' The interior is brightly decorated in yellows, rusty reds and greens, painted in patterns on the walls: 'All the furniture and decorations are based on Pompeii.'

As we inspect the sleeping quarters, Angus talks about his own military days. He served in Northern Ireland and is interested that I've been to Derry. 'I was in Derry on Bloody

Sunday – in the parachute division of the Seventh Royal Horse Artillery,' he says. 'I wasn't actually at the site when it happened, but I talked to people who were there.'

He pauses, and adds quietly: 'Someone described it to me as a turkey shoot.'

From the reconstructed west gate, we look out across to Wallsend, and Angus's bright style of commentary continues. 'Shearer and Beardsley [the footballers] went to Wallsend Boys' Club,' he says, pointing to the distance. Then we go down some stairs and enter the small museum in the building that looked like the changing rooms at a sports field. Here we take in a cabinet containing some rusty-looking armour. Angus stares at it intently.

I take the bait and ask, 'What are we looking at?'

'That is the most complete ring-mail suit ever to be found in Great Britain,' he declares proudly.

I stare at the old remains. Then I'm shown an ancient carved stone. 'That is not just any stone: it is the Regina Stone,' Angus pronounces. It is, he explains, the gravestone belonging to Regina, a freed slave from Hertfordshire who married a Roman soldier named Barates, a Syrian from Palmyra. It depicts her at a wicker chair holding her knitting and a jewellery box. The inscription is in Latin and Aramaic. 'The language of Jesus,' exclaims Angus. 'Right here in South Shields – Syrian merchants wandering the streets. That's how cosmopolitan South Shields was back then.' The gravestone was discovered fairly recently on the site of a nearby Asda supermarket, where there's now a plastic copy in the car park. Heritage sites at your local Asda… Unsung Britain has it all.

Angus loves to talk about the Romans. 'Septimius Severus!' he suddenly announces. 'Septimius Severus,' he repeats, as though he just loves the sound of the name of the Roman emperor, who ruled AD 193–211. Angus pauses, waiting for me to ask him about Septimius Severus: it's his style of delivery to present you with something and have you wonder what is going on. So I ask him about Septimius Severus.

'Oh well, you see, he was here, old Septimius. His wife's baggage shield was found, so we know he was here. He came with the emperor's entourage including his two sons. They took a ship from here to the continent to go to Rome.' Hardly pausing, he goes on to discuss the emperor's sons: 'Caracalla and Geta. Caracalla was a despot: he was an absolutely appalling person – there are baths in Rome named after him. You had good emperors and bad emperors. He was a bad one. An absolute maniac.' Then he suddenly says: 'I have a theory. When Septimius was here, all the known world was ruled from South Shields!' He pauses to let this sink in, and laughs. 'Imagine Septimius and his entourage, the reaction they must have caused in these parts. There's a Roman port somewhere down there.' We're outside now and he's pointing towards the Tyne. 'People are always looking for it. Archaeologists always get a first look when there's a development round here.' He pauses again. 'But isn't that great? Ruled from South Shields! The whole known world!'

He has another giggle. Lucy, a museum assistant who saw us begin the tour some time ago, puts her head out the door. 'He's not still going on is he?' she asks: Angus, I take it, has a reputation for letting his enthusiasm about Arbeia get the better of him. And she has a good laugh too.

The Sir William Fox Hotel is in Westoe village, a suburb of South Shields, and just like my train up from London, my taxi driver and Angus's tour guide delivery style, it has a quirky feel. The name of the hotel had caught my eye, and I discovered it was named after Sir William Fox, a four-time prime minister of New Zealand during the nineteenth century and a supporter of Maori land rights. He was born here in 1812. Who would have guessed that? It is 'a jewel in the heart of South Tyneside', so says its publicity blurb, and it looks rather nice from the outside: a distinguished old red-brick building with a red doorway with columns on each side. It is run by a friendly woman with auburn hair who meets me at the front door with a smile, and takes me up to my room along creaky corridors, passing a lounge on the first floor with an honesty bar, on which you jot down the drinks you've had on a pad and pay later.

After my afternoon at Arbeia Roman Fort, I head straight for the lounge, taking my laptop as there's an Internet connection. A couple are at the honesty bar drinking white wine, and the TV is showing a film starring Angelina Jolie. The auburn-haired woman has asked if I'm hungry and has recommended fish 'n' chips from a place called Colmans: 'It's the best fish 'n' chips in Tyneside,' she says. 'I'll order them in for you.' Everything feels very comfortable and friendly here, as though I'm in someone's plush living room: I'm glad I've discovered the Sir William Fox Hotel.

I call Anne, who hadn't been sold on South Shields in advance. But she's interested in the Roman fort. 'I didn't know there would be World Heritage Sites,' she says, sounding as though she wouldn't mind coming up as I describe the setting on a hill, with the river Tyne on one side and the North Sea beyond.

I also describe the train journey. 'It sounds wonderful,' she says.

South Shields has already been an adventure... and there is plenty more to come.

After saying goodnight, I open a can of Heineken from the honesty bar and reflect on the matter at hand: South Shields (population about 90,000). All I really knew about the town before coming was that South Tyneside had a reputation for high unemployment following the decline of mining and shipbuilding in the region. It had been that reputation that had made me curious: can you have a weekend break even in a place that so many people associate with mass unemployment and industrial hard-times? Have holidaymakers descended to the former mining towns of north-east Britain? I look at a website that shows that the last coal mine in the borough of South Tyneside, Westoe Colliery, closed with the loss of 1,200 jobs in May 1993, and the last shipbuilder, Readheads, closed in South Shields in 1984. For many years unemployment was higher here than anywhere else in mainland Britain, I learn, peaking at 16,250 people out of work in 1985 and standing as high as 12.8 per cent as recently as 1997.

Then I flick through a council-published booklet I picked up earlier at the library in town. This says that the decline in heavy industry from the 1980s onwards has meant that high unemployment has given the area the 'unenviable boast' of being a 'jobless black spot'. But the area's employment troubles, I read on the Internet, go back a long way further than the 1980s, with hardship in these parts being a constant concern ever since the Great Depression in the 1930s. I take a sip of Heineken and look up images of the famous Jarrow marchers taking their petition demanding the right to work to Parliament in 1936; Jarrow almost merges with South Shields, just to the west along the Tyne towards Newcastle. The march began after the closure of a major shipbuilder and a steelworks caused desperation, verging on starvation, among locals. Although according to one of the marchers, Cornelius Whalen, who is quoted in the council booklet: 'The march didn't achieve anything, except give the town a reputation for poverty that it never lost.' Unemployment in Jarrow was as high as 60 per cent during the Great Depression, says the booklet, and Whalen goes on to admit that one of his motivations for joining the 1936 march was simply that he was supplied with 'something to eat and cigarettes' when he signed up.

I'm supplied with something to eat too: my fish 'n' chips with mushy peas, delivered by the woman with auburn hair (whose name I never catch). It is absolutely delicious, and for a while I forget all about unemployment marches, and watch Angelina Jolie dashing about the screen. Afterwards, I help myself to another Heineken; what a wonderful thing an honesty bar is – no waiting about for service. And as Jolie fends off a baddie with a kung fu kick, I consider the general sense of doom and gloom on the Tyne that I've been getting from the booklet and the Internet. Is it really so bad now?

The next morning, after a good night's sleep at the Sir William Fox, I pop to the local library again, which is near a vast bingo hall, to get some answers. Here, in a slightly dingy basement research room, a very different, more hopeful picture begins to emerge, courtesy of a South Tyneside Council publication. During the past six years, at the time of my visit, unemployment has fallen by 17.8 per cent in the constituency of South Shields, according to the council. The area as a whole has performed better than any of the other twenty-three local authorities in the North-East during this period, it says. Unemployment stands at 4.5 per cent compared to a national average of 5.7 per cent.

And one of the big drivers of the turnaround *has* been tourism. Around the corner, I meet Gillian Quinn, the tourism officer for South Tyneside, at a cafe near the marketplace – a lively spot that seems to act as the centre of town, with stalls selling handbags for a couple of pounds, food and second-hand book stalls, and a ferry port to one side that takes you across the Tyne to the fishing port of North Shields. Gillian is (very) keen to stress the importance of tourist cash.

'But how important is it really?' I ask.

'Well, there are more than 3,800 people working in tourism in South Tyneside,' she replies.

'That sounds like an awful lot,' I say.

'Oh yes, tourism is worth £207 million to the region annually and we had five-point-eight million visitors last year. Unfortunately, ninety per cent of people are day visitors. We're trying to encourage people to stay longer. Newcastle and Gateshead is an emerging destination on the international stage. But we're only twenty minutes away from there.'

Gillian hopes that people will 'experience the city life in Newcastle' but stay in accommodation on the pretty coastline in South Shields. 'People think it's all whippets and people with caps up here,' she says, eyeing me closely. I am, after all, clearly a 'southerner', born and bred in London.

'They think it's all traditional industry,' she continues. 'There's the image of the North-East, that it's all industrial.' She eyes me again. 'Yes, heavy industry has been part of our history but there are emerging industries, like tourism, now.'

Gillian begins to fill me in on what to see and do, and tells me that Catherine Cookson, the romantic novelist who penned more than a hundred books, has been a big boost to the area's tourism. She is from these parts and based many of her stories here, Gillian says. Such is her popularity that back in the 1980s the council went as far as to declare parts of South Tyneside 'Catherine Cookson Country'. Street signs are still up declaring you are entering 'Catherine Cookson Country' – I'd seen them on the drive in with chatty Richard – and there are official tours of the places where she lived and that she mentions in her works. Not bad considering the fairly lacklustre efforts made on behalf of Larkin in Hull and Eliot in Coventry.

'They're really for older people. We used to promote Cookson Country, but really we don't do that as much now. There's not the same interest as there used to be,' says Gillian, who gives me a list of attractions and a glossy tourism brochure for my weekend break. 'That said we do get as many as two hundred groups a year. Her appeal is still quite amazing.'

After our conversation, I wander down the street to the South Shields Museum, which is on Ocean Road, close to the beach. I'm about to learn an awful lot about the remarkable life of Dame Catherine Cookson.

The museum is quirky and informative; just the type of museum you hope to stumble upon in an out-of-the-way spot. The section near the entrance is almost entirely devoted to

Cookson. The first display you come to describes how her mother was working away from home as a barmaid in a pub near Gateshead when she started her relationship with Catherine's father and returned home in disgrace. She was pregnant with Catherine, who was born Katie McMullen in Tyne Dock in 1906. The scandal deeply affected Cookson's childhood, and she left school at fourteen to enter domestic service, before working as a laundry checker at a workhouse, the display says. Later, she managed a laundry in Sussex, where she scrimped and saved to buy a house at which she took boarders, one of whom she married (Tom Cookson). She turned to writing at the age of forty-two on the advice of her doctor, as she had been 'suffering years of physical and mental illness and the heartbreak of several miscarriages'.

What a prescription that turned out to be. Her first book was published when she was forty-four and she went on to complete a total of one hundred and three. From 1983 to 2001 she was the most borrowed author from British public libraries. From 1950 to 1997 the prolific romantic novelist sold ninety-five million books worldwide at a rate that works out at 231 books an hour: no wonder there are so many tourists coming to find out about her. She wrote sixteen of her books in long-hand, scrawling her words so quickly that she began to suffer from writer's cramp and was forced to use a tape recorder, according to another display. She was made a Dame in 1993 and died aged ninety-one in 1998. As she grew older, she wrote even faster: towards the end of her life she had been going at 'such a rate her publishers could not keep up'. A cabinet contains her writing desk and a certificate from Pope John Paul II marking her golden wedding anniversary.

She is well-regarded locally as almost all her books describe the scenery and people of South Shields, says a sign by the cabinet. 'Like a great sponge I'd taken it all in,' she once wrote, talking about South Tyneside. 'The character of the people; the fact that work was their life's blood; their patience in the face of poverty; their perseverance; their kindness and open-handedness... I couldn't write with any strength about any other places.'

Beyond this shrine to Cookson there are displays that explain how South Shields was a thriving seaside resort until the 1960s, when package holidays in the Med attracted people further afield. There is also a moving section on the Jarrow March, explaining how the closure of Palmer's shipyard in 1933 was the final blow to a one-industry town. But Cookson is the museum's big attraction. I ask Hilary Jago, the kindly museum assistant, who is sitting by a shelf full of Cookson's books for sale, whether they get many romantic novelist visitors?

'Oh yes, people come in from all over the country because of her,' she says.

She pauses, then whispers: 'But she's not really my cup of tea, I have to admit. I much prefer biographies.'

From the museum I take a short taxi ride to a place where I'm about to learn something I'd never expected: that history was, literally, made in South Tyneside. During the seventh and eighth centuries the very first history of the English people was written by a monk living at a monastery in Jarrow: the Venerable Bede.

St Paul's Church, parts of which date from the time of Bede, is on a hill overlooking the Tyne. It may be damp, grey and not much to look at, but it was at this location at around AD 731 that Bede wrote the *Ecclesiastical History of the English People*. In this book, I'm soon discovering, Bede described the Roman occupation of England and the early Anglo-Saxon period, when the Angles, the Saxons and Jutes arrived in warships. *Ecclesiastical History* mentions ancient names from history such as Caedmon and Horsa that are only known now because of this text. Bede's stories are crucial to our understanding of the earliest days of English history. A museum display quotes him as writing: 'The race of the Angles or Saxons, invited by King Vortigern, came to Britain in their warships and by his command were granted a place of settlement in the eastern part of the island, ostensibly to fight on behalf of the country, but their real intention was to capture it.' Bede didn't quite match Cookson: he penned a mere sixty books. But it was enough to earn the title 'Venerable' and to have his remains taken to Durham, where there is a shrine to him at the cathedral.

All of this I learn in Bede's World, an interactive museum next to the church, where I spend an hour or so wandering round the displays. Then in the church itself, I meet Syd Harrison, the organist, who takes me into the oldest part of the building – the chancel, which dates back to 681. 'Bede lived from 673 to 735,' says Syd, who has a no-nonsense manner. 'He was only twelve when he came here and he stayed for the rest of his life,' he continues. 'Nobody travelled much in those days, you see.'

He sounds like a fascinating character – who began as a bit of a child genius. Bede started studying when he was seven, and the local monasteries were the 'Oxford University of that time', according to Syd. 'There was a maximum of six hundred pupils.' Bede was: 'A scholar, a monk, a priest, a writer, a poet, a historian, a geographer, a musician, a translator of the gospels. He was a lot of things.' Unfortunately, however, many of his books were destroyed by the Vikings.

The chancel is narrow, with walls believed to be made of stone taken from Arbeia and Hadrian's Wall, stained-glass windows, and rows of pews. A tiny circular window the size of a football is made up of delicate pieces of blue and green glass. 'That's the oldest glass in Western Europe,' says Syd matter-of-factly, adding: 'Bede worked out the present-day calendar. The one we use. Prior to that, we had the Roman calendar. He also worked out the tides. If it wasn't for Bede, a whole lot of things today could well be different.'

A church booklet that Syd gives me puts Bede's work in perspective. It explains that he dominated the intellectual life of Europe for four centuries. He was also responsible for promoting the idea of a unified England centuries before it happened, popularising the BC/AD dating system and calculating the date of Easter. His writings helped make sense of the sudden shift from Roman Britain to the Anglo-Saxon kingdoms.

As I'm finding so often, I'm the only tourist. Not many people, it seems, come here to find out about Bede. Syd and I stand by the gift shop in the quiet church… and start talking football. Syd is a Sunderland supporter: 'I'm a red-and-white man – never a blue. In 1973, when we won the cup, I saw that. I went to Wembley that year. It's been downhill ever since.'

Ray, a volunteer who's joined us, is a Newcastle fan. 'Jackie Milburn. In the early 1950s. Striker. Won the FA Cup three times. Wonderful!' he says.

We're joined by Ruth, another volunteer. 'Oh yes,' she says. 'Didn't that lift people's spirits?'

But then she turns to discussing Alan Shearer, the former England captain. 'He's always miserable,' she complains.

Yet another volunteer, Margaret, turns up; Bede may be short of tourists, but not volunteers. 'I just wish Shearer would speak grammatically,' she says.

'I like him,' says Syd, sounding put out.

Ruth turns to me: 'We don't really want too many people knowing about us or else we'll get all these awful southerners coming up and ruining it.'

'Like me?' I ask.

'Some of them are even more awful,' she jokes – or at least I think so.

Syd quickly adds: 'We don't mind if they come to the church.' Tourists are an important source of cash, of course.

As if proving this, I buy a copy of Simon Jenkins' book *England's Thousand Best Churches*, which features St Paul's. Then I go to an 'Anglo-Saxon-style farm', complete with vegetable patches and two enormous pigs, behind the building. At the far end of the garden, there's a grassy mound. I climb up this and find myself staring out across the Tyne. It is a wonderful view of an industrial landscape, the sort of view that might well have inspired Lowry, who actually visited South Shields many times. There are enormous cargo ships, looming silos, a vast oil rig that looks as though it is under repair, and thousands upon thousands of Nissan cars, creating a patchwork quilt of colour down by the docks. The cars are transported from here by cargo ship to Europe and were constructed at the Nissan plant in Sunderland, Syd had told me. I look across the river and there are pyramid-shaped piles of gravel and yellow diggers spinning about them.

I stand by a tall 'Northumberland cross' at the top of the mound, suddenly feeling amazed by how history works itself out. What on earth would Britain's first historian make of things now?

Then I go for a walk. Gillian from the tourist board had complained to me that the BBC's television series *Coast* bypassed South Shields: 'They went down the coast really quickly, totally ignoring us.'

They missed a stunning spot. I spend the afternoon walking south from the mouth of the Tyne to Souter Lighthouse. I stroll down Ocean Road to see an orange coastguard boat gracefully gliding out to sea in front of the cliffs of North Shields. It is so different from the view across the Tyne from St Paul's Church. Here, there is no sign of industry at all (save for a couple of cargo ships on the horizon). The elegant silhouettes of a ruin and a monument stand out on the cliff at North Shields, across the river, looking thoughtful against a lovely sky of pastel blues and pinks. A man is walking his dog along the curve of the beach, with slate-grey waters disappearing in the distance in a shimmer of sunlight. It's a very beautiful setting – one of the most picturesque so far in Unsung Britain. Lowry, on a trip from smoky Salford, did paint the scenery here (I saw the pictures at the Lowry Centre). Turner came, too. And you can definitely see why they were inspired by the setting.

I walk on, leaving the river and moving onto Sandhaven Beach. This stretches in a charming sandy curve beyond the Wonderland and Ocean Beach amusement arcades. A shelter near the arcade protects one of the country's oldest lifeboats, the *Tyne*, dating from 1833 (there is a rich lifeboat history in these busy waters). I take a look at this, and walk along to an area with a fountain and a curving windbreaker. A sign here says that George V once declared Sandhaven the 'finest' beach he'd ever seen. It certainly gives the one in Port Talbot, with its not-so-lovely slime, more than a run for its money.

There are lots of walkers about. It's a crisp, sunny Saturday afternoon. I climb a mound to reach the top of a small cliff with the remains of World War Two military defences. Beyond this in another bay, there is a former magnesium limestone quarry. This area is fenced off. A sign says that the quarry closed in the mid twentieth century but that it was filled with domestic and industrial waste during the 1960s and 1970s and that 'recent investigations have shown that some of the fill material contains pollutants'. South Tyneside Council and the National Trust, which owns this land, are in the process of preventing the spread of the pollutants.

Beyond this bay, I find myself on the cliffs of the Leas, where the landscape is flat and green. The cliffs twist and turn around a series of bays moving in the direction of Souter Lighthouse. I walk along, falling into step with a young man with a pit bull terrier on a lead. He's talking on his mobile. 'Oh aye man, **** that,' he says. 'Don't ***ing stand for that.' Then he ends his call and starts jogging along the path with his pit bull scampering alongside him. The Leas marks the finishing line for the Great North Run, the world's biggest half-marathon, which starts in Newcastle with 54,000 participants – perhaps he's in training. The event is so large it was recently named the official North-East Tourism Event of the Year.

Then I reach Marsden Bay. I walk down long steps to the beach. The scenery is wonderful. Marsden Rock, which once had a granite hoop in its middle, stands like a giant boulder in the gentle sea. The sun has turned golden, adding warmth to the cream colours of the cliff. I walk along the sandy beach, passing fishermen on fold-up chairs (who tell me they are after 'flat-fish and cod'), and head for the Marsden Grotto. This is an old pub dating from the eighteenth century when a former miner named Jack the Blaster set up home with his wife in the caves here.

I eat fish 'n' chips on the pub terrace – the fish 'n' chips in South Shields are second to none – and talk to the barman, who informs me that smugglers used to operate in these parts. 'This place oozes history,' he says. Then I take the lift to the top of the cliff, and walk on to the red-and-white hoops of Souter Lighthouse, decommissioned in 1988 and now run by the National Trust. The lighthouse oozes history too, I'm soon discovering. In 1869 more than twenty vessels were wrecked between South Shields and Sunderland, says a display. An urgent local meeting was held to discuss the disasters, and the result was the opening of Souter in 1871, Britain's first electric lighthouse.

Up a steep staircase there are views from the top of an empty field next to the lighthouse where there were once terraced houses for miners who worked at the Whitburn Colliery. This was closed in 1968, according to Emily, a young National Trust assistant sitting on a chair in the corner. 'On a good day you can see for forty-five miles in each direction,' she tells me, as I take a picture of the dramatic sweep of cliffs.

'Did the lighthouse bring an end to the shipwrecks?'

'Oh yes, there were a staggering number of shipwrecks but as soon as this was built it had an immediate effect,' she says proudly. Then she points at the lights: 'Guess how much they weigh.'

'I haven't a clue,' I admit.

'Well, the lights alone weigh four and a half tonnes,' she says. 'And they're placed in one and a half tonnes of mercury.'

Content that I now know the tonnage of the lights of the Souter Lighthouse, I catch one of the regular buses back to the centre of South Shields. As I do so I suddenly realise that the walk from the mouth of the Tyne to the lighthouse, perhaps alongside the Trans Pennine Way back in Hull's docks, was the most enjoyable so far on these weekend jaunts. What a lovely way to wile away a few hours, especially on a sunny day.

On my final morning, Sunday, I visit a place that does not count as an official 'attraction', though it did once lure the most famous tourist ever to venture to South Shields. In 1977 the world heavyweight boxing champion Muhammad Ali visited the Al Azhar Mosque in the Laygate area of South Shields, where he had his marriage blessed by the imam when he was visiting the North-East on a promotional tour. Angus back at Arbeia told me he remembered the day well. 'He came driving round the corner on an open-top bus,' Angus recalled. 'There he was: Muhammad Ali: the best-known person in the world! The best-known man in the world! And I just thought: "Oh my God".'

South Shields is home to a Yemeni community that dates from the 1890s, making it one of the oldest ethnic-minority communities in Britain. It all began when seamen were needed for the merchant navy and Yemeni crews were recruited by the British in Aden, I had already learned. There are now more than a thousand people of Yemeni descent living in South Shields, and the mosque was opened in 1972, making it the first purpose-built mosque in the whole of the country.

My taxi driver is interested in my destination. 'There were riots here in 1919. There was a lack of jobs, so there was rioting in the Yemeni community,' he says.

'Were the riots at all race related?'

'No, it wasn't to do with race,' he replies. 'I've been born and bred here and have lived here for sixty-odd years. I've never known any bad race problems. Most of them have married into the community now. That kind of proves they've been accepted.'

In fact, the riots were indeed race related; caused by disputes over jobs that involved white mobs attacking Arab boarding houses and launching prolonged campaigns against the Yemeni community. This tension continued well into the 1940s, with further notable riots in 1930, during which fifteen Arabs were jailed and deported, including a community leader who had not taken part in the disturbances at all. Another Arab leader at the time, Hassan Mohamed, wrote to the *Evening Chronicle* saying: 'I do not think the public knows the extent to which the Arabs are suffering. Many have to pawn clothing and other personal belongings to buy food. There are scores of Arabs who are living on one meal a day... they only want a chance to earn a living and believe that they only have the British flag behind them.'

We pull up by a building that looks as if it might be a sports hall. 'That's it,' says the driver, and I look at the building again.

At one end of the cream-coloured building there is a small onion-shaped dome next to two tiny minarets. There are grills on the windows. It does not look particularly welcoming as a place of worship, and it seems slightly odd sitting here on a hill above the Tyne: I can see the funnel of a ferry with seagulls circling above at the end of the street.

No one is about and I'm guessing the mosque is closed. But then a man wearing a woolly hat and an Australian cricket shirt walks up.

'Is the mosque open?' I ask him.

'Yes, I'm just coming for prayers,' says Muhammad Bakhtiar, who is in his fifties and tells me he is a marine engineer from Karachi. 'You should see this place on Fridays: packed. At least forty to fifty people every time. I've lived in South Shields since 2005 but first came to Britain in 1991. I like it in South Shields: it's a good, nice, peaceful, small place with quiet people. You can get halal food. It's very nice in South Shields. Let me go and ask if the imam is available for you.'

And off he goes, inside, leaving me sitting on a bench next to a black cat. A few minutes later his head appears out of the doorway and he waves me over. 'The imam is waiting,' he says. I take off my shoes and go upstairs into a room with a green carpet with an ornate pattern. The imam is dressed in white, perched on a chair. He doesn't speak much English, but another man named Ahmad, seventy-five, who used to be employed in a steelworks has better English.

'How long have you been living in South Shields – do you remember racial tension? Is there any now?'

'We've been here a long time, since before the first war,' says Ahmad, whose English, I now realise, is limited, making it difficult to get direct answers to questions. But it is interesting to hear his point of view nevertheless. 'South Yemen used to be a British colony,' he continues. 'And the government got us to work in the navy. We're also in Hull and Cardiff – the Yemenis. Many of us died in World War Two.'

There are just four people in the mosque, including the imam. Copies of the Koran are on a shelf and there is fluorescent strip lighting. The imam, also in his seventies, smiles at me. He seems pleased to have a visitor. Then Ahmad says: 'It's a good life… and it's a good death.' The imam smiles again. They're about to have prayers, so I gather my shoes and leave after thanking them for their time.

From burkas to Barbour. Before catching the Grand Central train back to London – while reflecting on just how random so many of my visits are becoming – I quickly stop off at a South Shields institution: the headquarters of Barbour, the outdoor clothing company. John Barbour began supplying sailors, fishermen and dockers with oilskins and other heavy garments back in 1894. He started with a stall in the South Shields marketplace, soon established a reputation for quality, and never looked back.

At the headquarters there is a factory supply outlet with clothes on sale at a 75 per cent reduction. Here, I meet Sue Newton, a marketing manager, who tells me how, almost thirty years ago, the company moved away from seafaring customers to a rather different type of buyer: the Sloane Ranger. 'It was in the early 1980s,' she says, showing me a booklet with a picture of an attractive young couple wearing flat-caps and Barbour jackets walking through the countryside with a Jack

Russell. This single advert had a remarkable effect: 'People wanted smart casual clothing to wear in the city as well as in the country, and this picture seemed to capture that.'

The look took off, with Princess Diana among others buying into the Sloane style created in the unlikely setting of an unemployment-ravished ex-mining town in the North-East of England.

'Are sales still going well?' I ask.

'Yes,' Sue replies. 'But now we're moving into another phase. Festival goers: people at Glastonbury like Peaches Geldof and the Arctic Monkeys. They've all been seen wearing them.' Barbour, she tells me, employs 180 locals. 'The majority are women, eighty-five to ninety per cent: you get two generations of the same family working together,' says Sue. 'We're one of the biggest employers in South Tyneside.'

After hearing this success story, of lots of jobs and a company that's doing well, I catch another taxi to the station. 'Why would anyone want to go to South Shields?' a colleague at *The Times* office had asked me when I told her I was coming here. Well, the World Heritage Site at Arbeia Roman Fort, the Venerable Bede and the origins of English history, the unusual life of Catherine Cookson, the quirky museum, some very good fish 'n' chips, comfortable hotels with pleasant landladies, extremely friendly people, and a beautiful coastline, all seem like pretty good reasons to me.

For my next foray into Unsung Britain I'm going 'down south' to a place that I'm just guessing might feel a little bit different to South Shields... and is very random indeed.

11

CROYDON: PLANES, TRAINS AND FRIENDLY FACES

Entering the Black Sheep pub on Croydon High Street on a Friday night feels a bit like passing through immigration into America. 'Excuse me, sir,' says an enormous man dressed in black. He's stepped across my path to block my entry and is gesturing towards a cigarette packet-sized unit with a wire attached to a computer screen.

'What do you want me to do?' I ask, perplexed.

'Standard procedure sir. Could you put your right index finger on that box?'

'Why do you want me to do this?' What's all this about... all I want is a beer on a Friday night.

'It's membership only here sir. We need you to register as a member,' he looks at me to make sure I'm not going to cause any trouble. 'Have you got any ID? Driver's licence or passport will do.' I give him my driver's licence and he goes to a booth where my details are added next to my fingerprint. I'm asked to stare at a camera. A digital picture is taken, and my membership file is complete. I may enter the Black Sheep pub to drink fizzy lager as a free man.

Another employee wearing black, with a motif of skulls on his shirt, comes over. He has a Salvador Dali-style moustache and introduces himself as Zak White. He's the assistant manager, aged twenty-five, originally from Lambeth. 'I see you've been introduced to our luvvly membership system,' he says smoothly. 'It's fairly unique in Croydon. I can't think of anywhere else with it. There are, I believe, sixteen clubs in Kent with the same system. The man who developed it, started there.' We're standing to one side away from the human brick of a doorman, next to a sign on a wall that says: 'HELP US KICK HATE INTO TOUCH.' The wallpaper has a black sheep pattern. Old school hip-hop music is thumping and breakdancers on a dance floor at the back are flipping about. There's a DJ wearing a black woolly hat. A guy next to him is in a hoodie and camouflage trousers. A barman wearing a red baseball cap tilted at an angle is observing me as I take notes. Another man with a bandana and an ink explosion of tattoos is ordering a drink.

'We call this "in-touch membership",' explains Zak, showing me the master computer. Two women who bear a passing resemblance to Kate Moss, the famous 'girl from Croydon', are just passing through. Their faces flick up on the screen as they press their fingers. 'If they were on our black list, a message saying "This member is banned" would have come up,' explains Zak. 'There are lots of implications for us,' he continues. 'Firstly, it encourages good behaviour as people won't be allowed in if they've misbehaved in the past. And we know exactly who everyone is. That's important. Most undesirables don't want to give details.'

'So it acts as a self-policing system, keeping the worst troublemakers away?' I say.

'Yes,' replies Zak. 'And of course, we're also able to contact someone if they leave a jacket or a wallet.'

'But isn't it all a bit Big Brother-ish?'

'Well, some people have complained. They've said it's an infringement of civil rights and some have tried to complain to lawyers that this kind of thing is covered by the Data Protection Act,' says Zak, twisting one side of his Salvador Dali moustache, as though making sure it is at the right angle. But nothing has come of these complaints, he says. As he does so, a group of lads enters and each of them presses his right index finger on the scanner. No 'banned' signs flash up and they are let through. 'The streets of Croydon can be quite harsh and despicable,' says Zak, all of a sudden. 'That's just the streets of Croydon. We're open till four in the morning and there's often no police presence on the streets after one. Our head doorman has just been to a meeting with the police to discuss this. The fact of the matter is: we have to look after ourselves.' The fingerprint scheme has 39,000 members and growing, and is believed to be responsible for an almost total eradication of violence at the Black Sheep, he tells me.

'So if that's the case, why don't more bars introduce it?'

'Simple,' he answers, tweaking his Dali moustache again and looking pleased with himself. 'A lot of the other venues are run by technophobes. And they're afraid of losing business.'

I buy a beer from the barman with the red cap. From a table by the wall I watch the breakdancing. Doug E. Fresh and Run DMC tracks are being played by the DJ with the woolly hat. It looks like a scene straight out of a film about hip-hop clubs in Brooklyn in the early 1980s, when breakdancing was in its infancy and gangsta rap had not really started. Zak introduces me to Keigan Westfield, a twenty-five-year-old English student at a local adult college who came to the UK seven years ago from Port of Spain in Trinidad. He's wearing a New York Yankees top and has just performed a handstand spin. His hobbies, he tells me, are dancing and photography.

'This place has a diversity and mixture of people,' he says, with a tinge of a Caribbean accent. 'It's fun. In other clubs you have fights 'cos everyone's too macho. "Why you lookin' at my girlfriend?" and all that. They should bring in fingerprints at all the clubs. Staff can go up to people here and say: "Please don't put your feet on the sofa." And they'll pay attention. It doesn't matter if you are black or white. This is one of the few places I can come to escape.'

Keigan remembers when he first came to Croydon: 'People would look at me 'cos I was black and had a strange accent. It was difficult. Even though it is a mixed culture, it is difficult for black people round here. And it's especially hard for a black man. If a black man is wearing a baseball cap and tracksuit bottoms, people think he's a rudeboy, a troublemaker.'

'How much of a problem have gangs become in Croydon?' I enquire – realising I've been asking a lot of questions in the Black Sheep without anyone seeming to mind. In fact, everyone is more than willing to talk. Welcome to Croydon on a (very) friendly, laid-back Friday night out. There's not a hint of trouble. I've been to pubs in quaint countryside villages with more of an edge (grumpy locals scowling at outsiders). None of that, or so it would seem, here.

Keigan is a case in point. 'Yes, there are gangs,' he replies, sounding thoughtful. 'I'm not denying that. But not everyone is in a gang.' He tells me that the best way to stop young black men turning into troublemakers is to introduce more youth clubs 'to give youngsters something to do'.

Keigan returns to his hand spins and I settle in a booth with my lager, thinking about my research into stabbings in Croydon at the public library round the corner this afternoon – and how it does not match what I see around me. The local website www.thisiscroydon.co.uk had a timeline on which 'CROYDON'S STABBING EPIDEMIC' is updated on an almost weekly basis. As I'd looked through the months I'd found that the longest period without a stabbing so far this year is twenty-seven days. In total there had been thirty stabbings in the year up to September, several involving fatalities. A fortnight before my visit the *Croydon Guardian* covered a 'SECOND TRAM STABBING IN TWO WEEKS' in which a seventeen-year-old schoolboy was 'stabbed in the face, legs and upper body at the Gravel Hill tram stop'. His injuries were not life-threatening. A teenage girl and an elderly man had survived a kitchen knife attack two weeks before this. At around the same time, Oliver Kingonzila, nineteen, a Croydon College student and a talented footballer on the books of Barnet Football Club, was stabbed to death outside the E Bar in South Croydon. His mother, Caroline Kingonzila, had told reporters: 'Whoever can take a knife and use it to hurt someone else is possessed by demons and needs help. I forgive that person, because my faith is strong, but only Jesus can help them.'

A group of friendly drinkers in their twenties sits at the table next to me and soon I'm chatting to Rachel, Tom and Harry. Just like everyone else round here, they seem open and charming. I get talking to them after one of the group asks if a stool on my table is free. They had seen me with Keigan earlier, and are curious about me. I don't – sadly – quite fit the younger age group here. I turned thirty-seven just before these journeys began (though I'm feeling a fair bit older now).

'What's it like living here?' I find myself asking.

They sound as though they are grateful to be able to let off some steam.

Tom says: 'It's horrible. I hate Croydon and I want to get out. I have been attacked in the street and got my nose broken. They threatened to stab me but they didn't get anything.'

Harry says: 'People are scared of Croydon – I am.'

Although Rachel says: 'I've never had any trouble myself.'

Tom tells me that he was threatened with a knife on another occasion: his eighteenth birthday. He was celebrating in a bar: 'I almost got stabbed. Apparently I had been laughing at somebody else's daughter who was doing karaoke.'

'It's lucky you weren't stabbed,' says Rachel.

Harry says: 'The problem with Croydon is just that there are some not very nice people about.'

Tom gives me some advice. 'Don't look at anyone. Be diplomatic. If someone asks you if you've got a problem, just say: "Not at all, I'm ever so sorry." There are gangs milling about: watch out for them.'

He's not the first person to offer safety tips for my visit. Already a senior member of the local council, who asked not to be named, told me: 'Don't go out on the High Street on Friday or Saturday night. Around the bars and clubs and things, I don't feel safe. Most of the people are under twenty-five. They all get drunk. I think that's everywhere. It's not unique to Croydon. Just watch out for hoodies. There can be quite a few around.'

But everyone is so pleasant at the Black Sheep, I'm thinking. The fingerprint scanner seems to work wonders to general sociability. For another perspective I cross the street and enter The Ship, a pub with an older clientele. On my way, I see a couple of people wearing hoodies near a bus stop. They look young, agile and furtive. Potential gang members, I suppose, who knows? Inside, I order a pint of Carling for £1.95 and somehow find myself talking to a man drinking with a pal at a bar stool. He's got clipped hair and a matching manner. 'Margaret Thatcher. Tony Blair. Gordon Brown. Have a guess what I do?' he asks.

'I've no idea,' I say.

'I'll tell you. Security. I protect them. I could tell you tonnes of ****. Don't get me wrong, I'm never going to tell you. Professional pride.'

He pauses and sips his pint. 'Paul Burrell,' he says. 'Diana's ex-butler.' He gesticulates in a rude way that leaves no doubt about his opinion of Paul Burrell. 'If you're in the SAS, you don't go out and bleat about it. I'm ex-military. I'd love to spill the beans, but I'm not going to go and write a book. Not allowed to. Official Secrets Act. I'm officially not talking to you.'

He's wearing a checked shirt and jeans – and is a bit flushed in the face. Regarding Croydon's recent violence, he says: 'Personally speaking, if you are sensible and wise, you will survive. It's the eleven o'clock bar fights you've got to watch out for. Sure, I've seen stabbings. Never heard a gunshot. You're not going to get involved in violence unless you're unlucky. Keep your head down.'

'I'm planning to visit New Addington tomorrow,' I tell him. It's said to be one of the bleakest estates in Britain (which may sound crazy on a weekend break... but I'm simply curious about it). Earlier in the year, I'd learned in the local library, Wayne Forrester, a thirty-four-year-old local HGV driver from New Addington, was arrested for murdering his wife using a kitchen knife and a meat cleaver after she posted a message saying that she was single on the social networking website Facebook, four days after they split up. He was jailed for life. This estate is, rather oddly, right next to Addington Palace, one of Croydon's few 'tourist attractions' and once a summer residence used by archbishops of Canterbury.

'I hope you put your stab vest on,' my neighbour says. 'I've lived here all my life and how can I say this without being racist? There used to be three black kids at my school. Now at my own kids' school it's fifty–fifty: white to black and Asian.'

'From what I've read, the ethnic mix across the borough is seventy per cent white, thirteen per cent black and eleven per cent Asian,' I say, realising that pedalling statistics like this might sound just a bit pedantic, if not downright anorak-ish, to him. I also realise that picking arguments with security men in pubs selling cheap lager in Croydon is not perhaps the best of ideas.

'Whatever. The demographics have changed. And so has the whole ethos. Croydon is a concrete jungle. You've got this cosmopolitan borough, but then five minutes' drive away, you're in the countryside and it's completely white.' After this 'non-racist' blast, he sips his pint once more: 'There's not a lot to be proud of in Croydon. When I retire, I'm moving elsewhere.' He looks out the window, where hoodies are still lurking by the bus stop. 'If someone wants a fight, I'm the last person you want to pick on,' he says, eyeing them. And I don't for a moment doubt it.

Like the journey into Coventry, the one into Croydon was not exactly spirit-lifting. From my local station, packed with commuters, I trundled towards Clapham Junction, seriously packed with commuters, pulling my black roll-along bag among the office masses, hardly believing that I was about to go on holiday in Croydon (London's largest and perhaps least-loved borough). From Clapham Junction, it took about ten minutes, in a carriage in which there were actually other tourists with bags – heading, rather sensibly I thought as East Croydon's dull business district appeared through a gloomy grey Friday in mid January, to Gatwick and distant shores. I'd been tempted to catch the train in from home each morning, but felt that would be cheating. I'm in for the long-haul: a weekend break in the depths of South London. Anne has already categorically said: 'I am NOT going to Croydon.'

That was the trip in, I reflect in my neat little hotel room – this is no adventure across the dangerous stretches of the Congo or expedition down little-known parts of the Amazon.

It is just Croydon, a couple of commuter trains away, via delightful Clapham Junction.

My hotel, however, is not so prosaic. In fact, it is wonderfully unusual. The Aerodrome Hotel is in a large, rectangular, white building on the A23, not so far from the former power station chimneys next to IKEA Croydon. The hotel was opened in 1928 on the site of Croydon Aerodrome, London's first proper international airport and the main airport in the capital until Heathrow was opened in 1946. I'd found out all this after running a Google search on Croydon hotels, wondering what on earth would crop up, expecting I'd end up in a downtrodden Travelodge, perhaps. I did not imagine I'd find myself in a quirky, historical building with an intriguing past and full of pictures of the early days of aviation in Britain.

From the outside, the hotel and the old airport terminal, housed in a similar-but-smaller building connected by a walkway and with a rusting propeller plane parked outside, look as if they might be art deco, though I am not quite sure how to describe the architectural style. Standing in front of the terminal, known as Airport House, I am put right on this matter, the Saturday morning after my Black Sheep night, by a short man with gold-framed glasses, a badge on his lapel saying Croydon Airport Visitor Centre, and an exhaustive knowledge of the airport that was here from 1920 to 1959.

Frank Anderson is chairman of the Croydon Airport Society. 'You think this is art deco?' he asks, beaming and tut-tutting. 'A very common mistake. Very. No, no – you are wrong. It is classical *retardataire*.' He beams at me, pointing up at arched windows and stucco work: 'Classical *retardataire* – a look of stripped classicism.' Frank, I learn (as one has to quickly in his amusing company), is a retired teacher. And he knows how to handle interjections by ignorant pupils. On this occasion: me.

We enter the building, where tables are laid out in the main hall beneath a grey Tiger Moth plane suspended from the ceiling of an atrium with an octagonal skylight. Near the front door a model of an Imperial Airways Hercules also hangs. 'Back then, they chose names from history or classical mythology for planes,' says Frank. 'We never worked out why the owners decided to use names that were unprounceable to ground staff. Maybe it was to baffle them and to show their cultural capital – to show they had a good education.'

On the far wall, clocks display the times in cities around the world, while on side panels black-and-white pictures capture the airport's heyday. 'Back in 1908 you'd have been standing in the middle of a field here,' says Frank. Now we are in the middle of business parks and storage depots, opposite a complex with a McDonald's and a cinema on the other side of the A23. We are also, Frank explains, near a gap in the North Downs, which is one of the reasons why Croydon grew up in the location it did: good transport links to the south coast. For a while in 1918, Hounslow Heath was used as the main airport for London, but it was soon discovered to be 'in the London fog belt – fogs and smoke from coal fires created smog', he explains. This was when Croydon's airport came to the fore.

At the time, there was a 'shed' that acted as the original control tower and a customs section, says Frank. He leads me to a picture on a wall showing two well-dressed women sitting on a wooden bench next to neat leather travel bags. Behind them there is a news-stand with a rack of postcards and a headline board for the *Daily Herald* that says something about 'British troops...' People wearing hats are peering at a 'LATEST WEATHER' board.

'From the picture I can see that the room's overall shape has not changed,' I comment. 'Yes, it's amazing how little has altered,' says Frank, before going on to explain that this was once a very glamorous place. 'Charlie Chaplin, Douglas Fairbanks Senior, and even George VI came here. Croydon was one of the most exciting spots in London: the main port of departure for Britain for the adventurous wealthy,' he says.

'They were not trying to promote mass travel in those days,' says Frank. 'It was only for the rich.' And it was also for the Empire, he adds. 'A lot of diplomats came here – and of course there was mail. At the time India was four weeks away by steamboat, Australia was six weeks away and New Zealand was seven. Flying, you could get to India in seven or eight days. Knowledge is power, you see. To some extent the flights were adding to imperial cohesion.' We look at a picture of an Imperial Airways booking desk: 'In the early days they actually weighed you,' Frank says. 'If you were too large for the seat on the flight about to go, they'd say: "Sorry you can't fly, but you can go on the next one."'

Outside, we reach the spot for which the old airport is perhaps best known. But before telling me why, Frank looks out across a car park towards ramshackle warehouses that seem to stretch on, depressingly, forever. 'If we'd come here before 1959 all we would have seen would have been an expanse of green here,' he says quietly. 'It makes a man cry to see what's happened.' He pauses before taking me to a disabled parking space and saying: 'Right here is where she started from.' He's referring to Amy Johnson, who became the first woman to fly to Australia in 1930. She travelled solo in a Gypsy Moth plane bought by her father, taking nineteen days to travel 11,000 miles to reach Darwin, Frank tells me. Previously, her longest flight had been 146 miles to Hull, where she was brought up in a street very close to Larkin's flat in Pearson Park. 'She was a very unusual lady,' says Frank. 'In 1930 a normal career path for a woman was school, work, marriage, motherhood – not flying round the world.'

Her Australian trip was not without mishaps: 'She crash-landed near Rangoon. She was looking for Rangoon racecourse but landed in error on a field next to a technical college. Her plane ran into a ditch and had a slightly bent propeller, but luckily she had a spare one.' Students from the college gathered round, wide-eyed, Frank explains. 'They gave her their shirts so she could repair the canvas.' When she returned to the UK 'thousands of people were waiting to greet her in Croydon... right here'.

In the control tower at Airport House there's a small museum that opens on the first Sunday of each month (Frank is showing me round as a favour this Saturday). We go up to take a look. I really had not expected to find a quirky little museum like this connected to my hotel in Croydon, I'm thinking, as we take in a display by the door that contains a battered old leather holdall.

'What is that?' I ask.

'Oh, that belonged to Amy. She had it with her on her last flight in 1941,' Frank replies. 'It's a sad story. She had broken a rule and flown above the clouds on the day she died. But there had been a duff forecast and the weather hadn't improved in the way it had been expected to. The result was that she got hopelessly lost, ran out of fuel and had to parachute out. Unfortunately she was over the Thames Estuary, and she ended up drowning.'

We explore the many wonderfully higgledy-piggledy cabinets, which are full of old timetables, goggles, model planes, and menus from years ago – this is an aviation buff's dream. The Imperial Airways dinner on one flight in August 1935 consisted of a grapefruit starter, followed by mock turtle soup; a choice of cold roast chicken, lamb cutlets, or veal and ham pie for main courses, with an odd 'orange and onion side salad'; and a pudding of stewed raspberries and apples with cream, with cheese, biscuits and coffee after that.

'Sounds pretty good for a short hop over to Paris,' I say.

'They knew how to do things then,' Frank replies.

On the balcony of the control tower, we gaze across Croydon. 'Horrid, isn't it?' says Frank, staring towards IKEA, beyond the warehouses that were once the site of the runway. And I find myself having to agree. Croydon, I can already say with some certainty, is definitely not the most picturesque of my stop-offs in Unsung Britain. But the history of Croydon's airport, Frank and his terrific museum have been completely diverting. You *can*, after all, be a tourist in Croydon – the excellent Croydon Airport Visitor Centre is well worth a visit on a day trip.

Next I catch a bus to East Croydon railway station, where I take a tram on the green line to New Addington. This passes the Gravel Hill stop where the seventeen-year-old schoolboy was recently stabbed. On board there are several 'hoodies', and I get the sensation that people are generally trying to avoid making eye contact with anyone else. There is very little conversation. Elderly folk clutch shopping bags. A guy sitting near me is dressed as if he's just appeared in a gangsta rap video; slumped in his seat as though his posture is making a statement. His bright sports gear, including pristine trainers, must have cost a small fortune. We slide on wordlessly past a dull housing estate under a grey suburban sky.

Then we reach the end of the line: New Addington. The first non-passengers I see in this housing estate dating from the 1930s are a pair in police uniforms standing with folded arms, wearing fluorescent jackets, and watching us leave the tram. Kat Griffiths and her partner are community support officers. I go up and ask if there is a community centre where I might ask people what it is like to live in a Croydon neighbourhood that even people in other parts of Croydon are rude about. I am not trying to poke fun at the place: rather like my trip to Chalvey back in Slough, I am simply intrigued about it. I realise this is not the 'normal' way to be a tourist – and I do not want to be a voyeur of the troubles of others. I am just somehow drawn to New Addington. I want to see it with my own eyes – to see all of Croydon. By this stage of my journey, on my penultimate trip, I realise that there is often very little that is 'normal' about being a tourist in Unsung Britain.

The officers point to a building about a hundred yards away and then Kat tells me about problems with local gangs. 'Anti-social behaviour. Kids with nothing to do. That's a big issue,' she says matter-of-factly. 'A lot of kids won't get involved in organisations like the cadet forces as it marks them out. They don't want to look like saddos. Others might mock them. They don't want to be different.

'The gangs and hoodies are especially difficult for the elderly,' she continues. 'Yesterday there was a big group of lads round here. They were behaving OK. But they looked as though they could cause trouble. An elderly woman who had been playing bingo at the community centre came up to us. She needed some money but was too scared to cross the street and use the cashpoint over there.' She points to a dull row of shops. 'She asked us whether we would accompany her there and back to the centre – which we did.'

Kat's partner tells me about another fatal stabbing that recently took place in Gravel Hill. Billy Ward, a twenty-one-year-old roofer, was stabbed ten times on a night bus heading for New Addington on a Saturday night last winter. I'd read a report about this at the library. The two suspects, Starfield Badza and Junior Lumbango, both aged nineteen, were found guilty at the Old Bailey. The British National Party, which attracts strong local support, had used Ward's death to say that 'racism works both ways' as Ward was white and his attackers black. 'Billy's mum has started an anti-stabbing campaign,' the officer says. 'So at least some good has come out of it.'

Over at the nondescript Addington Community Centre, which is a short windswept walk from the station across a nondescript plot of land with the dreary shops on one side and a couple of walls covered in graffiti, the Bethel Prayer Centre International Ministries is meeting. Through doors into the main hall I can hear a preacher saying: 'You need to cry out to the Lord!' To which a congregation replies: 'Amen!' There's a noticeboard advertising a judo club, bingo meetings and tea dances. Sweet singing voices emanate from a side-room: 'Alleluia… we worship you.'

'We are just Christians,' says Marcia Sharpe, a member of the prayer group, who I meet in the hall. She is dressed in a white shirt with black embroidery, silver earrings and red painted nails. 'It's a challenge to motivate people to do something positive round here,' she says. 'We try to say: "Yes, you *can* do it" to the youngsters. But most of the time people are not interested in giving our kids a chance.' Too many kids, she says, join gangs. 'We've got to get beyond seeing [these youths] as "trouble".' But then she pauses and adds in a voice that suggests that it's all a bit hopeless really: 'Even older people are scared of gangs. It's difficult to approach them in case they have knives or guns.'

I listen to the gospel music, suddenly realising that I've never heard live gospel before. If I closed my eyes, I could be somewhere in America's Deep South. Croydon may have its difficulties, but it definitely feels as though it's got community spirit and soul, in a way that Milton Keynes, with its pretty villages, cheap houses and shopping malls, for example, just did not. Then we're joined by Beverley Beckford-Barry, the pastor, who has a simple gold chain over a black polo neck. We start to talk about the chances that youngsters from this area have of making a good life for themselves – it is such a burning issue that it is hard to avoid the topic in New Addington.

Beverley is angry at the lack of help offered to youngsters from the estate. 'They are forgotten,' she says simply. 'There are not enough facilities and the things we do have, like the swimming pool, are too expensive.'

'Is anything being done to change this?' I ask.

'That would require politicians actually doing something,' she replies. She believes politicians do not have their priorities right: 'They put a lot of money into fighting unnecessary wars. Yet for people, like myself, on a low income they put up the council tax.'

The result of kids having little to do is boredom, she says.

'Is it safe to walk around here at night?'

Just from strolling over from the station, and seeing a few teenagers hanging about, it feels edgy on the streets. 'Vandalism is chronic and people are scared,' she replies. 'Kids join gangs. At eight o'clock there will be gangs with people aged six and seven on the streets.'

Her group provides youngsters with help completing job applications, as well as maths and English. 'They call New Addington the armpit of Croydon,' she tells me. 'If you say you live here, people pull faces 'cos it's part of Croydon that nobody wants to live in.' She pauses, and then changes tack: 'But I love it. It's like a village... everyone knows each other and looks out for each other.'

After listening to more of the beautiful music and saying goodbye to the pastor in Croydon's little-known 'village', I catch a tram back towards the centre. But I get off a couple of stops down the line at Gravel Hill. This is right next to Addington Palace, an old summer house of the archbishops. I walk through grand gates and am confronted by a boisterous party of people in suits and dresses with glasses of white wine, attending a function at the fancy clubhouse of the palace's golf course. A wedding reception is on and laughter rings out across the twisting driveway. I walk up and come to a fine stone, grade two listed building dating from the 1770s. This was the summer residence of six archbishops of Canterbury during the nineteenth century. Now it holds corporate functions and provides an attractive backdrop to the golf course. Shiny Bentleys and Mercedes are parked outside... and yet we are not far from one of the most deprived areas with one of the grimmest estates in London. It all feels very odd indeed. I go up to the building and enter a reception filled with richly coloured oil paintings and ornate furniture.

'Can I have a look around?' I ask.

'Sorry, I would but there's a birthday party on,' replies a tight-lipped woman, pointing to a sign that says: 'Happy 70th birthday Cynthia.' The building is not officially open to the public, but you can sometimes ask for a peak around and there are a handful of open days each year.

'Can't I just have a quick look?' The party has yet to arrive.

'Sorry, no.'

'Please?'

'No.'

And that is the closest I get to seeing one of Croydon's greatest attractions. Is this one tourist spot too far, even on this adventure, I'm beginning to wonder?

What am I doing here? I'm still thinking as the tram pulls into East Croydon station and I head for my next appointment, in the late afternoon. Is the whole idea of tourism in Croydon totally mad? If stab vests are the order of the day, and it's not considered safe to walk around the high street at night in case you happen to look at someone in the wrong way, surely you'd be better off taking a break just about anywhere else? But then again, I have by now come to terms with the hit-and-miss nature of my adventures – there are ups as well as quite a few downs. The Aerodrome Hotel is a wonderfully unusual, and comfortable, place to stay, with a sense of history that still hangs in its corridors – the ghosts of its former glory days with the likes of Amy Johnson and Charlie Chaplin; the sense that it is a forgotten place. But the trouble with gangs and the anonymous warehouse sprawl of so much of Croydon is, let's face it, not going to have too many people rushing back.

This is the reality for Liz Hollowood, who has worked for seventeen years at the tourist information office on the ground floor of the Croydon Clocktower, a Victorian building close to the high street. I find her behind a counter selling postcards of trams and civic buildings. When I arrive, Liz is patiently listening to a man who is enquiring about how to catch public transport *out* of Croydon to reach Southampton. 'Ah Tom! Good to see you!' she exclaims, leading me towards a cafe at the far side of the building.

We buy coffees and sit at a table next to a woman eating tomato soup. A poster on the wall asks: 'Do you have dreams you don't understand? Are you uncertain about your life? Then come to The Event: Indian head massage, life readings, eyebrow readings and dream interpretations.' Liz, who is bright and helpful, peering at me through spectacles and, wearing a pink top, cuts to the chase: 'If I'm being honest, one of the most difficult questions I get is: "I've got three hours to kill in Croydon, what can I do here?"'

This makes me chuckle. And Liz chuckles too: she knows she's got a job on her hands.

There is now, Liz continues, a local museum – upstairs in this building – and she mentions a few churches. The council has created a pamphlet called *A Walk Round Central Croydon* that highlights these main sights and takes about an hour to complete. One of the attractions Liz mentions is Surrey Street Market.

'What's sold there?' I ask.

'It's mainly fruit and veg,' she says.

She pauses for a moment. 'And they've also got things like fifty pence for three packets of Rizla,' she adds, as though the citizens of Croydon exist on salads and roll-ups.

'Do you get many tourists?'

She pauses again and smiles: 'We've had the odd one come by.' But from the tone of her voice, I don't think that means very many.

There are plans, however, to open a new visitor centre near the train station; part of a multi-million pound scheme to revamp the business district. The majority of the enquiries she receives, she admits, are from people like the man trying to get to Southampton: 'Local people who want to go off to London usually. What are the best hotels for families? Is there a good exhibition for my kids?' As cheery as she may be, it sounds as though the chances of a tourism boom in Croydon are pretty slim.

I thank her for her time, and then go upstairs to the museum. Here I discover that the composer Samuel Coleridge-Taylor lived in the borough, as did Hablot Knight Browne, also known as 'Phiz', the illustrator of ten novels written by Charles Dickens. The famous IKEA opened in 1992, a display says. Another section entitled 'Croydonisation' shows a dramatic model of what the business district will look like by 2020, with a wild array of futuristic new buildings in dramatic shapes. The renowned urban architect Will Alsop has been enlisted, and there are hopes to create a vibrant new centre; already Croydon has the third biggest business district in London after the Square Mile and Canary Wharf. It's this type of plan that inspired the French President Nicolas Sarkozy to suggest recently that the suburbs of Paris could learn a thing or two from this part of South London. 'CROYDON-SUR-SEINE' ran the headlines at the time.

Perhaps. But a display with small plastic balls that visitors are invited to use to cast votes, seems more telling to me. 'Will Croydon become the new Barcelona?' it asks. There is not a single vote for 'yes'... and a whole container full of 'no's.

Whitgift Shopping Centre is a short walk away. This is named after John Whitgift, a sixteenth-century archbishop of Canterbury, who spent much time in Croydon Palace, another summer retreat for archbishops, which is just round the corner and now a private girls' school. In centuries gone by, there were a series of such palaces leading all the way to Canterbury, spread about ten to fifteen miles apart and acting as staging posts for the archbishops, I read earlier at the library. But the palace in Croydon, being the closest to central London, was the most used, and Whitgift became fond of the area, helping to fund hospitals, almshouses and schools.

Near the shopping centre's entrance there are stalls selling sweets, cured meats and cheeses. Inside, all the usual brands, and sales posters, are there. But then I come across Funky House Ltd.com. This is a one-off fashion shop selling baseball caps, hooded jumpers, baggy jeans and T-shirts with cartoon figures of 'street' people. It's the same type of clothing worn by the man I'd noticed earlier on the tram. Reggae music plays. A youth with dreadlocks mans the counter. As I look around, a large sales assistant wearing a black T-shirt and a silver baseball cap comes to ask if he can help. It turns out that Bigzie is the owner of Funky House and is also the airbrush artist responsible for most of the clothing designs. Bigzie, he says, is his 'airbrush name' and he would prefer if I use this. He is twenty-four and began his business, operating on a smaller scale at a shop on Church Street, three years ago. Last Christmas he had such good sales that he decided to relocate to bigger premises in the Whitgift Centre. 'It's been a big move,' he says, grinning. 'All the paperwork, the solicitors… Getting in here was so difficult and time-consuming.'

Bigzie exudes entrepreneurial spirit. 'We are not a hip-hop store, this is an urban store,' he says quickly. 'The concept of the shop is to promote airbrush artists. Most of it has been done by me but we're getting more people coming through. We've got embroidery coming soon, and we customise T-shirts.' One of his latest customised T-shirts, he says, was made in protest against an extension of a tramline with the slogan: 'Give us back our green.' Another was in memory of Oliver Kingonzila, the teenager who was on the books of Barnet Football Club when he was stabbed dead. 'It happened in front of a club. There's a campaign to stop the stabbings,' Bigzie says.

About the stabbing epidemic, and there does not seem to be much getting away from the subject during my visit, he adds: 'Authorities don't seem to be bothered. The police don't want to be dealing with the problem. The system we have now does not operate properly.'

'Do you think there is a big difference between growing up white or black in Croydon?'

'Of course,' he says. 'To be a young black man in Croydon is tough. The media portrays young black males in a very bad light,' he says. Bigzie believes that prejudging young black people is very common. 'If I wasn't in the Whitgift Centre, where people feel safe, for example, it would be very different. A lot of white customers might feel threatened. But it's getting better,' he says.

To give youngsters a first taste of life in the workplace, Funky House runs a rolling work experience programme. 'We're doing something different,' he says. 'What with the stabbings and the youth of today, if we can give work experience to people who might fall into bad ways a chance – a realistic experience of work – then we will have achieved something.' Wayne, twenty-one, is one of the T-shirt printers, wearing one of his own creations, which shows an evil-looking Bugs Bunny. He says: 'It's been very enjoyable working here. I was in IT at college and I'm glad I've been able to use some of the skills I learned there.' Being black himself means that his black employees feel that they might go on to run their own businesses, says Bigzie. But he's worried about the economy. 'I just pray this shop works,' he says looking about. Funky House is empty of customers. 'I really pray it works.'

Around the corner, a shop that is not working, but really deserves to, is Beano's. This is the largest second-hand record shop in the world. It was started thirty-two years ago and has attracted the likes of David Bowie and Diana Ross as well as hundreds of DJs, who stock up here on rare tracks and vinyl records. The shop used to run over three floors, but now only the ground floor is open, as Internet downloads and record-buying on websites such as eBay have all but killed the business, I'd read in the local newspaper.

Beano's is wonderful. Through a purple arched doorway next to a sign saying 'Come in: CDs from 10p!' Jimi Hendrix is singing 'Come On (Let the Good Times Roll)', with guitar solos reverberating around the warren of shelves stacked with records and CDs. Walls are covered with old album sleeves. There are Beatles albums, Aretha Franklin, Buddy Holly (£600 for an 'almost extinct' record), Simon and Garfunkel, Elvis Presley, The Supremes: just about every artist under the sun must be here. A dozen or so customers look as though they are in record heaven. I join them, passing a neon Wurlitzer jukebox and going down steps onto the shop floor that holds most of the records.

At the counter I ask if the Hendrix track that was playing is for sale. It is. And I've soon got a CD copy of *Electric Ladyland*: £5. The assistant says she's 'really worried' the shop will close. She calls over her boss, David Lashmar, who takes me upstairs to a former cafe on the now-closed third floor. The walls are decorated with hundreds of old seven-inch singles. There's a model of a hippy-chick 1960s woman suspended from the ceiling. A neon picture of Elvis is next to a parking metre, beside the grill of a Cadillac emerging from the wall by a staircase.

'At our peak we had twenty-four employees, now it's four,' says David, who is sixty-four and looks like an aging rocker. 'The market has gone. We can't compete with the Internet. We used to have bands playing here on Saturdays. People would come from all over England. There was a real buzz.' He now has plans, he says, to open a market similar to Camden Market over the three floors of the building, but he is waiting for the right economic moment. He says that the giant shopping centres in the borough disappoint him: 'I'm not anti-Croydon, I'm anti how suburban towns are developing. I find that I have to do everything "in spite of Croydon", and I mean that in both linguistic senses.' When his market opens he intends it to be 'the antithesis of elsewhere... of everything looking the same' – which reminds me of J. G. Ballard's take on life and my weekend in Milton Keynes.

The most expensive record he has is 'God Save the Queen' by the Sex Pistols (£8,500) and the highest-value sale he's ever made is £20,000 for an entire collection of Beatles originals. 'That was to an American,' he says. 'He was just doing it as an investment and I didn't really like that.'

Why? 'Well, I want people to enjoy the music: to be music fans,' he says. 'Music shouldn't be about money. It should be about music.'

From Beano's (which sadly closes not so long after my visit), I walk round the block to two of Croydon's main tourist sights: St John's Church, which is next to the slightly ramshackle, higgledy-piggledy buildings of old Croydon Palace (the school is locked as it's Sunday), even though one of the record shop assistants had warned: 'Don't step on any needles if you're going round there.' Past a Jamaican food shop and a Poundstretcher, I turn into a street that leads to the church. Three skinny men holding cans of Strongbow cider are on a corner. They are so skinny, like matchsticks, that it's difficult to imagine them coping in too strong a wind. Their expressions are hollow and empty, and their clothes are filthy. I don't think they're tourists.

At the church, which overlooks the noisy A236, there's a wedding. Inside, I can see that it's a mixed marriage, one half of the church is mainly black, the other mainly white. Six archbishops of Canterbury are buried here including Whitgift, and royal visitors, during better Croydon times, have included Henry VIII and Queen Elizabeth I, says a sign. It is a lovely old church in the middle of a touching ceremony. I go outside and walk through the churchyard, where a gang of youths is drinking Jack Daniels and smoking roll-ups on a bench.

Croydon, I very well know by now, has both hidden histories… and unhidden problems.

My last 'tourist attraction' – well it is clearly marked on my map from the tourist information centre, so I suppose you could say it's one – is Lunar House. And it is probably Croydon's biggest single draw, but perhaps not for typical tourist reasons. This building brings in tens of thousands of visitors from across the globe to the borough as it is home to the UK's main immigration office.

Slough Trading Estate looked prettier than this. The tower block looms bleakly at the north-east corner of the shopping district, reached via a subway under a busy street. A wind sweeps across the forecourt. Fumes from double-decker buses waft by. Pigeons poke at old sweet wrappers. The concrete tower block shoots upwards into the grey Sunday sky. For a first taste of Britain, Lunar House is not a sweet one.

Watching the news on the TV at the Aerodrome Hotel last night, I had listened to Phil Woolas, the immigration minister, announcing strict new limits on immigration. He said that he did not want the population of the UK to rise to above seventy million during the next twenty-five years (the population currently stands at just over sixty million). Many of the papers today are running articles saying the UK should not become a soft target for immigrants and that it is about time the government acted. In a windy corridor with a long, snaking queue of people at the base of Lunar House, I ask a few people whether they are worried about this crackdown.

The first person I speak to is from Sierra Leone. He is twenty-one and won't give his name. He looks frightened by the prospect of the interview he is about to have in the immigration office. 'It's not easy getting into the UK,' he says peering forwards. 'All I want to do is join my father here. But it is so hard.'

Next to him, I talk to Sarah, who is in her thirties, from Lahore in Pakistan. She says she is concerned about the day's news: 'It is the first time I have tried for a visa extension: I am very worried.' A couple from Malaysia, who work at a major city bank and initially give their full names but then feel nervous and ask me not to mention them, are also agitated: '"Easy" is not the word I would use to describe this place – our visa application is taking months.' A woman from Dakar in Senegal sounds desperate: 'I have children, but I can't get benefits because I don't have status. So it's a struggle. Social services do help a bit. I definitely do not want to go back to Senegal.'

From Lunar House I walk to the station, passing a newsagent with a bleak headline board: 'SHOPPER STABBED IN FACE.' I have never been anywhere with so much talk of stabbings and casual street violence, even though I haven't witnessed so much as someone raising their voice this weekend. A Metropolitan Police advert near the newsagents says that there are now a hundred more uniformed officers on the streets in the centre of Croydon: yet another sign of concerns about public safety.

As I buy my ticket back to the centre of London, I'm certain that of all the places I've visited, I'm least likely to return to Croydon, even if it has had its moments. As much as I did not like parts of Coventry near the ring road, it was in a different tourist league to Croydon.

I call Anne. She is amused when she hears of my exploits in housing estates, trams shared with hoodies, and pubs with fingerprint scanners. 'I'm so sorry I couldn't make it,' she comments, with the muffling sound (of laughter) starting up again.

'You were advised by someone from the council not to walk about the city centre at night?' she says, after I tell her about that. More muffles.

'Yes, but actually, there were bits I liked.'

'Which bits exactly?'

I explain about the friendly atmosphere and the sense of community spirit, despite all the headlines about violence. I tell her about the Aerodrome Hotel, the history of the early days of flight, the gospel music, the peaceful vibe at the Black Sheep, the archbishops' summer homes (even though they are difficult to enter), the pretty church that Henry VIII visited.

'Oh lovely,' she says, not quite sounding convinced.

We end the call as my train arrives at the platform. My final stop in Unsung Britain does not require fingerprints to get in.

12

HELL: NOT SUCH A
BAD PLACE...

Coming to the Scilly Isles is, I admit, a bit of a stunt. I started in Hull and I'm ending in Hell: Hell Bay on the tiny, little-known island of Bryher. I've travelled from Hull to Hell, with all else (including Coventry and Croydon) that fell in between. But it is a happy stunt because I've always wanted to visit the Scilly Isles and the trip here also means I will have covered most of Britain, from South Shields in the North-East near the Scottish border, to Derry in the west of Northern Ireland, to Norwich in the east of England, and now here in the far South-West.

So it is with a sense of adventure that the train from Paddington to Penzance leaves, bang on time – to be fair to Britain's privatised and weirdly fragmented train system, it hasn't let me down once so far. It is an early evening departure arriving at Penzance late. And as I'm settling into my standard-class seat, a one-sided conversation begins and just does not stop; turning into one of the longest, almost continuous, oddest, at times amusing (and totally hopeless) chat-up attempts I've ever overheard.

As we leave West London, a bald man in his early thirties with trendy glasses starts chatting to a polite woman in a purple dress, who happens to be sitting opposite. They are a few seats away from me as the man, who anyone within earshot quickly learns works in food preservatives, begins his spiel. 'Dunkin' Donuts is one of our customers,' he says, as though this will get her interested. 'Very good they are, Dunkin' Donuts. So are KP Crisps – but they've been harder to please.'

'Oh really,' she replies, desperately trying to fix her eyes on a magazine.

'Omelette makers in Japan: now we'd really like to sign up them,' he smiles at her, looking very content with his progress. 'If only we could get them on board.'

The young woman's eyes begin to look as though they are swivelling independently. There's nowhere else to sit. She's trapped.

And on he goes via 'mineral water treatment' (as we pass friendly Slough, which doesn't seem to want to go away), tomato soup (in Reading) and types of custard (in Taunton). 'But is custard a solid or a liquid?' he asks in a poignant tone, to which she shrugs looking non-committal and slightly suicidal. It's quite a performance, full marks for effort… but it doesn't get him anywhere. She disembarks at Plymouth; phone numbers are not exchanged.

It's dark outside and we slip away further south-west – there always seems to be a nice, escapist feeling coming down to this part of the country. We reach the fabulous Royal Albert Bridge over the river Tamar on the boundary between Devon and Cornwall. The bridge was designed by Isambard Kingdom Brunel and opened in 1859, the year of Brunel's death. The train slows down. Even though it is dark on this Friday evening in early February, the structure looks superb, with the vast grey wrought-iron support tubes snaking on either side of the carriage. It feels as though we're travelling through a giant, elaborate cage. Everyone peers out in admiration. It's just as impressive in its own way as the Humber Bridge way back in Hull: four (very packed) months ago, now.

It is past 11.30 p.m. by the time we reach Penzance, where I'm booked into a cute, cheap and slightly chintzy hotel near the ferry port. And after a sound but short sleep, I walk down a steep hill early the next morning on a bright, cold day passing The Dolphin pub and The Buccaneer gift shop to the ferry, the *Scillonian III*. It's a sleek-looking vessel (far sleeker than the rusty old *Lagan Viking* from Birkenhead to Belfast) with a yellow funnel with a black-and-white Cornish flag painted on it.

With three blasts of the horn, we are away. There aren't many other passengers and I stand on the top deck, looking out towards the distant pyramid of St Michael's Mount – the former priory that from the twelfth to the fifteenth century had its own laws and was run by the abbey of Mont Saint-Michel across the Channel in France. To the right I catch a glimpse of Penzance's impressively big art deco lido, and then we are moving swiftly along the coast, passing Land's End, where gannets drop like stones into the liquorice swirling waters, and entering the Atlantic Ocean proper.

I eat a ham and tomato sandwich in a cafe that smells of bacon, after being served by a friendly assistant who tells me: 'There's a twenty-knot westerly with twelve-foot waves. That's gale force five or six. We won't depart if it's gale force ten.' There are adverts for Scilly flower farms on board. Helicopters buzz past every now and then – flying to the Scillies takes twenty minutes, while the ferry is two and a half hours. And I read a booklet from the small giftshop about the legend of the lost land of Lyonesse that is said to have existed in ancient times between Cornwall and the Scillies. Somewhere beneath these waters there may be the remains of a city named Lions with a castle looking out across a land punctuated with the steeples of 140 churches, it says. Some Scillonians apparently claim to hear bells from these churches ringing during storms.

Another pamphlet says that the islands could be the final resting place of King Arthur, and that there was a Bronze Age settlement in the Scillies 4,000 years ago. Then, the sea level was lower and it was possible to walk between what are now the main five inhabited islands. There are fifty islands altogether, and the name 'Scilly Isles' comes from 'Sulli', which means the 'Sun Isles' and dates from the Middle Ages.

Land appears in the form of sweeping beaches, a cliff bathed in golden light and a hillside covered in confetti-like seagulls. As we approach the cute little harbour of St Mary's, I'm surprised to read that until just over twenty years ago, these beautiful islands (I can already tell they are beautiful) were officially at war with the Netherlands. During a period of particular lawlessness in the seventeenth century, piracy against Dutch merchant ships had become such a problem that Holland declared war on the Scillies. This period of 'conflict', which never amounted to much, ended when the Dutch ambassador visited to say that bygones were finally bygones, I learn. If only all wars could be conducted, and concluded, so peacefully.

From St Mary's harbour – where a postman is wearing shorts, and it's noticeably warmer than back in Penzance – I catch another ferry to Bryher. It's a short journey, about twenty minutes, and we stop at a pretty white-sand beach on the island of Samson on the way. The boat literally pulls up to the beach, with passengers getting off via a ramp onto the sands. And then we arrive at Bryher, which at least has a tiny jetty. And soon I'm being whisked away in a tiny van driven by a Hungarian named Tibor to my hotel, a service the hotel arranges. 'I like it here,' is all Tibor says after introducing me to a spaniel named Sophie who joins us for the ride.

And so I made it to Hell... and the Hell Bay Hotel.

But before I settle in (I only really have time to drop my bag in a very smart room), I'm off for a meeting on the neighbouring island of Tresco. I'm soon in the van with Tibor again, back at the jetty and taking a boat on the short journey – little more than a stone's throw – across the water. I'm about to be introduced to a modern-day Lord Proprietor.

I'm led by an employee of the Tresco Estate to a manor house down a lane, and taken to a library with shelves stacked with leather-bound books. There's a curious oriental frieze on the wall near my chair, and a very comfortable, lived-in feeling to the room. A black Labrador enters and comes up to me as if to say 'hello'. And then so does Robert Dorrien-Smith, who runs the estate which employs all the people who work on Tresco. 'This is the only proper private island in England,' says Robert, almost as soon as we meet, making sure I get this point early on. 'There is one employer: the estate. We provide mains electricity and education.'

Robert tells me he took control of the 735-acre island on the death of his father in 1973, when he was twenty-two. He explains that he comes from a family that has a lineage back to Augustus Smith, who acquired the lease on the Scilly Isles from the Duchy of Cornwall in 1834, taking the title 'Lord Proprietor'. The lease to the Dorrien-Smith family continues to this day on the island of Tresco. Though when I ask how long it has to run, I'm cut short.

'A long time,' Robert replies firmly. 'That's nobody's business.'

The building we're in, he goes on to explain, is named Tresco Abbey, and was designed by Augustus back in the 1840s. As we drink coffee I ask, 'How many rooms does it have?'

'A lot, about thirty,' he replies.

At first, Robert keeps his answers short and to the point. But when I explain my mission in Unsung Britain – 'I'm visiting the parts that most people don't reach... it's a bit like the Heineken advert, only it's a journey around Britain...' – Robert seems to like the idea.

'There has been a mass exodus to the Med, but the UK has the most fascinating history, there is so much of interest everywhere you go.'

'That's what I like to think,' I reply.

'It's true. I really hold hope that there's a tourism resurgence in Britain: people love things that are old-fashioned, and Britain is full of that.'

Robert is soon opening up, telling me the remarkable story of Augustus. 'He was an eccentric philanthropist, a benevolent autocrat; not a bossy megalomaniac,' Robert says, settling into his armchair. He is wearing a green jumper and blue trousers, looking a bit like Roger Moore from his later Bond period.

Augustus was from a wealthy banking family in Hertfordshire, he tells me. 'He was a young new thinker after the Napoleonic Wars,' Robert says. 'He came here to demonstrate that if you educate people they will become self-sufficient. The islands were effectively starving. It was a national scandal of the 1820s. There was murder, mayhem and piracy. It had got out of hand.' After a visit to assess the state of affairs, Augustus – who was himself educated at Harrow and Oxford – went to the Duchy of Cornwall who enlisted him to help sort out the problems. The original lease, which cost Augustus £20,000, was subsequently altered in 1922 so it covered the island of Tresco alone, Robert explains.

'There was unrest and he came here to do something about it,' he adds. 'In the politics of that time, he was a socialist, but he was probably more right-wing than we can imagine.' One of his schemes ended the practice of sub-dividing land between sons, instead giving all inherited land to eldest sons, Robert says. Anyone who complained about this policy was exiled. On top of this, he would not allow young people to marry unless they had property – upsetting lots of men who were not eldest sons. He also ordered the depopulation of the small island of Samson – upsetting the inhabitants there, too. This annoyance was compounded when Augustus made an extraordinary decision to repopulate Samson with black rabbits. Another island was filled with white rabbits. This was some sort of peculiar experiment, highlighting the Lord Proprietor's eccentric streak.

Augustus also built churches and schools (with lessons in navigation 'so people could become pilots not pirates'), Robert continues. There was compulsory education that hit the poor hard in the pocket: the system worked by charging parents one penny a week if their children went to school and two pennies if they did not. Grass, gorse and saplings were planted to add substance to the sandy terrain and block the wind whipping off the ocean: sand blown onto crops, fields and into houses had been a big problem during winter storms.

'What was he like as a person?' I ask.

'He was energetic. He had vision. He was a very busy man,' Robert answers, sipping his coffee from a delicate china cup. 'He also had hanging powers from the Crown. He could banish and punish. He was authoritarian, but in those days people were used to it. People had respect.'

'Did all these draconian measures turn around the island's fortunes?'

'Yes,' Robert replies. 'After a number of years it was obvious that the pain was going to be worth it.' Navigational tuition was particularly successful and locals soon acquired a reputation for being 'good pilots who raced out to ships on gigs and were paid good fees'.

One of Augustus's most remarkable achievements was the Tresco Abbey Gardens, which I am about to visit. As the Scilly Isles have a milder climate than mainland England, and as many ships passed by carrying exotic plants from far-away shores, Augustus was able to cultivate cuttings and create a unique garden with species that cannot survive in the open anywhere else in Britain. He never married – the woman he is said to have loved married his brother – and my guidebook suggests that his love of plants acted as a substitute for a romantic life. People from far and wide came to see the garden including Lord Alfred Tennyson and George Eliot, who said she was 'enchanted with the delightful island' on a break from her work on the *Westminster Review*.

'Did he have any children?'

'Augustus had no *legal* children,' says Robert, implying that there was quite a lot of romantic life after all. But it was his brother's son who inherited the islands when Augustus, by then dubbed 'Emperor Smith', died in 1872, he explains.

Tourism has of course been the big local earner in the Scilly Isles for years now – the Scillies are not strictly speaking unsung, although few people I've talked to about the trip had heard of Bryher or Tresco. On Tresco, there are timeshare cottages, self-catering apartments (costing as much as £4,000 a week), a hotel, and B & B rooms for £70 a night above an inn. 'Officially tourism is eighty-five per cent of all the islands' income,' says Robert, pouring more coffee. 'Honestly I think it's more than that. If tourism ended, we would be bereft and the islands would become uninhabitable.' There are 180 full-time employees on Tresco and 100 seasonal; the population of the Scilly Isles as a whole is 2,100, although this is believed to go down to about 1,700 during the winter.

'Do you enjoy living here?' I ask Robert.

'I do immensely, it is a varied life,' he replies. He also enjoys the offshore perspective. 'We can look at this financial crisis [the global economy was in meltdown during my visit], all these headless chickens running around, all the media people hopping about loving it. I don't get the hysteria. I have a detached point of view.'

'In what way detached? What do you mean by that?'

He pauses. 'In modern life everything is so instant. Nobody has time to consider things. People just press buttons. They spend their whole lives in front of computers. It's not like that here.'

The Hell Bay Hotel is run by Robert. I mention to him that I am staying there and have paid for a room with a sea view.

'Oh yes, Hell is beautiful,' Robert says, gazing at the rows of leather-bound volumes on the library shelves. 'It's probably the most beautiful situation of anywhere in the islands. Luxury in the wilderness.'

My time is up. We shake hands next to an oil painting of Augustus, who looks plump and is wearing Masonic regalia. I give the Labrador a pat and go in a tiny green van (there are no cars on Tresco or Bryher) to the Abbey Garden. The van moves along a twisting, tree-lined lane the width of the driveway of a suburban home. A pheasant crosses ahead. As we turn a corner, I look back at the Abbey. A Union flag is fluttering on the roof. 'That's when he's in residence, it's a bit like a king or a queen,' says the driver.

By the entrance to the garden, there is a courtyard full of vividly coloured figureheads collected by Augustus from the many wrecks around the islands. A woman with plaited hair, a necklace and a considerable bust peers across the yard. She's from an 'unidentified vessel', says a sign. A man with a sword held before him is from the *Palinurus*, which was wrecked in 1848 with the loss of all seventeen crew, according to another display. Next to this, a woman with a red flower attached to her dress is from the *Jane Owen*, a schooner that sank in 1889.

The figureheads are exquisite, and give a taste of what life must have once been like in the Scilly Isles: not just the danger from the treacherous sea, but also the adventure and glamour of its former days. In the nineteenth century, when the wind blew easterly, as many as 200 ships would anchor in the safe water between Tresco and Bryher, making this an incredibly lively spot. Then, there were a dozen inns on Tresco (now there is just one). These islands often acted as an exciting and busy first port of call to Britain for ships arriving from the New World.

As I'm taking in *Jane Owen*, Mike Nelhams, the head gardener, introduces himself. He is wearing a red ski jacket and has his arm in a sling. 'What happened?' I ask.

'I fell down some stairs,' he says, grimacing at the memory. Mike first came to Tresco as a Royal Horticultural Society student on a scholarship, he says. That was back in 1976 and he has been running the garden since 1984. He is extremely laid-back and tells me straight away: 'I'm not a gardening nerd, but there's not a day when I don't get excited about coming here.'

We turn through a gate and I soon understand why. It feels as though we've stepped into an incredibly well-kept jungle. There are mini palms, tropical bushes, plants bearing fruit, and beds overflowing with yellow and pink flowers. Beyond these are shrubs with flower-heads the size of hubcaps, corridors of vast hedges, and strange trees that I've never seen before. It is a kind of fantasy garden, with around five thousand species of plants. 'About ninety-five per cent of these would not grow outside anywhere else in the UK,' says Mike, leading me between the huge hedges: 'We need a whacking great ladder to get to the top of that. Health and Safety have a splendid time with us.'

Being in the middle of the Gulf Stream and further south, the winter temperature on the Scilly Isles is about two degrees warmer than on mainland Britain. 'The temperature doesn't fall much below eight or nine Celsius in the winter, and it rises to about twenty-two or twenty-three in the summer,' says Mike. 'The breeze off the sea cools everything in the summer. We've got stuff here from the Med as well as from South Africa, Australia, New Zealand, California, Mexico, Chile, Peru – lovely places around the world.'

The garden is surrounded by Monterey pines and cypress trees from California, which act as windbreaks. There are stone archways and half-built walls that were once part of a Benedictine monastery here for three centuries from 1120. We stop by a tall thin plant that looks like a test tube cleaner. 'That's actually a weed,' says Mike. 'We've got some amazing weeds here. They'll grow to twenty feet in height in a year. They're from the Canary Islands.'

We pass a bed of emerald succulents. 'Succulents are plants that retain water,' Mike says, beginning my own horticultural crash course. We stop by a bed of pink flowers. 'They look as though they belong on another planet,' I comment.

'They're protea from South Africa,' Mike explains. 'We've got the best protea garden in Britain.' Nearby there's a plant with red leaves that look like eyes: 'That originates in the Pitcairn Islands, it can get so vigorous we have to hack it back with a chainsaw.' There are cacti that might come from an

American West desert, next to an agave plant from Mexico: 'We've had that forty years and it hasn't flowered yet. It only flowers once in a lifetime, then it dies.'

We pause on a terrace next to a bench covered in ash-grey lichen: 'Lichen is a great sign of clean air; the air we're breathing here has come all the way from America, about two thousand miles away,' Mike says. The terrace is on a hill at the top of the garden, which tumbles greenly below. From here we can see two of the garden's prize specimens: a Norfolk Island pine, with eerily symmetrical branches that point upwards, and a New Zealand Christmas tree: 'When the flowers come out, they're like huge great red blobs, you can see them from the golf course on St Mary's.'

'Before Augustus, the island had no vegetation beyond bracken and heather,' says Mike, who requires a large team of gardeners to keep today's vegetation in check. Like the plants, many of his employees come from overseas. 'We've had Hungarians, Bulgarians, Poles, people from the Czech Republic,' he says. 'They are brilliant and hard-working and don't get pissed and into fights. Other people from Bury, Manchester and Plymouth come here too. They tend to blow their cash each week on booze and end up duffing each other up.'

We've completed a circuit of the grounds. 'This is one of the most fabulous gardens in the world,' says Mike, not boasting, merely marvelling at the historical quirk of Augustus having started off the collection in this micro-climate. 'It's in one of the most fabulous locations. I feel very lucky to be here.'

Back at the hotel after my meetings over on Tresco, the sun is beaming and waves are being whipped up by a wind, creating a salty ocean mist. Through this mist and the glare of the sun on the choppy metallic water I gaze out across a series of jagged islands that look like a mariner's worst nightmare. The islands seem to stretch out forever. Hell's Bay Hotel is named after a stretch of coast just to the north of the property where dozens of ships have come to their end against its rugged granite rocks. The sun is illuminating the peaty landscape and turning bracken on a hill near the shore bright orange. There are rows of elegant mini palm trees in the neat garden of the hotel. Two brown cows are munching grass near a pond. Croydon feels a very long way away. This is the most beautiful place I have visited in Unsung Britain, by a long shot.

My room is tastefully decorated in white and pale blue, with a balcony overlooking the ocean. It is without a doubt the best room I've had during my entire trip (it cost £150 a night, so I guess you might expect it to). I go to the hotel lounge. The walls are plastered with modern art – bright abstract splashes of colour, paintings of ships, and circular drawings by Barbara Hepworth. There are piles of *Country Living* and *Harper's Bazaar*. The latter's cover headline reads: 'VINTAGE STYLE: DECORATING WITH DAMASK', and there's certainly a lot of style here. Orange lilies are arranged in a vase near a fireplace decorated with shards of blue and yellow glass. Wicker chairs with cushions and little coffee tables surround the fireplace. I sit on a pale-blue corduroy sofa and a polite barman from the Czech Republic brings me a fresh coffee. I call Anne and tell her about the hotel.

'Oh,' she says – and the line goes quiet. If one thing about my trip has kept Anne particularly happy, it's been hearing news of me slumming it in Wit's End guesthouses, Best Westerns by

Port Talbot's beach and B & Bs with smallpox wallpaper in Coventry.

'We'll come back some time, I promise,' I say. Anne has been more than understanding over the past four months (which is a bit of an understatement). 'When all this is finished.'

'Can you write that down somewhere,' she replies. 'Maybe on a postcard?' She pauses. 'And post it!'

The deal is agreed.

Then I meet the manager, Philip Callan, in the trendy lounge. He is wearing a blue-and-white checked shirt and jeans. He has combed his hair with a neat side-parting that never seems to ruffle, even when outside in the breeze. The hotel opened in the 1980s and for many years it was 'almost like a posh little Butlins', says Philip. 'It was really quite weird. But ten years ago Dorrien-Smith bought the hotel and literally gutted it.' Now there are twenty-five rooms spread across a series of buildings, he says. There is a smart seafood restaurant, a pool and a spa. Wi-fi was recently introduced in Hell, Philip adds.

He goes on to tell me what almost everyone tells you on Bryher – population eighty. 'We don't have to lock our doors here,' he says. 'In fact there are no locks on the door to my house. Even when I go away for three weeks, it's OK. This is a very safe place: our children can run around freely.' He worked for many years at the hotel on Tresco, before getting a job at a five-star pad on London's Park Lane: 'But the grass was not greener in Hyde Park.'

'Do you enjoy life in Hell?'

'Absolutely, I love it here. Every other day I go out to check my lobster pots. It's like playing a game of squash or something: it's like a hobby. You can't do that in Park Lane.'

The hotel has two pigs that are being fed for slaughter, Philip tells me, and chickens will be introduced soon. Rainwater is collected and guests are urged not to waste water in the bathrooms. 'Bryher is a place where you learn about yourself,' he says. 'It is a good place to come and realise what life is all about,' he adds, looking out at the rugged coastline through a window.

After Philip leaves to deal with new guests, I watch the sunset from the hotel terrace. The sky is a blue-grey and the sun is orange, sliding with remarkable speed towards the liquorice sea. An elderly man wearing a jacket and tie joins me on the terrace.

'Amazing, isn't it?' I comment.

To which he replies: 'Yes, it's always amazing.' And the two of us stand there wordlessly, in awe of the lovely sky, as the sun drops beneath the ocean.

In the lounge before dinner, a group of birdwatchers is re-living their day. A man in a polo neck says: 'I spotted that one because I happen to know its call.' He squawks loudly several times imitating the bird.

Another group of birdwatchers arrives. The Scillies are prime twitcher territory. 'We've been to St Agnes [one of the other islands, just to the south] today,' says a middle-aged woman wearing pearls. 'A warbler. We definitely saw a warbler.' Someone else says: 'And a red-breasted flycatcher.' A man who appears to be a bit of an expert says: 'We've got a south-westerly; with a south-westerly we should get the birds in from America. They get blown over here. Shouldn't be here of course.' The woman with pearls cuts in and comments: 'An American bird took my son!' They laugh and sip their wine.

The dining room has wicker chairs and grey-slate tables. I eat smoked trout with creamed leeks and an excellent turbot in between chatting to the head waiter, a South African who married a local woman. What does he make of Hell Bay? 'Coming from South Africa I really appreciate the lack of crime,' he says. 'That makes a big difference. There are trade-offs: no cinema, for example.' He pauses: 'But Hell is a lovely, addictive place to live.'

It does seem that way, and on a walk around Bryher, about two miles long and one mile across, the chances are you'll bump into most of the island's population. The islanders seem eager to know about outsiders. The next morning as I head out to explore the island, a receptionist at the hotel says: 'This is a close community that likes gossiping. Everybody knows everything within an hour.'

I take an anti-clockwise tour of the coast along easy to follow paths, heading for the dramatic cliffs of Hell Bay, and start by stumbling upon Ruth Jenkins who, with her husband Paul, runs Hillside Farm, round the corner from the hotel. Outside the farmhouse, there is a green wooden container holding butternut squashes for seventy pence, onions for twenty pence and bags of potatoes for a pound. There is a payment box with a few coins inside. 'People are pretty honest,' says Ruth. 'It is really true: we don't ever lock things up on Bryher.' She invites me in for a coffee, after showing me the fields at the back of the property. The small plots of land are marked by rows of thick bushes that act as wind barriers, she tells me: 'Those bushes come from New Zealand. They grow quickly and are salt resistant. So when we get sea spray, it doesn't affect them.'

Her husband's family, she's soon saying, dates back to 1735 on Bryher. But Ruth was brought up in Leicestershire.

'So how did you end up here?' I ask.

'I just wanted to get away. I wanted to work on an island,' she says. 'So twenty-six years ago I applied for jobs in Mull, Sark and Tresco. I had a phone interview for the Island Hotel on Tresco. I got the job and met Paul there.' Paul comes in and says: 'We're just ticking along,' when I ask him how the farm is doing. Then he swiftly departs. 'Paul is not a people person,' says Ruth, with a twinkle in her eye, before explaining that most of their income comes from three holiday apartments on their property.

'Living here is like a dream: the changes in the colour of the rocks, the shadows, the movement of the sky, the rainbows, the winds. Nature has so many different moods,' Ruth says. 'When I moved I wanted to be with the elements. On the mainland people have become so removed from nature. They live in bubbles. They step out of their doors into their cars and go to an indoor shopping mall.' Which makes me think of Milton Keynes and Croydon. 'Here nature is part of your life,' Ruth continues. 'The weather, the tides... I couldn't leave.'

Beyond, there's a field covered in sea mist, with a path along the swirling ocean and rocks that remind me of Henry Moore sculptures. A fast-moving walker scurries by surprising me with: 'Morning!' Up Samson Hill, I follow a path between gorse bushes. At the top there is a sweeping view of all the Scillies, which are much more compact than I'd realised before coming. The ferry is heading towards St Mary's; not so far away really. A green fishing boat with a decorative orange sail is chugging towards the channel between Bryher and Tresco.

I can see the Abbey Garden, with its explosion of green near Tresco Abbey. The Scillies feel as though they are a walker's paradise, with so many islands to explore, as well as quaint little places to visit.

Down the hill, I pop into the island's only shop. The owners are away, according to a scraggly haired man who seems shocked to have a customer. He tells me he usually works in 'water supplies and water management, boatbuilding and maintenance and whatever else they want me to do'. The shop sells basic food supplies and maps. Outside, I meet a tourist wearing red trousers, who is with a friend in a Barbour jacket. He's heading for Hell Bay Hotel.

'The road to hell is paved with good intentions,' jokes the man with red trousers. 'Who said that? Jesus?'

Then the man in the Barbour says: 'On this occasion it is paved with concrete.'

They have a laugh and I leave them at Fraggle Rock pub, where the landlord, Chris Hopkins, serves me a lager at the bar on the first floor of a modern building decorated with models of old sailing boats. How does he get supplies to such a remote spot? 'I get a lot of my stuff from Tesco,' he replies. 'They do deliveries from Penzance. Tesco does massive business round here.' The name of the pub, he says, came from the children's television show of the same name: 'The boatmen from St Mary's used to call the island Fraggle Rock as they thought the inhabitants looked like the small hairy characters in it. I was looking for a name and thought: "Why not?"'

There are three other drinkers at the bar. One says that there is a local nickname for 'posh' people from Tresco: 'TTT... Typical Tresco Twats.' Another, referring to Robert Dorrien-

Smith, says: 'We just call him Mr Robert, then doff our caps as we go by.' They cannot believe that I have been to see him at the Abbey. 'You were honoured if it was in the Abbey: usually it's in the office.' Regarding people who go on holiday on Tresco, one of them says: 'You can normally hear them before you see them.' They express concern about high house prices. A small house near here would cost about £300,000: 'Who can afford that? That's why young people are moving to the mainland.' Prince Charles, who runs the Duchy of Cornwall, is mentioned. The consensus is that his rents are high: 'Some are extortionate. The rent for a headmaster's cottage on St Mary's was £17,600 for the year. That has to come from the local education authority's money.'

I walk up a hill to Shipman Head Down. There are views here of Hangman Island, where Royalists were hung by Parliamentarians during the Civil War. On the wide, open top of the down, I can just make out stone remains of Bronze Age graves. A short walk from here I come to Hell Bay for real – not the hotel. It's quite a sight. Giant waves smash at the foot of Shipman Head and Badplace Hill. Spray leaps as the waves hit land, and then fizzes in a vast white foam among the rocks, looking like a million gallons of milk. The sky is grey with a fine line of lilac on the horizon. It was here many years ago that locals spotted the *Marion G Douglas* ship floundering in a storm. When it was reached by a rescue vessel, they discovered no one was on board... just like the *Marie Celeste*. Shetland ponies are clipping grass on the slopes of Badplace Hill, where there are a handful of walkers. I sit on a broken wooden bench on the cliff of Hell Bay. This is the last full day of my journey and I suddenly feel exhilarated, looking out across the choppy waves and letting the wildness and beauty of the scene sink in.

And I begin to think back over the past four months.

When I set off to explore Unsung Britain, I knew it was a gamble. What if the Hulls and Sloughs of Britain just didn't make the grade? Maybe the *Crap Towns* books would be right. Maybe the journey would be one travel adventure too many. Maybe there wouldn't be hidden stories and things to do in Salford and Milton Keynes, after all. Maybe I'd get bored. Maybe I'd just want to go straight home, and plan trips to more usual holiday spots. Places where it's all a bit warmer, with things like beaches and jungles and verandas with waiters serving G&Ts (places Anne would actually want to visit without arm-twisting).

But as I quickly found in Hull – with charming Jean Hartley and her tales about Larkin, and the beautiful walks beside the Humber along the Trans Pennine Way – it did not work out that way. And when I look back over my unusual breaks and try to put my finger on what made it all so enjoyable (and I have enjoyed it, even the most out-of-the-way reaches of Croydon), I realise what made all the train journeys and interviews and meetings and poky guesthouses come together for me.

While you might think that a journey to such overlooked, unsung places is plain crazy – and plenty of my friends and colleagues have continued to say as much, the sense of *Schadenfreude* never, ever, far away – I now know that this has been the whole point. By going to the spots that so few others bother visiting I have begun to get a sense of Britain as a whole that has somehow emerged from the sheer randomness of the mission I set myself.

Yes, I have seen places that tourists will not, and in many cases cannot, go. I always knew I'd do that, as I wanted to get a deeper understanding of each place than I would by merely seeing 'attractions'. Casual visitors cannot see all the mad-looking cargo ships piled with second-hand holiday homes heading for Russia in Hull. I had to make an appointment for that. Most people are unlikely, perhaps at all, to venture to Slough, and certainly not to go to the neighbourhood of Chalvey to witness Romanian families living in overcrowded houses. And my last-minute whirlwind night in a police car on the streets of Derry is definitely not what most tourists are expecting (unless something has gone horribly wrong).

This sense of randomness has extended to the people I have met, too. From Delia and her love of Julian of Norwich, to the headmaster of Eton and his defence of public schools, to the strange and very orange Captain Beany in Port Talbot – I have talked to some extraordinary folk, I reflect, looking out across the waves. All the way along people have shared their time with me, and talked up Unsung Britain. They have made uncovering the 'hidden gems' possible.

Most of the time, I have simply not known what to expect next. Croydon's history of aviation. The real story of the Russia Revolution in Salford. The joys of mountain biking in Port Talbot. The pretty villages of Milton Keynes. This is what has made the journey so fun… setting off and being prepared to be surprised. And without wanting to sound pretentious, I believe this is what turns mere travel into adventure: leaving home with an open (and curious) mind.

As I think about this, a huge roller crashes against the hellish rocks in Hell Bay. This really is a dramatic spot. I had definitely not expected Hell to be so beautiful. Voices are rising on the path from Badplace Hill. Two women in anoraks appear, and stand by my bench admiring the view. They see my notebook and ask what I am doing. 'He's writing a book called *To Hull and Back*,' says an elderly woman with a well-spoken voice to her friend, who couldn't quite hear because of the wind. 'When are you going back to Hull?' she asks, as they make their way onwards.

Tourists have been everywhere in Unsung Britain (well, everywhere if you don't count Croydon). Earlier today, I read at the hotel that a group called the World Travel and Tourism Council estimates that tourism is responsible for one in every ten jobs across the globe. Even in heavily industrial areas such as Port Talbot there are tourism 'strategies', devised by people with very long job titles working on the local authority. Coventry has a tourist information centre. So does Milton Keynes. While other industries decline, holidaymaking seems to grow and grow.

Is this a good thing? Or are tourist information centres just a desperate attempt to sell Heritage Britain when we've run out of other ideas? Who knows? All I can say for sure is that tourism certainly seems to be happening all over our shores (even in poor old Slough).

I spend the afternoon relaxing at the hotel, and eat a good final meal in celebration of nearing the end of my journey: pheasant, parsnips and roast potatoes for the main course, washed down with a good red. Why not take it easy, and put my feet up a bit? And from the hotel the next day I catch the ferry to St Mary's, where I have a few hours to kill before the

Penzance ferry. I walk along the quaint high street, passing a Methodist church, and climb a hill to find the extraordinarily modest holiday home where Harold Wilson stayed every summer when he was prime minister. The small grey building is not much bigger than a garage. I knock on the door of a neighbouring pink cottage to ask the owner if I have found the right place. In these days of politicians visiting millionaires' villas in Tuscany and Barbados, it is hard to imagine a prime minister going on holiday in such a simple spot. A man wearing a cardigan says: 'Yes, it's the right house. Mary [Wilson's wife] still comes three or four times a year.'

Further on, past a cute bay, an area marked on my map as 'Nowhere' (I've moved from Hell to Nowhere), and a helicopter port, I come to Tremelethen Farm. Here I meet Keith Hale, a flower farmer. He is a tall man, doing the *Daily Telegraph* crossword puzzle in his kitchen when I arrive. He makes coffees and tells me he has been running the farm since 1973 when he took over from his father. Tremelethen produces four million stems of narcissi (small yellow flowers with multiple heads) every year, making it the biggest flower farm in the Scillies. Keith's trade has picked up recently. 'Competition from abroad is not as strong now as supermarkets have started focusing on local growers,' he explains. 'They have had to start listening to what their customers say – the ethical side of things. You can't get away from the fact that, if you are flying in from Africa, there are massive carbon emissions.'

His farm covers fifty acres and has three full-time staff. Keith met Harold Wilson 'a couple of times' when he was playing golf, he tells me. 'I nearly hit him once,' he says. 'I said "Sorry about that, nothing to do with my political inclinations", and he replied: "Well if it was, it must be that you are from the far left." You see, it had been a big hook.' We talk about travelling closer to home, and 'staycations'. And Keith says: 'That's all very well, but I'm not giving up the Caribbean. I love the sea and the sand and the warmth and the sunshine. I jump on a sailing dinghy and just blow around.'

Then I walk back to the pier. The *Scillonian III* is about to depart. A steward agrees to put a lobster I bought on Bryher in the galley fridge, jokingly asking as he takes the bag: 'Do you have any garnishes and some white wine to go with that?' As the ferry slides away from St Mary's past Rat Island, I look back from the deck and see a man on the pier. He is standing on a wall waving a skull and crossbones to a friend somewhere on board, reminding me of Augustus Smith and his scheme to bring order to the islands. I buy a pint of Scuppered beer from the bar and hang on to it as the vessel begins to tilt on the waves. The sun breaks through speckled grey clouds above St Mary's as the island disappears in the distance. I've been to Hell via Slough, Croydon, Milton Keynes and Hull, and I've had a highly unusual, rewarding and sometimes downright bizarre adventure.

It's been fun while it lasted. Now I'm looking forward to going home.

13

POSTSCRIPT: BACK IN HULL

But first I'm heading north again. The woman who'd asked when I was going back to Hull on the cliffs by Hell Bay had been spot on. I am going to Hull and back, literally – sooner than I'd expected.

It feels incredibly odd to be returning to Hull's Paragon station, and meeting Jean Hartley once again, this time in the reception of the Royal Hotel Hull. As I was coming back from the Scilly Isles, it was announced in the papers that Hull plans to commemorate the twenty-fifth anniversary of Larkin's death with a series of lectures and exhibitions in the city. There is to be a Larkin Trail with audio MP3 recordings of his poetry. There is to be a statue of Larkin at the station. There is even talk of a 'major community art event' with '100 Larkin toads' placed around the city – a reference to his sharp poems about 'the toad work' that squats on our lives. It is certainly no longer true that the poet is being 'shoved in a corner' in the city, as Jean had said four and a half months back. Instead, he is being given pride of place. Larkin tourism is all go! Hull seems to have fallen in love with Larkin since my visit.

Jean has been a key figure in this turnaround as it is her booklet *Philip Larkin's Hull and East Yorkshire* that is being used as the basis of the MP3 tours. She is wearing a fur-lined overcoat and shivering slightly in the lobby. She smiles and is soon saying: 'People say: "Oh, Larkin didn't like Hull." But he did. Why would he have lived here so long? He was productive and happy here, and he did wonderful things like arranging the building of two libraries.'

'I wonder what he would think of the MP3 player tours – they seem very un-Larkin-like,' I comment.

Jean smiles again. 'Well, he would deride them,' she replies. 'But he would be secretly pleased.'

We are in an appropriate place to meet. The Royal Hotel Hull, a sturdy limestone building connected to the station that was formerly the Royal Station Hotel, the subject of Larkin's poem 'Friday Night at the Royal Station Hotel'. In this poem he describes salesmen heading back to Leeds 'leaving full ashtrays in the Conference Room' and a dining-room with 'a larger loneliness of knives and glass'. Jean tells me and Anne, who is a big Larkin fan and has joined me on this trip, that 'all the salesmen went back to Leeds because Leeds was where it was all at' and that Larkin loved this hotel.

'Hull is so isolated, but Larkin saw this hotel as a symbol of civilisation,' she says. 'It was a place to go for tea or coffee or booze. It was a welcoming place, a little intimate corner of Hull to take his guests in the city.'

We get into a shiny black Chrysler limousine that's been laid on by the Yorkshire Tourist Board (no expense spared for Larkin these days), and head off on our mini Larkin tour. We pass the Hull Royal Infirmary, the subject of his poem 'The Building' ('he saw a lot of this in the last few years'), and head on to Spring Bank Cemetery, which Larkin once described to John Betjeman during a 1964 BBC *Monitor* programme as 'the most beautiful spot in Hull'. The two poets were filmed sitting by gravestones overgrown with weeds. We take in the peaceful setting. 'This was where he came when he wanted to sort his head out,' says Jean. 'It was a wilderness. A natural cathedral. I think it answered something in the spiritual side of him.'

'Why is there so much sudden interest in him?' Anne asks Jean, as we walk past a grave topped with a broken stone angel. 'Is it because there is something very modern in his poetry?'

'Yes, younger people always liked him. He always said that he felt that it was important to appeal not just to poetry readers, but to everyone. He wanted people in pubs to read his work.'

We go to the Hull Nuffield Hospital, where Larkin died – the unassuming red-brick building is tucked away on a side street next to a roundabout with an ornate fountain decorated with mermaids. 'He told me when I visited that he was very amused that two of his nurses were called Thatcher and Scargill,' says Jean, who last saw him two months before his death. 'I thought he would look quite pale. But he was sitting on the edge of his bed, as beautifully dressed as ever. He didn't seem like a patient at all. We went for a walk round the garden: a perambulation. He said: "OK, well you'll be able to say that you were one of the last people to see me alive." He loved to make comic comments about his health.'

Just round the corner we stop outside his Pearson Park flat, which is as run-down as ever. Jean says: 'I met the owner the other day: Mr Mills. Normally he keeps himself to himself but we had a chat. He said that soon after he bought the house, he let out Larkin's flat to two young men, who managed to pull enormous numbers of birds. They all wanted to say they had slept in Larkin's bed, you see.' And after seeing his next house in which he lived with Maeve Brennan (who apparently kept all his clothes in his wardrobe after he died, as though he was about to pop back at any moment), and passing the library (where Larkin is said to have hidden in students' cars to avoid unwanted visitors), we reach the municipal cemetery in Cottingham, and find his grave. Jean tells us simply that what she likes most about his poetry is that 'it deals with the decisions we make, about life and love – he was not a cynical man, as people like to make out'.

It has been a terrific tour, and the next morning on the train home, it is Larkin's thoughts about the river Humber and his choice of home, as told to Betjeman in the BBC programme, that spring to mind. As our train moves along the estuary, I look up what Larkin said about this view and his adopted city. 'You get some very fine effects of light, particularly in the evenings when you have the sunsets building up westwards down the river. You get magnificent pilings up of clouds, all golden and rosy and so forth,' he said. 'That again is not the sort of thing you see in the average mid-England provincial town. And that's the sort of reason I like being in Hull.' And with that, Anne and I head south on this sunlit Sunday. The journey is now complete.

ACKNOWLEDGEMENTS

Many people kindly shared their time during my journey around Unsung Britain, and it was their enthusiasm and insights that carried me along. I don't believe in travelling with a notebook and keeping a distance – merely observing as a silent outsider and passing on by. Without talking to people and engaging in their stories (which I would otherwise miss), I feel lost. So I am very grateful to all those who showed me about along the way. I have mentioned many people in the text, but I am also especially indebted to Roger Bailey, Kate Taylor, Lucy Pennington, Nigel Massey, Simon Ward, Tess Sullivan and Stephanie Boyle. My colleagues at *The Times* have been very supportive, particularly Jane Knight, Kate Quill and Kathleen Wyatt. I also owe thanks to Frank Barrett, Stephen McClarence, Rupert Wright and Mark Ellingham – and to my parents Robert and Christine Chesshyre, for their excellent advice. I am extremely grateful to Jennifer Barclay at Summersdale for her encouragement, as well as to Lucy York and Leah James for their sharp-eyed editing. Lucy Luck helped set me off in the right direction, and has provided great support. Friends and family – as well as sometimes wondering 'why?' – have also patiently listened to my mutterings about the likes of Milton Keynes and Slough. Without Emma Woolf, who has backed me throughout (and been a great inspiration and editor, too), I doubt I would have made it to Hull and back.

Have you enjoyed this book? If so, why not write a review on your favourite website?

Thanks very much for buying this Summersdale book.

www.summersdale.com